Domain Architectures

Domain Architectures

Models and Architectures for UML Applications

Daniel J. Duffy

Datasim Education BV, Amsterdam, Netherlands

John Wiley & Sons, Ltd

Other Wiley Editorial Offices

John Wiley & Sons Inc., 111 River Street, Hoboken, NJ 07030, USA

Jossey-Bass, 989 Market Street, San Francisco, CA 94103-1741, USA

Wiley-VCH Verlag GmbH, Boschstr. 12, D-69469 Weinheim, Germany

John Wiley & Sons Australia Ltd, 33 Park Road, Milton, Queensland 4064, Australia

John Wiley & Sons (Asia) Pte Ltd, 2 Clementi Loop #02-01, Jin Xing Distripark, Singapore 129809

John Wiley & Sons Canada Ltd, 22 Worcester Road, Etobicoke, Ontario, Canada M9W 1L1

Wiley also publishes its books in a variety of electronic formats. Some content that appears
in print may not be available in electronic books.

Library of Congress Cataloging-in-Publication Data

Duffy, Daniel J.
 Domain architectures : models and architectures for UML applications /
Daniel J. Duffy.
   p. cm.
 Includes bibliographical references and index.
 ISBN 0-470-84833-2 (alk. paper)
 1. Computer software—Development. 2. Business—Data processing. 3. UML
(Computer science) I. Title.
 QA76.76.D47D84 2004
 005.1—dc22   2004002216

British Library Cataloguing in Publication Data

A catalogue record for this book is available from the British Library

ISBN 0-470-84833-2

Typeset in 10/12.5pt Times by Laserwords Private Limited, Chennai, India
Printed and bound in Great Britain by Biddles Ltd, King's Lynn
This book is printed on acid-free paper responsibly manufactured from sustainable forestry
in which at least two trees are planted for each one used for paper production.

Contents

Preface

The last two decennia have witnessed many advances in the area of software development. The advent of object-oriented programming languages and modelling languages such as Unified Modeling Language (UML) has increased our ability as developers to design and realize large and enterprise-wide software systems. However, software engineering, as a discipline seems to be lacking in its support for reference models that can be used in order to help developers create new systems quickly and efficiently. The software development process is still a very context-sensitive and idiosyncratic process. Whereas disciplines such as chemical engineering and mathematics have developed domain models for a range of problems, the IT industry is in general lacking in such models. Software development tends to be a very personal experience and in many cases how a system is to be developed is a product of a single person's insights. This is a potentially dangerous state of affairs because there is no guarantee that the resulting model reflects the problem domain well.

This book introduces a number of so-called models (we call them domain architectures) that act as 'cookie-cutters' or reference models for more specific real-life applications. Working with domain architectures demands a shift in thinking because when designing a new software system we try to categorize it as an *instance system* of one or more domain architectures. Having done that we can reuse and specialize the requirements, viewpoints and generic architecture to the specific systems. This results in massive reuse at the architectural and design levels while the risk of failure is reduced because the reference models in this book are based in real-life applications and experience. They have been used on real projects with real customers.

The reference models can and should be used in much the same way as people reason about the world around them. This is the Ausubel subsumption theory: when developing software systems we relate new knowledge to relevant concepts and propositions we already know.

ACKNOWLEDGEMENTS

Although many of the results in this book are based on my own work it would have been impossible to write this literature without the support and feedback from many organizations and individuals that I've come in to contact with during the last 25 years. First, I would like to thank Datasim's customers who have attended our analysis and design courses since 1992. It is impossible to name them all and we wish to thank them for their feedback. Particular thanks goes to the following individuals (in random order): Paul Langemeijer, Hans Plekker, Henry Rodenburgh, Marten Kramer, Wim van Leeuwen, Robert Demming, Adriaan Meeling, Martijn Boeker, Vladimir Grafov, Jeff Keustermans, Teun Mentzel, Ilona Hooft Graafland and many more. For all others who have had some form of involvement with me throughout the years, many thanks to you as well.

This work has been importantly influenced by several major sources. Firstly, Michael Jackson who is the originator of Problem Frames and who sparked a number of ideas that led to *Domain Architectures*. Secondly, the researchers in the Design Patterns movement (too many to mention) who realize that software development is a repetitive process and that a multitude of patterns can be discovered, documented and used in many different contexts. Finally, to Bjarne Stroustrup, the inventor of C++ for his efforts in making OO more accessible to a wide audience. A word of thanks is due to the 'three amigos' Booch, Jacobson and Rumbaugh for their hugely successful efforts in making UML the *defacto* standard for object-oriented analysis and design.

A special word of thanks is due to the staff at Wiley in Chichester who had infinite patience with me.

Finally, I wish to thank my family, Ilona Hooft Graafland and Brendan Duffy for their patience during the preparation of this book. They probably wondered when the book would finally be finished. Hopefully as I write this sentence...

Daniel J. Duffy
Datasim Education BV, Amsterdam
February 2004
dduffy@datasim.nl

PART I

Background and fundamentals

1 Introducing and motivating domain architectures

> *'Architecture is born, not made—must consistently grow from within to whatever it becomes. Such forms as it takes must be spontaneous generation of materials, building methods and purpose.'*
>
> Frank Lloyd Wright

1.1 WHAT IS THIS BOOK?

This book describes how to analyse large enterprise systems. In particular, we define a process that maps high-level business concerns and business processes to artefacts in the Unified Modelling Language (UML). This is one of the first books that explicitly links the business world with the IT world. We achieve this end by first of all providing the reader with a number of ready-made reference models that he or she can use as a basis for specific applications. These reference models are called domain architectures in this book. Second, and just as important, we adopt, adapt and (hopefully) improve current understanding on how software systems are analysed and designed. In particular, our interest is in creating flexible and maintainable software systems using proven technology. We document the products of our endeavours using the visual notation in UML. This adds to the usability of our process because UML is a *de facto* standard and we shall use it as a universal communication language.

A domain architecture is a reference model for a set of applications sharing similar functionality, behaviour and structure. It describes the essential features in some business domain. In this book we introduce five major domain architecture types. These types describe recurring themes in software development. We could loosely define a domain architecture as a pattern that describes structure, functionality and behaviour in the earliest stages of the software lifecycle. We discuss generic architectures for *management information*, *process control*, *access control*, *manufacturing* and *tracking* systems. We devote a chapter to each of these five architecture types. Specific instances of these architectures occur in real-life software development projects and we describe a number of such instances in this book.

Our domain architectures are models in the so-called *problem domain* (roughly speaking, the domain of the sponsor and user of the system) while design and system patterns are models for the *solution domain* (the domain of the object-oriented analyst and designer). Domain architectures fill the gap between the business and the IT worlds. In short, we provide the reader with a set of documented reference models that he or she can specialize to produce analysis artefacts for specific instance systems. We devote six chapters to show how this specialization works; each chapter deals with a well-known application.

1.2 WHY HAVE WE WRITTEN THIS BOOK?

The main reason for writing this book was to describe and document a number of recurring patterns and models that we have discovered in software projects. These models describe a set of applications having similar structure, functionality and behaviour. Each model is documented in handbook form and the reader can use the handbook to 'clone' specific applications. We are primarily interested in large enterprise systems because we have seen that traditional object-oriented technology is not suitable as the driving force for systems of this magnitude. The old maxim of 'looking for the objects and the rest will take care of itself' is not applicable in these situations, in my opinion. It becomes very difficult to manage the object networks that result from this approach. Furthermore, it would seem that the levels of reusability with the object paradigm are quite low; we are interested in reusability at system and architecture level. For example, a system that we have already analysed and designed can be used as a first approximation to some new system that we suspect is similar to it in some way.

Another reason for writing this book is that we wish to integrate the world of business processing modelling, requirements analysis and UML into a coherent whole. In particular, we create a well-defined and hopefully seamless path that maps high-level requirements and business concerns to analysis artefacts such as class diagrams, interaction diagrams and other artefacts in UML. We are not aware of such a process in the literature. This is why we have created the Datasim Development Process (DDP) that *does* provide a step-by-step plan to get you to the UML finish line. The DDP describes the following phases: business processing modelling, architecture, requirements analysis, object-oriented analysis in UML and design. It is a lightweight process and can be used by novice developers. We give an introduction to the DDP in Chapter 3. Each of these topics is discussed in this book with the exception of design.

Finally, we have written this book because we wish to improve the communication lines between customers and developer.

1.3 FOR WHOM IS THIS BOOK INTENDED?

This book is aimed at software architects, (structured and object-oriented) analysts and other software specialists who are involved with the creation of stable architectures for medium and large systems. We describe a step-by-step process that takes the system goals and business processes and maps them to a software architecture consisting of a network of interrelated systems and classes. We describe how to decompose the systems into subsystems and classes. To this end, we use a subset of the UML syntax that is sufficiently rich to allow a detailed design. Thus, this book is also suitable for those developers who analyse and document systems using UML and who wish to integrate them with the 'Gang of Four' (GOF) and system (POSA) patterns. In general, this book focuses on that part of the software lifecycle between business process modelling and object-oriented analysis and it provides a stable architectural framework on which to place customer requirements.

This book is also of interest to analysts who are involved in requirements determination activities and who need to align functional and non-functional requirements with architectural models.

1.4 WHY SHOULD I READ THIS BOOK?

We think that this is one of the first books that attempts to use UML for large enterprise systems. It provides the reader with tools, concepts and advice on how to map the business world to the IT world. We use standards wherever possible, such as UML, standard architectures, business process modelling and patterns. We also improve these standards whenever necessary.

This book should help you produce stable, understandable and high-quality software systems. New key features that we see as important are:

- A defined software process from A to Z
- Integration of proven technology with our software process
- Ready-made reference models that you can use in projects
- Using the UML artefacts in a predictable and usable way
- Reference models that are based on real-world experience
- Software development as a continuous improvement process.

1.5 WHAT IS A DOMAIN ARCHITECTURE, REALLY?

A domain architecture is a reference model for a range of applications that share similar structure, functionality and behaviour. It is not an application as such but

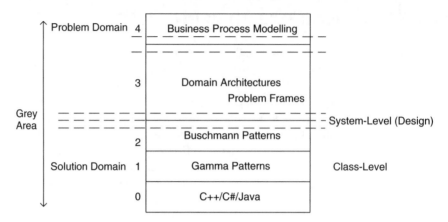

Figure 1.1   Taxonomy of domain architectures.

is in fact a meta model that describes how more specific instance systems ('real applications for real customers') are created. A domain architecture subsumes much of the current techniques in software development and is positioned between a number of other methods as shown in Figure 1.1. This diagram should help the reader position domain architecture in the galaxy of methods. For a discussion of the methods in Figure 1.1 and how they have influenced our work, we refer to Appendix 3 at the end of this book. We thus see that our work and results are positioned between the problem domain and the solution domain. Once you have determined in which domain architecture type (or types) your application falls, you can then use the ready-made templates to map the business artefacts to UML artefacts. You have a foot in both camps, as it were. This can't be a bad thing.

We discuss five basic forms and one 'composite' form in this book:

- *MIS* (*Management Information Systems*): Produce high-level and consolidated decision-support data and reports based on transaction data from various independent sources.
- *PCS* (*Process Control Systems*): Monitor and control values of certain variables that must satisfy certain constraints.
- *RAT* (*Resource Allocation and Tracking*) *systems*: Monitor a request or some other entity in a system. The request is registered, resources are assigned to it, and its status in time and space is monitored.
- *MAN* (*Manufacturing*) *systems*: Create finished products and services from raw materials.
- *ACS* (*Access Control Systems*): Allow access to passive objects from active subjects. They are similar to security systems.
- *LCM* (*Lifecycle Model*): A 'composite' model that describes the full lifecycle of an entity; an aggregate of MAN, RAT and MIS models.

We realize that some of the above names may be confusing to some readers, or that readers may infer some wrong conclusions based on those names. For example, the author once spoke to a software engineer who developed reporting functionality in the telecom industry. For example, the system to be developed should create invoices at different levels. The author suggested analysing the system as a MIS category. The response from the engineer was 'Oh no, my system is technical!'.

In order to fit domain architectures in a hierarchy that improves understandability and discovery we create a semantic network model as shown in Figure 1.2. This is an application of well-known techniques in cognitive psychology (Eysenck and Keane 2000). There are three main categories:

- *Superordinate level* (level 1): This is a high level of abstraction in a conceptual hierarchy and corresponds to a very general type. In our case we have categories for object creation, aligning objects in some structure, and modelling object behaviour. The basic assumption is that these three categories model the lifecycle of *any* object in any phase of the software lifecycle.
- *Subordinate level* (level 3): This is the lowest level in the conceptual hierarchy and contains specific objects and systems. This is, for example, where all the specific applications that we discuss in Part III of this book are to be found.
- *Basic level* (level 2): This is an intermediate level of abstraction in the conceptual hierarchy and fits between the superordinate and subordinate levels. This is the level where the current domain architecture types are placed.

The reader can use the hierarchy in Figure 1.2 as a navigational aid. For example, he or she can try to place a system to be developed as a subordinate level system under a more general basic level category. For example, a system that produces invoices

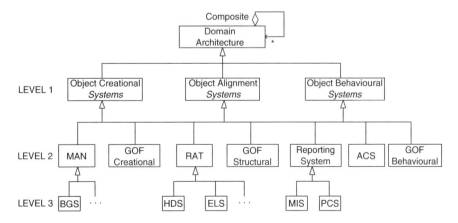

Figure 1.2 Hierarchy of patterns and reference models.

on mobile telephone usage is seen as an instance of an Object Reporting System. This can be refined by modelling the system as an instance of a MIS category.

The domain architecture types are fully documented in Part II. The documentation style is similar to how the patterns community document their design and system patterns (see GOF 1995, POSA 1996). The structure is roughly as follows ('DA' stands for Domain Architecture):

- *Motivation section*
  - — Background to DA and its history
  - — Motivational examples (one small example, one larger example)
  - — The general applicability of the DA
- *Functional modelling, architecture and structure*
  - — The goals, processes and activities for the DA
  - — Context diagram, system discovery and system decomposition
- *Behavioural modelling*
  - — Stakeholders and their viewpoints
  - — Requirements and use cases
- *Object-Oriented Analysis (OOA)*
  - — Class architecture UML classes in the DA
  - — Use cases (and possibly sequence diagrams)
- *Extensions to the DA*
  - — Specializations of the DA
  - — Using the DA with other systems (as client, server, collaborator).

Each of the artefacts in the above list is documented using UML whenever possible.

1.6 THE DATASIM DEVELOPMENT PROCESS (DDP)

This book would not be complete if we did not pay some attention to the actual process of mapping high-level concepts and requirements to lower-level artefacts that we use in UML. We describe a step-by-step *constructive* process that actually shows you *how* to do this. This topic is discussed in Chapter 3. In particular, we develop processes for the following important phases:

- Architecture discovery and decomposition
- Requirements analysis
- Object-oriented analysis.

Furthermore, we discuss the integration problems when we wish to align the artefacts of the different phases. We note that it is possible to use the DDP as described here without having to refer to domain architectures at all! This makes the book useful for those readers who do not have the time to study the domain architectures in detail but who will still want to use a solid software process.

A full treatment of project management issues for DDP is outside the scope of this book.

1.7 THE STRUCTURE OF THIS BOOK

This book consists of four main parts and 18 chapters. In Part I (Chapters 1–4) we motivate domain architectures by describing what they are and how to use and document them and by giving examples. In Part II we discuss and document the six basic forms of domain architecture. We discuss these categories in Chapters 5–10. Each chapter in this part is documented using a standard template structure. Part III analyses six instance systems of the domain architecture types from Part II and these instances are described in Chapters 11–16. The cases are well known in the software literature or have been distilled from real-life software projects in the past. Finally, Part IV contains two chapters that summarize the similarities and differences between the different domain architecture types and how to use them in your software projects.

The chapters in Parts II and III have been written in handbook form. We have written several chapters and appendices to help the reader understand the rationale behind the structure of the book.

An important feature in this book is that we resurrect information models that have been used for many years to help systems analysts design software systems and we have dressed them in a more object-oriented suit. In this way we hope to save these useful models for future applications.

How do we use this book? We attempt to answer this question by posing a number of standard questions that we hope will encompass those that readers might ask, and then directing the reader to the most appropriate chapters:

- *Question*: Where can I find a summary of domain architectures and their instance systems?
  Answer: Chapter 2.
- *Question*: Where are domain architectures and UML artefacts documented?
  Answer: Chapter 4.
- *Question*: Where are domain architectures and their instances documented in detail?
  Answer: Parts II and III of this book. Furthermore, Chapter 17 summarizes the domain architectures and the client/server relationships between them and their instance systems.
- *Question*: How do I start?

Answer: Chapter 18 discusses the different ways of tackling software projects. We develop a number of practical techniques to help you get up to speed.

- *Question*: Does this book help me to develop interviewing skills?

Answer: Yes. Please read Appendix 1.

1.8 WHAT THIS BOOK DOES *NOT* COVER

First, this book is not a UML tutorial and we assume that the reader has experience of UML syntax. Second, this book is not concerned with design issues or design patterns, although the artefacts can be mapped to the GOF and POSA patterns. This topic is beyond the scope of this book.

Finally, this book does not deal with component technology, although it is possible to first model domain architectures using this technology and then create systems in which the component and object technologies dovetail. We thus see the object paradigm evolving into something to adapt to the realities of the modern software development environment.

2 Domain architecture catalogue

> 'Any problem in geometry can easily be reduced to such terms that a knowledge
> of the lengths of certain straight lines is sufficient for its construction. Just as
> arithmetic consists of only four or five operations, namely, addition, subtraction,
> multiplication, division and the extraction of roots ... so in geometry, to find
> required lines it is merely necessary to add or subtract other lines.'
>
> René Descartes, *The Geometry*

2.1 INTRODUCTION AND OBJECTIVES

This chapter summarizes the major domain architectures that we discuss in this book as well as several instance systems in each category. It has been included mainly for reference purposes and it may be skipped on a first reading. The added value of this chapter is that the reader can use it as a kind of *Yellow Pages* to help find applications that are similar to his or her current applications. This topic will be further developed in Chapter 18 when we develop some guidelines to help us discover the structure and functionality of an application by comparing it with known applications. This is called *analogical reasoning*.

In short, this chapter is a quick reference to the domains and instance systems in this book. It is *not* meant to be read from start to finish but gathers all the domain architectures and their instances in one place for perusal and reference.

We assemble all the domain architectures, their instances and exercises in one place. This is where you can begin before you consult the chapters in Parts II and III because your specific application will hopefully be analogous to one or more categories or instances. You can use this chapter as you would a real catalogue, namely by browsing until you come across something that interests you.

One of the assumptions in this book is that each new application is similar to an instance of some domain architecture (or category as we shall sometimes call it). In order to help the reader determine which category is 'best' we have introduced domain architectures and their instances. A domain architecture encapsulates the assumption that all applications in a given domain have a central description that then stands for all of them. An application is a member of the category if there is a good correspondence between its attributes and that of the more general architecture. For example, we suggest that the following applications are good prototypes for their respective domain architecture types:

- Manpower Control (MPC) is a prototype for MIS
- Home Heating System (HHS) is a prototype for PCS
- Order Realization System (ORS) is a prototype for RAT
- A compiler is a prototype for MAN
- The Reference Monitor model is a prototype for ACS
- The Product Lifecycle Model (LCM) is a prototype for lifecycle and composite models.

We note that the domain architectures themselves may be used as prototypes for new systems. The disadvantage is that it may not be possible to fit your application to a prototype. Then we must resort to the so-called *exemplar-based view*. Rather than working from an abstraction of the central tendency of all the instances of a category, people simply make use of particular instances or exemplars of the category (Eysenck and Keane 2000). For example, some exemplars in the RAT category are:

- Help Desk System (HDS)
- Order Realization System (ORS)
- Call handling systems.

People relate to instance systems more quickly than to abstract reference models. However, you have a choice! Basically, we choose between one representative application and several exemplars as the target when using analogical reasoning to help us discover the architecture and behaviour of the system under discussion (SUD). A prototype approach assumes that there is a single 'best' system that is representative of all other systems in the same category, while the exemplar-based view contradicts this assumption. Instead, we need several instance systems to help us discover system structure and behaviour. We discuss prototypes and exemplars in more detail in Chapter 18.

In order to focus on the problem at hand we attempt to define the major defining features of a system or domain architecture type. We reduce the scope by focusing on the initial business and analysis phases of the software lifecycle. To this end, we think that the following set will provide a good starting point:

- C1: What are the main goals of a system?
- C2: What are the main core processes and key systems?
- C3: What are external stakeholder systems and their viewpoints?
- C4: What are the most important use cases?

For point C3 we are using the term 'viewpoint' as defined in Sommerville and Sawyer 1997, for example. This is a term that we use in the very early stages of the software lifecycle to denote perspectives taken by different system stakeholder groups. We give a fuller definition in Chapter 3.

Note that these questions are mainly of relevance during the early analysis phases. Unfortunately, these are the problems that tend to get glossed over in large systems in the rush to UML nirvana.

Answers to Questions C1 to C4 should be forthcoming as soon as possible and before commencing with object-oriented analysis. The risks are great if you gloss over or 'fudge' these issues.

2.2 MANAGEMENT INFORMATION SYSTEMS (MIS) (CHAPTER 5)

Management Information Systems produce decision-support information that can be used as input to other systems such as data mining, statistical analysis and executive information systems. The motivation and vocabulary for MIS date from the 1960s and 1970s (see Section 5.2 for a description) and we have subsumed the corresponding models under an object-oriented framework. The core process is to produce decision-support information based on low-level or transaction input data from various sources. The output is presented in various ways. The main activities in the core process are:

- Register, validate and create basic transaction objects
- Consolidate and aggregate transaction objects
- Present, dispatch and report on consolidated data.

The MIS category subsumes many industrial, technical and administrative applications. The word 'management' should not be interpreted as just being of relevance to business domains. It has a broader scope.

We now give a brief discussion of the MIS instances in this book. These are useful for reference purposes.

1. Simple Digital Watch (SDW) (Section 5.3.1)
SDW accepts pulses (one pulse every second). The pulses are buffered until the number of pulses reaches 60. Then the current time (in hours and minutes) is (re)calculated and the new time is displayed on an output panel. SDW can be configured on a 12-hour or 24-hour time regime.

SDW contains a panel consisting of two buttons for setting the time. We see the current version of SDW as an instance of MIS for a number of reasons. First, low-level data (seconds) is registered and merged to high-level data (time, that is hours and minutes). Second, we need different kinds of merging and consolidation algorithms to create this high-level data. Finally, this data is displayed on a LED and is in fact decision-support information (for example, it's time to get up!).

2. Instrumentation and control systems (Section 5.3.2)

This technical problem occurs in many industrial applications. Nonetheless, it can still be modelled as a MIS instance. All instrumentation and control systems convert physical quantities and display the converted information on a recording device or recorder. The recorder stores the results of the measurements. The difference between a recorder and a display is that the former produces a permanent (persistent) record while the latter shows the results in volatile form. In general, we use a database system to store results permanently while displays can be implemented by some kind of light-emitting diode (LED) display or a graphics screen.

3. Noise control engineering (Section 5.10.1)

This is another technical example of MIS. In this case we imagine a petrochemical plant consisting of various noise-producing equipment. The equipment is grouped into various areas, clusters and assemblies. The system calculates noise levels (in decibels) in the petrochemical plant and the main goal is to produce high-level decision information for health inspectors and local authorities. Typing reporting functions are:

- What are the noise levels at various distances from the plant?
- What are the noise levels caused by various assemblies?
- Compare actual noise levels with levels allowed by the law.

4. Reporting activities in the 'Rent-a-machine' system (Section 10.3.1)

This system is an instance of a lifecycle model (LCM) and its core process is the tracking of a customer request from A to Z. The lifecycle system has the following subsystems:

- Reservation: create the basic customer order (MAN instance)
- Contracting: create a binding contract between the customer and garden centre (RAT instance)
- Reporting: marketing and sales information on rented equipment (MIS instance).

This last system is an instance of a MIS because we are interested in monitoring the status of each rented machine. Some typical questions to be answered are:

- Report on the usage levels for a given group of machines
- How many machines need repair?
- What is the garden centre's profit in the last six months?

5. Manpower Control (MPC) system (Chapter 11)

An engineering company works on projects for internal and external customers. A project represents the sequence of activities that are executed by the different departments. The project is deemed to be complete when each activity has been completed. An employee works on several activities in a project and is allocated a certain number of hours and other resources for each activity. Each department has its own area of expertise.

Departments are grouped into divisions. Customers are the sponsors of external projects. The resources (in this case hours) are allocated to departments and employees on a project basis.

A system needs to be built that registers, validates and monitors project resource usage (in this case man-hours). In particular, the following requirements must be supported in the system:

- MPC processes transaction data (resource usage) once per period (e.g. per month)
- Resource utilization must be monitored
- Status reporting capabilities must be available to stakeholders.

We model this problem as a MIS instance because we wish to monitor project status. We could have modelled this as an instance of RAT (a kind of time-tracking) but the fit may be less clear. For example, RAT does not say much about high-level reporting and consolidation algorithms, while MIS does.

6. Portfolio management

A financial instrument (or instrument for short) is an entity that can be traded in the marketplace. Examples of instruments are cash, equities, equity options, index options, bonds and futures (see Jarrow and Turnbull 1996). We can create MIS systems for a given instrument type, for example:

- Calculate the value of the instrument
- Get the instrument history (historic prices of a selected instrument).

Thus, we can monitor instrument behaviour using a MIS, albeit at the level of a single instrument. You could also model it using a RAT, in which case you have a competing solution.

A portfolio is a set of instruments. We now wish to monitor the performance of the portfolio so that we can generate an optimal return on the portfolio. In particular, we wish to calculate a strategy of buys and sells and we achieve this by using simulation techniques, for example using the Monte Carlo method (see Wilmott 1998).

The main reporting functions in a portfolio system are:

- Get portfolio history (display the historic values in a graph)
- Calculate performance (sum performance of instruments in portfolio)
- Calculate the Value At Risk (VAR) of the portfolio.

Some other examples of MIS applications are discussed in Section 5.10.

2.3 PROCESS CONTROL SYSTEMS (PCS) (CHAPTER 6)

Process Control Systems model differences between the scheduled and actual values of certain attributes and variables in a system. The main objective is to keep these two sets of values within close proximity to each other. The system monitors the values and corrective or control action is taken if the values drift too much away from each other. Process control systems are well understood and we discuss the basic model and its variants in Sections 6.4 (reference model and main components) and 6.4.2 (control engineering). We subsume these models under a domain architecture that we call PCS. The core process in PCS is the activation of actuators that ensure that the system returns to equilibrium. The main concurrent activities are:

- Monitor disturbances and other changes in the system's environment
- Activate actuators to bring the system to a steady state
- Monitor and control the life of the system (for example, via an operator panel).

As we shall see in Chapter 6, we map each activity to a subsystem that contains the necessary structure, functionality and behaviour to approximate the corresponding activity.

Process Control Systems occur in many industrial, real-time and business domains. In fact, any application where part of the problem is to monitor and control disparities between actual and ideal values of some variable will almost certainly be a candidate for one or more PCS instance systems.

1. Water level control (Section 6.3.1)
The water level in a tank must be monitored and controlled. If the water level is too high we open a valve to let the water escape, while if the level is too low we close the valve and start a pump motor that consequently delivers water to the tank in order to increase the level.

2. Bioreactor (Section 6.3.2)
This problem is similar to the previous problem. Instead of monitoring water level the bioreactor system monitors and controls the temperature of the water (or other liquid) in the tank. An example of a bioreactor system is a sewage plant.

Real applications monitor several variables such as temperature, pressure, pH level and percentage of oxygen in the liquid. We then speak of a *multi-parameter* problem.

3. Barrier options (Section 6.3.3)
In this case we are interested in situations where stock price fluctuates between critical 'barrier' values. Upper and lower barriers may be defined and stock value is measured against these scheduled values. For example, a so-called knock-out option becomes worthless if its underlying stock value reaches the barrier value.

Whereas a plain option is unconstrained, a barrier option is constrained by the predefined barrier values of the stock. Control action is executed when these barriers are reached, thus confirming that we are indeed looking at an instance of the PCS category.

4. Control engineering (Section 6.4.2)

This is a specialized discipline and it is concerned (among other things) with the definition of models that ensure that a system behaves in a certain way. We distinguish between open, closed, feedback and feedforward systems.

You can skip this section on a first reading. It may not be to everybody's taste.

5. Complexity of object-oriented applications

Systems built using objects and classes tend to become more complex and difficult to maintain as time goes on. In particular, classes may have associations with several other classes. The more relationships a class has with other classes, the less understandable and maintainable this class becomes. In order to redress this problem, we can define a number of so-called *software metrics*, define target values for them and describe the problem of defining the resulting system as an instance of the PCS category. For example, we could define an upper threshold value for the number of attributes in a class; a warning message is sent to the software risk manager if this value is exceeded. Of course, risk and quality managers are interested in risks and potential calamities. Modelling their world using PCS systems may not be a bad idea after all because these systems inform the managers when things start to go wrong.

6. Home Heating System (HHS) (Chapter 12)

This system is a prototype for the PCS category. It is a standard benchmark case in the software literature. Our approach to the HHS is unique, in our opinion. Some of the issues that we address in a comprehensive manner are:

- Integration of HHS with process-control terminology (from Chapter 6)
- Benchmark previous analyses of HHS (Booch, Hatley and Pirbhai)
- Thorough description of behaviour with use cases
- Integration of the PAC model with use cases.

Furthermore, we have used HHS as a reference model for new systems. We can employ a form of analogical reasoning to 'morph' HHS into the current system under discussion. This is easier than approaching the analysis of HHS using traditional object-oriented technology and its related methods such as using nouns for classes, CRC cards and so on. Our approach is better because we have decomposed HHS into loosely coupled systems and each system encapsulates a difficult and volatile design decision. Furthermore, we have integrated this approach with the object paradigm.

2.4 RESOURCE ALLOCATION AND TRACKING (RAT) SYSTEMS (CHAPTER 7)

The main added value of the RAT category is that it provides us with a model for registering and tracking entities in a system. It must be possible to query the status of the entity at all times. The primary input to RAT systems is some kind of request. The core process produces status information and the main activities are:

- Register and verify the request
- Assign resources to execute the request
- Monitor the status of the request and present this to stakeholders.

RAT systems occur in many industrial and business applications and we consider the RAT category to be one of the most important categories in our repertoire. We now summarize the specific RAT instances that are discussed in this book.

1. Help Desk System (HDS) (Section 7.3.1)
This is a good prototypical instance of a RAT category and it contains enough information to allow us to generalize it to other applications. We discuss the viewpoints and requirements of a number of stakeholder groups. Furthermore, we create a context diagram for HDS that is able to support stakeholder requirements and that can be used as a prototype for other applications in the same category.

2. Discrete manufacturing (Section 7.3.2)
This real-life problem discusses the process of trimming and forming computer chips once they have been manufactured. To this end, pallets of chips are loaded into a machine, the chips are trimmed and formed and finally unloaded. There is a clear tracking metaphor in this problem.

3. Tracking systems in financial risk management (Section 7.11)
This is a large system in general but there is a strong tracking element and this is modelled as a number of 'layered' RAT systems. One layer tracks real-time market data, the next layer tracks individual portfolios, while the highest-level layer tracks all portfolios in an organization.

4. Elevator Control System (Chapter 13)
We devote a chapter to this problem. We discuss how the RAT category is a good fit to this problem. We analyse the problem as three loosely coupled RAT instances, one for elevator reservation (by would-be passengers), the second for elevator utilization (by passengers) and finally a RAT system that is responsible for the actual scheduling and dispatching of physical elevators.

A thorough discussion of goals, processes, stakeholders and requirements is given in this chapter and we document these artefacts using the standard templates as discussed in Chapter 4.

5. Order Realization System (ORS) (Chapter 14)

This is a RAT instance that is embedded in a Lifecycle Model (LCM). We create the context diagram for ORS in order to reduce scope and risk. Furthermore, we show how to construct a PAC model for ORS and we integrate this model with the requirements and use cases. We also discover a number of critical classes in ORS and we document them using UML. Finally, we discuss how ORS should be designed and we place particular emphasis on database design and how the software components actually communicate.

6. Rent-a-machine (Section 10.3)

This is an application from the retail industry. We wish to track the whereabouts of a machine that is rented from a garden centre.

2.5 MANUFACTURING (MAN) SYSTEMS (CHAPTER 8)

This category defines applications where there is a clear idea of *creating* products and services. In general, a MAN instance creates a product from raw materials. This is the core process and its activities are:

- Process and check raw materials
- Convert raw materials to 'half-products'
- Package and dispatch half-products.

There is a clear idea of procuring raw materials, designing a product based on these materials and packaging the product for different kinds of customers. We are not interested in tracking the manufacturing process as such (this is done by a RAT system), nor in historical information concerning the product (this is done by a MIS system). We could say that a MAN is a MIS or a RAT without memory; in other words, we create a product but we have no historical data on it and we do not know how, when or by whom it was created. Of course, complementary RAT and MIS systems will be needed in real applications if we do wish to model these requirements.

The MAN category is needed by other applications because we must first create objects before we can do something with them.

1. Reference models in manufacturing domains (Section 8.2)

Models for manufacturing processes are well known in the literature. We use these models to describe and document the MAN category. We note that there are many flows in MAN systems, for example material, cost and information flows. We must model these flows.

2. Compiler construction (Section 8.3.1)
This is probably the prototypical MAN instance. Compiler models are well documented in the literature.

3. Graphics and CAD applications (Section 8.3.2)
These are applications that create entities that are then displayed on a screen. The raw input data is usually an ASCII or binary file that describes graphics objects.

4. Human memory models (Section 8.3.3)
These are models that describe how long-term memory works and how we remember events based on sensory perception. We see this problem as a MAN instance because we are interested in how long-term memory is created and stored.

5. Rent-a-machine (Section 10.3)
This is a lifecycle model and it has an 'embedded' MAN component. In this case we create a basic request object. This object will then be assigned to resources in an upstream RAT system.

6. Tracking plastic manufacturing processes (Section 16.3)
This is a lifecycle model and it has an 'embedded' MAN component. In this case we create a basic request object. This object will then be assigned to certain resources in an upstream RAT system.

We note that there are many similarities between this problem and Rent-a-machine; in the latter case we are tracking rented machines while in the former case we are tracking a customer request for a supply of processed plastic film.

2.6 ACCESS CONTROL SYSTEMS (ACS) (CHAPTER 9)

This class of applications includes security systems and systems where controlled access to valuable resources must be defined. These systems are well understood because there are many reference models for them. There are two main processes in ACS systems:

- Authorization: securely identifying principals
- Authentication: controlling which principals can execute which operations on which resources.

The main activities in the Authentication process are:

- Accept a request from a subject to gain access to an object
- Check whether access is allowed
- If successful, execute the request on behalf of the subject.

ACS systems are 'helper' systems for other applications because they realize requirements such as Security (a sub-characteristic of Functionality) and to a lesser extent Reliability.

1. The Reference Monitor model (Section 9.3.1)
This can be seen as the original model for this class of problems. We can learn a lot about ACS systems by looking at the model and its corresponding architecture. We have modified this model to suit an object-oriented context. In particular, we have mapped the architecture in the Reference Monitor model to a context diagram in ACS.

2. Security issues in Web applications (Section 9.10.1)
Here we give a short description of some modern versions of the Reference Monitor model from Section 9.3.1, including role-based access mechanisms that we conveniently document by an UML class diagram.

3. The proxy design pattern as a special ACS system (Section 9.10.2)
We subsume the well-known proxy pattern under the ACS banner. In particular, the different kinds of proxy as described in POSA 1996 are discussed in relation to the ISO 9126 quality characteristics.

4. Drink Vending Machine (Chapter 15)
A classic! This problem is discussed in many books on software development. We model the problem as an instance of ACS and we show how our solution compares well to the somewhat *ad hoc* approaches taken to analyse this problem. Just looking for the objects is no longer good enough!

2.7 LIFECYCLE AND COMPOSITE MODELS (CHAPTER 10)

The systems in this category have three components, namely a MAN instance, a RAT instance and a MIS instance. Lifecycle Models (LCM) are very important because most real-life applications are in fact composed of multiple lifecycle models.

Many reference models exist for this class of applications. These models have been standardized and institutionalized in mature disciplines such as retail, manufacturing, marketing and oil (where the author got the model).

1. Product lifecycle in general (Section 10.2)

This is a general discussion of the lifecycle model for any kind of product. The reader should consult technical marketing literature to understand just how organizations view this problem.

2. Rent-a-machine (Section 10.3)

This problem discusses the lifetime of a request from a customer to rent a machine at a garden centre. We sketch the core processes in this system as well as the context diagram and main activities in each subsystem. Special emphasis is paid to how customer-defined features (which are always a bit fuzzy) are mapped to more concrete requirements.

3. Order Processing System (OPS) (Chapter 14)

This is a large chapter that discusses a lifecycle model that tracks a request or order from the moment that it is created to when it is completed and archived. We concentrate on the structure of the subsystems and the different kinds of stakeholders that have their own specific viewpoints on the system.

4. Plastics extrusion (Chapter 16)

This chapter describe how we have applied the LCM to an industrial application, namely the production of plastic film. We pay attention to defining robust context diagrams and black-box interfaces between the systems and components in this problem. Some design topics are introduced to show the reader how the artefacts from the DDP map to design patterns. Special emphasis is paid to how user-defined features (which are always a bit fuzzy) are mapped to more concrete requirements.

3 Software lifecycle and Datasim Development Process (DDP)

'There should be as many types of house as there are types of people, and as many differentiations of the types as there are different people.'

Frank Lloyd Wright

3.1 INTRODUCTION AND OBJECTIVES

This chapter is a summary of the underlying software process that we use when developing applications using UML and domain architectures. We are really in the realms of project management and a full treatment is outside the scope of this book. The Datasim Development Process (DDP) is minimalist in the sense that we employ those artefacts in UML that we need for the task at hand. It can be seen as a competitor to the heavyweight Unified Process (UP) that is used for large UML projects. UP is fine if your organization is large and has a lot of resources to set up a UP-based application. In general, the author has found UP to be less suitable for many applications and organizations. This is not to say that the method or the organization is wrong. What we are saying is that the 'mix' is not optimal.

In this chapter we define and elaborate the concept of *software lifecycle* and how it relates to domain architectures. We have developed a software process called DDP (Datasim Development Process) that describes and documents this software lifecycle. DDP is a lightweight process in the sense that it can be used for software projects and does not introduce too much overhead. We see DDP as an alternative to the Rational Unified Process, RUP (see Kruchten 1999 for an introduction to RUP).

In general, a software system is born when a list of system needs and wants is drawn up. Then high-level features are transformed to more detailed specifications and eventually to a working system. This is the core process and we describe it as a network of related activities. Each activity produces artefacts based on input from other activities. In this chapter we document this process by describing what these activities are precisely, what the intermediate and final artefacts are and how domain architectures are related to them. This will be important when we document domain architectures and their instance systems in Parts II and III of this book, respectively. This chapter will give the rationale for why and how we have documented domain architectures.

Is it possible to use this book without using domain architectures? The answer is yes because we have developed a defined process that transforms high-level features into a set of UML artefacts. This chapter describes this process. We assume that the reader is conversant with UML.

This chapter discusses the following issues. In section 3.2 we give an overview of the software lifecycle in the DDP and the main activities and artefacts that we need to understand in order to appreciate the intent of domain architectures. In Section 3.3 we reduce the scope by focusing on that part of the software lifecycle that we discuss in detail in this book. Section 3.4 is an overview of high-level business modelling, while Section 3.5 discusses a defined process for object-oriented analysis (OOA) in UML.

3.2 THE SOFTWARE LIFECYCLE

In this section we take a high-level view of the software process by viewing it as a workflow system. The process is shown in Figure 3.1 as a UML activity diagram.

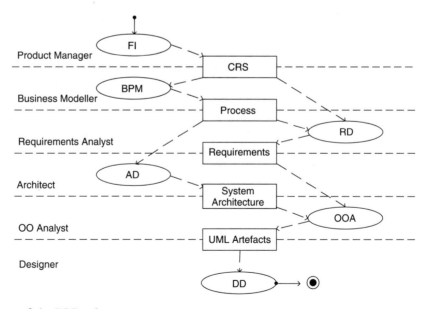

Figure 3.1   DDP software process.

The process has a Customer Requirements Specification (CRS) as input and a set of analysis products (documented as UML diagrams) as output. In general, the CRS contains a list of features that the system should provide and the analysis products include artefacts such as UML class diagrams, interaction diagrams, statechart diagrams and activity diagrams that describe the conceptual design of the system. The main activities are:

- Feature Identification (FI)
- Business Processes Modelling (BPM)
- Requirements Determination (RD)
- Architecture Discovery (AD)
- Object-Oriented Analysis (OOA)
- Detailed Design (DD).

Please note that this activity diagram does not include design, implementation or deployment. Furthermore, the precise details of each activity in Figure 3.1 do not concern us yet. The most important conclusion at this stage is that there are several activities that collaborate to create the final product.

The main responsibilities of each activity are:

- FI: Produce an initial list of system features and high-level requirements
- BPM: Find the goals and main business processes in the system
- RD: Find the system stakeholders, their viewpoints and requirements
- AD: Create a context diagram or 'super' system map
- OOA: Map the output of RD and AD to UML artefacts
- DD: Create design blueprints and patterns (outside the scope of this book).

The boxes in Figure 3.1 are in fact placeholders and they can be expanded to show their inner object structure.

3.3 REDUCING THE SCOPE

It is not possible or desirable to discuss all the activities from Figure 3.1 in a book of this size. We list the activities again and we state to what extent they are discussed in this book:

- FI: Not discussed in any great detail
- BPM: Very important in this book
- RD: Main concepts explained: integrated into the software process
- AD: Very important in this book
- OOA: Main concepts explained: integrated into the software process
- DD: Not discussed in this book.

We thus see that the focus is on structural and functional elements; for example, in BPM we concentrate on scoping the system by determining what its neighbouring systems are and we also describe how information flows between the systems. Furthermore, the products from BPM will be elaborated and sharpened in AD and it is in this latter phase that we lay the foundation for an object-oriented analysis. Of course, we must also pay attention to requirements if we wish to model the behaviour in the system. Much has been written on the subject of behavioural modelling for object-oriented systems. We content ourselves by using known results and then aligning them with our architectural models. This is not a book on requirements determination although we use the results of other authors (see, for example, Sommerville and Sawyer 1997).

We give a number of definitions in order to make things as unambiguous as possible.

Definition 3.1: *Software development process*. This is a set of procedures, policies and patterns that a software architect or analyst uses to produce software artefacts.

Referring to Figure 3.1, the current software development process creates UML artefacts (paper models of a given problem) based on the Customer Requirements Specification (CRS) (see below). Thus, the input to the software process is a CRS and the delivered product must be UML artefacts. The process has a number of major activities and produces several intermediate artefacts that are of interest to various (developer) stakeholder groups.

We first define the work products in Figure 3.1 and then the activities that use these products.

Definition 3.2: *Customer Requirements Specification (CRS)*. This is a description of the main features that the system to be developed should have. Normally, the product manager creates a CRS document after initial discussions with the customer and the sponsor of the software project.

Feature Identification (FI) is the activity that maps the experience of initial customer interviews to a CRS. A discussion of this activity is outside the scope of this book.

Definition 3.3: *Processes*. A process (or business process) is a set of activities that achieve a specific result for a given stakeholder group. There are three main types of process: first, a *core process* produces results for stakeholders external to the system; second, a *supporting process* produces results that are visible to internal stakeholders; and finally a *management process* is an enabler for core and supporting process. It does not produce tangible results as such but it provides the 'go/nogo' for these other processes. Business process modellers are responsible for creating the Process artefacts.

Business Process Modelling (BPM) is the activity that maps a CRS to the artefacts in the Processes product.

Definition 3.4: *Requirements*. A requirement is a statement of some capability that the system must deliver without actually stating how to achieve it. It can also be a capability needed by the user to solve a problem to achieve an objective. Finally, a requirement can be a capability that must be possessed by the system in order to satisfy a contract, standard, specification or other formally imposed documentation.

The Requirements artefacts consist of a description of all the stakeholders, viewpoints, requirements and use cases in the system. Requirements Determination (RD) is the activity that maps the CRS and Processes artefacts to Requirements artefacts.

Definition 3.5: *System architecture*. This is a description of the structure of the system that realizes the core, supporting and management processes. Each process will be mapped to a system while the inter-process relationships will be mapped to logical connectors and interfaces between the corresponding systems.

Architecture Discovery (AD) is the activity that maps the Processes artefacts to the System Architecture artefacts.

Definition 3.6: *UML artefacts*. These are the end products of the work in this book. They contain enough detail to be used as input to a Detailed Design (DD) activity.

Object-Oriented Analysis (OOA) is the activity that maps Systems Architecture and Requirements artefacts to UML artefacts.

We now list those stakeholders that are involved with each activity in Figure 3.1. It is important to note that these stakeholders are roles; a person can play different, multiple roles at any given moment in time and a role can be played by different persons:

- Product manager (PM): create a CRS
- Business modeller (BM): create Processes from a CRS
- Requirements Analyst (RA): create Requirements from Processes and CRS
- Software Architect (SA): create System Architecture from Processes
- Object Analyst (OA): create UML artefacts from Systems Architecture and Processes.

We summarize the software lifecycle by showing two concept maps for the high-level activities and detailed activities that we are concerned with in Figures 3.2 and 3.3, respectively. In general, a concept map is a kind of semantic network that depicts concepts in a given domain as nodes while the edges connecting the nodes are structural relationships such as generalization/specialization, association and aggregation. A good introduction to concept maps and the concept mapping process is given in Novak and Gowin 1985. The present author used concept maps in the past as a simpler variant of UML and OMT class diagrams (see Duffy 1995).

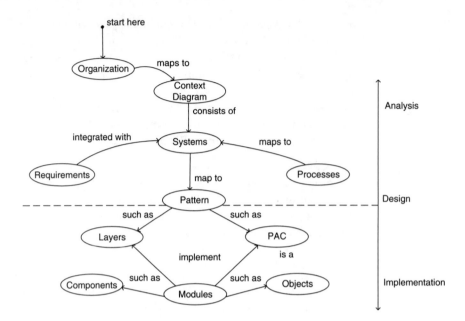

Figure 3.2 Concept map for structural artefacts.

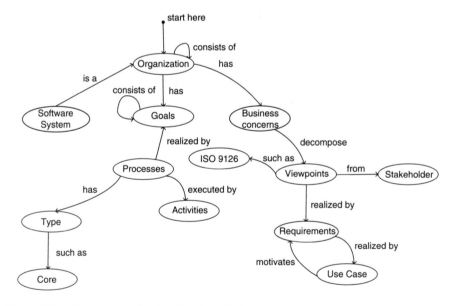

Figure 3.3 Concept map for functional artefacts.

3.4 THE REQUIREMENTS/ARCHITECTURE PHASE IN DETAIL

Figure 3.4 shows the activity diagram for the Requirements process. It consists of three activities. First, Registration transforms the CRS into a super-system map that contains the systems corresponding to the core, supporting and management processes. We must discover and document the viewpoints in a given system. These are then aligned in activity Assignment with the systems already found. Finally, activity Presentation transforms these aligned systems to use cases in UML.

A more detailed view of this activity diagram is given in Figure 3.5 and shows the steps and intermediate products in the core process:

1. Use the CRS to determine the goals in the system.
2. Each goal is realized by several core processes.
3. Map each core process to a system. Decompose each system into its subsystems.
4. Use the CRS to determine the viewpoints in the system.
5. Determine stakeholders and viewpoints.
6. Map viewpoints to requirements. For example, we can discover requirements using the questions in the Inquiry Cycle model (see Appendix 1).
7. A given requirement is realized by several use cases.

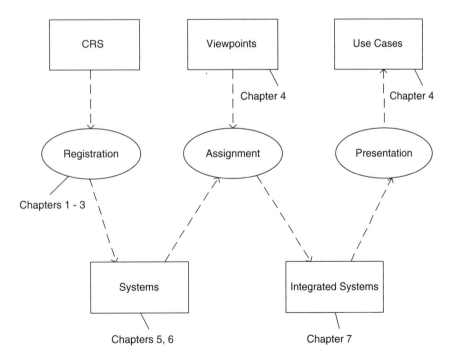

Figure 3.4   Activity diagram for requirements phase.

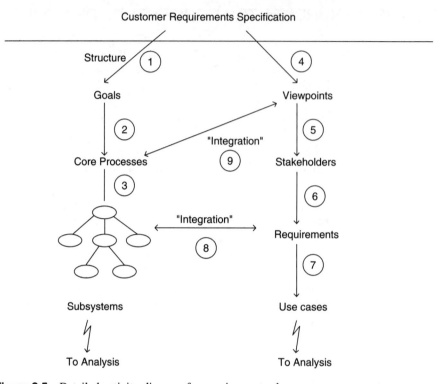

Figure 3.5 Detailed activity diagram for requirements phase.

The next two steps are optional. Both steps are concerned with the alignment of structure and functionality, albeit at different levels:

8. Align viewpoints and core processes. This is an N:N relationship in general.
9. Align requirements and (sub) systems. The ideal multiplicity between requirements and (sub) systems is N:1 because this tactic promotes loose coupling between the systems.

The postcondition is that all requirements artefacts have been created. We can now begin with analysis.

   We have described steps 1–9 above in a sequential fashion. We hasten to add that you do not have to execute them in the given order. You may skip certain activities if they do not add enough value to the artefacts.

3.5 THE OBJECT-ORIENTED ANALYSIS PROCESS

Figure 3.6 shows the activity diagram for the Analysis phase. It consists of three activities. First, Registration transforms the systems corresponding to the core,

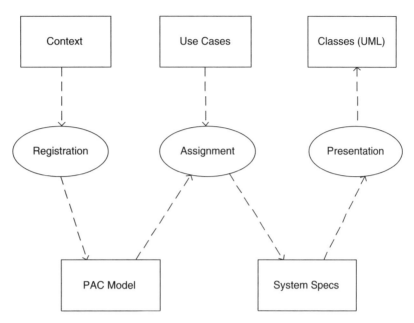

Figure 3.6   Activity diagram for analysis phase.

supporting and management processes to several Presentation–Abstraction–Control
(PAC) models (for more on PAC, see Appendix 2). These models are then aligned in
activity Assignment with the use cases already found. Finally, activity Presentation
transforms the system specifications to classes, class relationships and statecharts.

A more detailed view of this activity diagram is given in Figure 3.7 and shows
the steps and intermediate products in the core process:

1. The high-level system architecture (the context) is mapped to one or more
   detailed architectural models (for example, PAC model or a Layers pattern).
   We may be able to discover some candidates for Boundary, Entity and Control
   classes here. Life is easier if you are able to categorize the systems in the context
   diagram as instances of one or more domain architectures. (This latter activity is
   an optimization step.)
2. We map each use case to sequence diagrams. The participating objects are found
   from step 1. In general, look for the nouns in the use case text as these will
   be candidates for classes. For example, you could use concept-mapping techniques here (see Duffy 1995). Sequence diagrams may also lead to new objects
   and classes.
3. We create a 'precise' UML model using aggregation, association and generalization relationships. Care must be taken with validation efforts, in particular
   checking the consistency of classes and sequence diagrams.

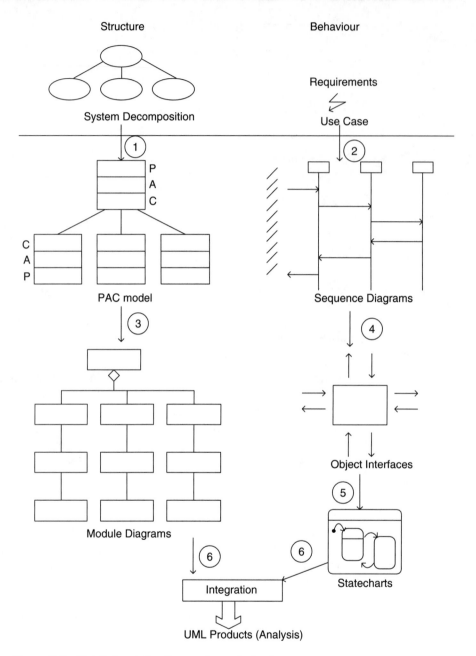

Figure 3.7 Detailed activity diagram for analysis phase.

4. Find the input and output messages for each object from the sequence diagrams in which this object plays a role. A possible optimization step is to standardize message names and to define object interfaces using already found interfaces and protocols. Collaboration diagrams are useful in this regard.

5. Create (nested) Harel statecharts for each object based on the input from step 4. (Harel charts represent and model an object's run-time attributes.) This is an optional step; it may be 'overkill' for certain types of applications.

6. Integrate the structural sub-processes. In particular, we discover object operations and the corresponding design-time and run-time attributes.

The postcondition is that all analysis artefacts (such as classes, their attributes and operations and inter-class relationships) have been created. We can now begin with design.

We have used the above process during training courses in order to integrate the different notations in UML into a coherent whole.

We have described steps 1–6 above in a sequential fashion. We hasten to add that you do not have to execute them in the given order. You may skip certain activities if they do not add enough value to the artefacts.

3.6 PROJECT CULTURES AND DDP

The DDP advocates an incremental approach to software development with domain architectures and UML playing the unifying roles. We shall discuss the risks involved in real-life projects. In particular, we introduce the concept of an organization's project style and how it relates to the artefacts in the various phases of the software lifecycle. For example, some styles are focused on documentation while others tend to be obsessed with performance. A good discussion can be found in Booch 1996 where five different project cultures have been identified:

- Calendar-driven
- Requirements-driven
- Documentation-driven
- Quality-driven
- Architecture-driven.

We discuss each of these styles in some detail in this section. First, we define what each style is and we give some possible reasons why organizations use such a style. Second, we describe what the consequences of using the style are.

3.6.1 Calendar-driven projects

Calendar-driven projects are projects that are driven by an obsessive focus on schedule. The development team moves from one milestone to the next and all decisions are based on short-term expediencies. Some organizations use this style in an attempt to satisfy the customer. The objective is to show the customer some new functionality. Little attention is paid to niceties such as process and product improvement, documentation and creating a stable architecture for future requirements enhancements. The consequences of using this approach are:

- It will not lead to a sustainable business solution.
- The long-term cost of ownership is (very) high.
- It has a high social cost (morale, burn-out).
- The project is driven by short-term expediencies.

It is advisable to look closely at projects that are managed in this way; in particular, the code that has been written should be retired and not given a lease of life longer than a year or two! Experience has shown that it is very difficult to maintain and extend such code. Remember the friendly hint: it takes a lot of money to create bad products!

3.6.2 Requirements-driven projects

This style is driven by the system requirements (or *features*, as they are sometimes called) and in particular by the system's outwardly observable behaviour. The focus is mainly on functional requirements (because they are observable) and in this respect non-functional requirements such as scalability, portability and maintainability (ISO 9126 characteristics) tend to be forgotten or given a low priority. All decisions are based on the local needs of each requirement and completeness is much more important than other issues such as schedule, for example. The project schedule is allowed to slip as long as the requirement is realized. This style may not be so bad for stable requirements or requirements that do not change. However, the style is highly sensitive to requirements perturbation effects; a slight change to a requirement may signal disaster for the stability of the system. The consequences of using this approach are:

- There is little motivation to deal with the ISO 9126 'ility' quality requirements.
- Lack of stable architecture: systems are built on shifting sand.
- Each requirement tends to be mapped to one or more physical components.
- It is unsuitable for problems with 'emerging' requirements (that is, requirements that arise when the project has already started).

A number of organizations have attempted to apply this style to object-oriented software systems (with disastrous results). Finally, it is not always possible to define at the outset of a project what all the system requirements are or will be; some emerge as we gain more insights into how the system really works. This is neither good nor bad. You cannot avoid or pretend that this eventuality will never happen by writing a watertight contract wherein all the requirements are embedded in cement.

Some features associated with this style are:

- Some developers believe that there is a 1:1 correspondence between a requirement and a user screen.
- This style does promote requirements traceability (this is advantageous).
- It is useful for disposable/throwaway applications.
- It is not for long-term projects.

Finally, it is surprising how many organizations still use this style. This may be for largely historical reasons, because many of those who create and document requirements had their training in the 1970s and 1980s.

3.6.3 Documentation-driven style

This is a common style that can be found in many organizations, for example government, defence and large commercial organizations. It can be seen as a degenerate form of the requirements-driven style and the focus is on producing documentation before the next deadline. The real work has to stop at some time before the deadline because it is at this time that developers have to down tools and get down to writing documentation! At this moment in the software development process there are more writers than programmers in the organization. The big challenge is to determine which documentation to produce next. This unhappy state of affairs is caused by management (who in general do not know and sometimes do not want to know what the software process is). They force programmers to produce documentation so that they can control the situation. Another misguided vision is that managers have been led to believe that CASE tools for UML are a must for every project because, as they have been told, CASE tools increase productivity, programmer happiness, and the general well-being of the organization. The consequences of using this approach are:

- Development work ceases when nearing a deadline.
- The customer never reads the document anyway!
- Documentation costs may be higher than the software costs.
- This style is a sign of management weakness and insecurity.

If your project is in this category, look out! On the other hand, writing documentation is good but it should not be the driver in the project.

3.6.4 Quality-driven style

This style has its own obsessions. In this case, the obsessions tend to be quantifiable measures for characteristics such as performance, reliability and security. Some examples are:

- Less than one second of down-time per year
- Mean time between failures (MTBF) is 100,000 years
- Five percent efficiency improvement
- Response time of five seconds.

The focus on these measures is poison for the other ISO 9126 characteristics such as portability, maintainability and scalability. In some cases it is absolutely essential that a project satisfies its quality requirements and measures. For example, there can be no compromise on human safety in an avionics software project. However, some developers are obsessed with performance in all cases. The consequences of using this approach are:

- The wrong things are sometimes optimized.
- Redirecting the system to a new focus may be extremely painful.
- All emphasis is on throughput.
- Understandability and changeability will suffer.

Some features of this style are that documentation is usually very prolific, applications are brittle and optimization is local, which is to say that some components are optimized while others are not. The style tends to lead to a conservative mindset; no changes or modifications will take place if they adversely affect the quality measures.

3.6.5 Architecture-driven style

This is a relatively mature form of project style. The focus is on creating a framework that satisfies all hard requirements and the requirements corresponding to the core processes. On the other hand, the framework should be resilient enough to accommodate new requirements. This style attempts to mitigate the shortcomings of the requirements-driven style. When compared to the calendar-driven style, the current style tends to optimize for the long term.

Completeness is addressed because users can experiment with different versions of the system; the style lends itself to incremental and iterative development. As Booch notes, 'completeness is in the mind of the end user', and we should not be surprised if new requirements emerge as time goes on. A useful tactic is to use the current style as a stable baseline structure that supports new system requirements. The consequences of using optimization in the long term are:

- Immediate time-to-market considerations can still be addressed (there is always an increment available).
- It supports the construction of adaptable frameworks.
- The frameworks are tuned to suit customer requirements.

We now discuss how to actually realize a stable architecture-driven style using domain architectures in combination with the Datasim Development Process.

3.6.6 Process-driven style and the DDP

It would seem that the architecture-driven style is the most stable and robust style for object-oriented development. But is it optimal and should it be replaced by more flexible solutions? Before we propose a solution, we examine a number of the (implicit) assumptions underlying the architecture-driven style. First of all, by 'architecture' we invariably mean the architecture as perceived by the software development team. It is not necessarily the way customers view their organization. It is common to hear IT people speak in terms of the following kinds of (software) architectures when referring to customer systems (Shaw and Garlan 1996):

- Layered architecture
- Blackboards and repositories
- ModelViewController architecture
- Client–server architecture
- Two-tier and three-tier models.

We must realize that these architectures describe the topology of the systems in the solution domain. There is no guarantee that this topology is flexible enough to support existing and future customer needs and wishes. The sad news, however, is that many software projects start their life when a senior developer proposes one or more of the above architectures and uses them as the 'driver' for all future development activities.

The two main risks associated with blind faith in software architectures are:

- There is no guarantee that the software architecture is a 'good' approximation of the problem architecture (traceability problem).
- The software architecture will need to change if the hard requirements change.

The first risk is caused by the development team's failure to align the software with the problem domain. In particular, an implicit assumption is that a plausible software architecture will probably be a good approximation to the current problem. We call this developer risk. The second risk has to do with so-called requirements volatility; this means that requirements can change. For example, our software architecture style was motivated by the vital hard requirements, but what happens to the architecture if any one of the following situations should occur?

- The hard requirement is no longer a requirement.
- The hard requirement is relaxed (for example, less stringent constraints).
- New and higher priority requirements need to be supported.
- The hard requirement becomes 'even more hard'.

Each of these scenarios can occur. The main source of risk in this case is the requirement itself. In general, requirements originate from a stakeholder and thus represent a specific view of the system. Creating an architecture based on requirements alone will lead to specific and brittle solutions. Processes, on the other hand, are more stable than requirements and less likely to change. This is because processes (especially core processes) are realizations of system goals and these tend to be less volatile than stakeholder-based requirements. The rate of change of a requirement is many times greater than the rate of change of processes or even goals.

We conclude this section with a summary of the advantages of choosing for a process-based business architecture:

- We have defined a strategy in this book to help us create process architectures for a wide range of problems (see, in particular, Parts II and III).
- Examining architectures from a process viewpoint leads to stable systems in general; creating architectures based on hard requirements will not necessarily lead to software systems that are future-proof. Even worse, this approach could lead to systems that do not realize core processes.
- There is a good chance that a smooth mapping can be found between the process architecture and its software equivalent. Traditional approaches tend to equate architecture with software architecture. An example of the latter is the original 4+1 View Model of Architecture (see Kruchten 1999). This model may have its uses but it is not suitable for modelling the business domain, in the author's opinion, for the simple reason that the vocabulary and jargon are different from what a customer is used to. One of the challenges for the Object Management Group, in the author's opinion, is to define domain architectures and software architectures, the differences between them and the mappings between them.

3.7 SUMMARY AND CONCLUSIONS

We have given an overview of the software lifecycle according to the Datasim Development Process (DDP). The main activities, artefacts and workflow are discussed. We pay special attention to the mapping of business processes to a stable architecture that is subsequently mapped to UML artefacts.

DDP is not really new but it is based on common sense, experience and a wish to make the software development process easier rather than more complicated. IT people sometimes have the tendency to make things more difficult than need be.

The DDP may be used either in conjunction with domain architecture descriptions and documentation or as a stand-alone process that we describe in a step-by-step fashion. We have created a lightweight and customizable process for object-oriented analysis.

One last remark: we have modelled the processes in Figures 3.4 and 3.6 as instances of the Resource Allocation and Tracking (RAT) domain architecture type. This is because we see software development as a tracking problem, in this case tracking the life of software artefacts as they progress from one software phase to the next.

4 Fundamental concepts and documentation issues

'Just the place for a Snark! I have said it twice.
That alone should encourage the crew.
Just the place for a Snark! I have said it thrice.
What I tell you three times is true.'

Lewis Carroll, *The Hunting of the Snark*

4.1 INTRODUCTION AND OBJECTIVES

This important chapter introduces a number of key concepts and definitions and also discusses how we document domain architectures and their instance systems. In particular, we introduce the following topics:

- The structure of a domain architecture description
- The ISO 9126 quality characteristics
- How to document architectural and analysis artefacts.

In short, this chapter lays the foundations for the other chapters in this book and should be read carefully. We have tried to be as clear and accurate as possible.

A UML model for the structure of a domain architecture is shown in Figure 4.1 while the ISO 9126 product quality taxonomy is shown in Figure 4.2. A nice project would be to write a database system that could store the different artefacts in these figures as well as the relationships between them. In this way we could generate documentation automatically (including chapters in books!).

Continuing, this chapter defines and documents the following key artefacts:

- Goals and core processes
- Stakeholders and viewpoints
- Requirements and how to document them
- Use cases and how to document them.

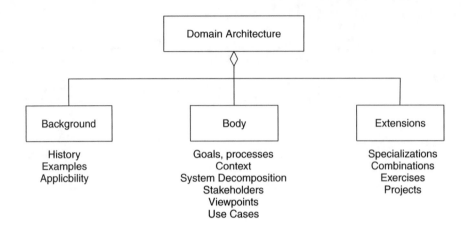

Figure 4.1   Documenting a domain architecture.

	MIS	PCS	RAT	MAN	ACS
Functionality	⊘	△	○	○	⊘
Reliability	○	⊘	△	○	△
Efficiency	○	⊘	○	⊘	○
Portability	○	⊘	○	○	○
Maintainability	○	○	○	○	○
Usability	⊘	○	○	△	○

⊘   Strong

○   Medium

△   Weak

Figure 4.2   Domain architectures and ISO 9126.

This chapter describes the rationale for the chapters in Part II (domain architectures) and Part III (specific applications). In particular, Part II introduces the five basic forms (MIS, PCS, RAT, MAN and ACS) as well as one composite type, the Lifecycle Model (LCM). Part III discusses a number of well-known problems. We base our style of documentation on how the design patterns movement document design and architectural patterns (GOF 1995, POSA 1996).

We give guidelines and templates to show how to document the artefacts in the DDP. The reader can use the results in this book in three different ways: by studying definitions (in this chapter), by examining classes of applications (Part II), and by delving into specific and detailed examples (Part III).

4.2 HOW WE DOCUMENT DOMAIN ARCHITECTURES

Chapters 5–10 describe and document the domain architectures in this book. Each chapter is structured in the same way in order to promote understandability. We structure the chapters in Part II using the following template structure:

Introduction and objectives: A general section that introduces the domain architecture and discusses its role in the software development process.

Background and history: This section discusses how the domain architecture was born, which reference models from other sources influenced it, and its relevance to object-oriented software development.

Motivational examples: In general we take two examples, one small and compact and the other larger in scope, in order to show the applicability of the model in a specific context. We give technical and administrative examples in general, although this distinction is rather artificial, in the author's opinion.

Reference models from the past for the given domain architecture: We draw on experience from the past as a source of inspiration. In particular, we use well-known models for process control, management information, manufacturing and access control to help us construct object-oriented models. This process is called *analogical reasoning*: comparing our current problem with a problem that we have already solved and documented. Successful models from the pre-OO era help us structure our domain architectures.

General applicability of the domain architecture: Having given a number of examples, we now need to describe the applicability of the domain architecture in general. We describe the situations where the architecture can be applied. The reader consults this section to determine whether the *checklist* questions and answers fit into her current problem.

Goals, processes and activities: This section describes the main reasons for the architecture, the objectives and goals. It also describes the main business processes that *realize* the goals. Finally, we apply UML activity diagrams to describe the information flow in the business processes. Emerging classes and class architecture can be discovered from these activity diagrams.

Context diagram and system decomposition: We describe the system under discussion (SUD) as a black box that is surrounded, as it were, by other systems that cooperate with it to ensure that its goals can be achieved. The discovery of the context diagram in real applications is very important because it is a foundation for the discovery of other artefacts such as stakeholders, viewpoints, requirements and contractual interfaces between SUD and its satellite systems. Furthermore, it is an indispensable tool for project managers and risk managers who must determine project size and risk. Once the context diagram has been found, we decompose the

SUD into subsystems using the information flow as criterion. Further decomposition inevitably leads to classes and objects.

Stakeholders, viewpoints and requirements: In this section we list the major stakeholder and actor groups who receive services from the SUD, deliver services to the SUD or collaborate with the SUD in some way. Once we have made an inventory of these groups we can then start thinking about their viewpoints and requirements. To this end, we consider the ISO 9126 characteristics and sub-characteristics as good candidates for viewpoint discovery: Functionality, Reliability, Usability, Efficiency, Maintainability and Portability. We note that five of these characteristics are non-functional and we address these up-front in the early stages of the software development lifecycle. Traditional object-oriented technology tends to focus on functional requirements; in particular, use cases take this approach. For example, how do you create a use case for an efficient system? To answer the question, one way is to *transform* non-functional requirements to functional requirements that are subsequently realized by use cases.

Use cases: We document those use cases corresponding to the core processes in the category. We use the standard use case template structure (see Section 4.9) whenever possible. We have not documented the use cases corresponding to supporting and management processes, although you should probably do so in real projects. There has been a lot of hype concerning use cases in the past. We see them as useful tools for making requirements more explicit.

UML class architecture: In general, we employ the Presentation–Abstraction–Control (PAC) pattern to help us decompose the SUD into loosely coupled classes and objects. PAC is not the only model that we could have used and there are other candidates. We identify Boundary, Entity and Control classes.

Specializations of the domain architecture: This short section gives some examples of special sub-categories of the domain architecture. A general classification is an open problem at the moment of writing. In general, we specialize a domain architecture to produce 'real' systems as discussed in Chapters 11–16.

Using the domain architecture with other systems: Enterprise systems are usually a network of interconnected systems, each system being an instance of one or more domain architecture types. In this section we give some clues as to how the domain architecture under discussion fits into such a network.

4.3 CHARACTERISTICS OF ISO 9126 AND ITS RELATIONSHIP WITH DOMAIN ARCHITECTURES

We wish to model system behaviour at a higher level of abstraction than is possible with use cases and UML actors. To this end, *viewpoint-oriented requirements analysis* is a suitable solution to the problem. A viewpoint is a perspective taken by a group of stakeholders. Discovering viewpoints and stakeholders can be a time-consuming task and we may run the risk of overlooking vital stakeholders and viewpoints. There is some hope if we can identify a set of *standard* viewpoints that can be applied in each new project. To this end, we propose the ISO 9126 as a candidate.

The ISO 9126 standard (see Kitchenham and Pfleeger 1996) is a description of a set of characteristics that measures the quality of software products. It consists of six orthogonal quality characteristics that describe how good a product is. We discuss them because they are very useful in all phases of the software development lifecycle (in particular, business modelling and even during design) and not just in the more solution-dependent stages such as design, coding and maintenance. In fact, many managers think in terms of these characteristics, albeit implicitly. The relevance of ISO 9126 to this chapter is that it can be used as 'testers' or attention grabbers to determine whether they are possible candidates for goals, viewpoints and requirements. Furthermore, each characteristic has several sub-characteristics. The six characteristics are:

- Functionality
- Reliability
- Usability
- Efficiency
- Maintainability
- Portability

Functionality refers to the capability of a system (in fact, the software that implements the system) to satisfy user needs. These needs may be explicitly stated but they can also be implicit. This characteristic has five sub-characteristics:

- *Suitability*: has to do with functions for specified tasks and their appropriateness for their tasks.
- *Accuracy*: has to do with the problem of producing correct and agreed results or the agreed effect.
- *Interoperability*: has to do with the ability to interact with other systems. An important proviso is that the systems are predefined.
- *Compliance*: refers to whether the system adheres to standards and conventions such as regulations, domain-related standards and the law.
- *Security*: has to do with the ability of the system to prevent unauthorized access, whether it be deliberate or accidental.

Reliability is concerned with how a system maintains a given level of performance over some given period of time. We must also state the conditions under which the system performs. This characteristic has three sub-characteristics:

- *Maturity*: has to do with the frequency of failure in the system. Most failures are caused by so-called faults.

- *Fault tolerance*: refers to the ability of the system to maintain a specified level of performance. We must specify the duration of time for which that level is to be maintained. Disturbances compromise this level of performance. These disturbances are caused by software faults and bad interfaces, for example.
- *Recoverability*: refers to the capability to re-establish previous levels of performance. For example, we could consider the time and effort it takes to recover information and data after a system crash.

Usability refers to the effort that is needed in order to 'use' an application or system. Of course, there are many kinds of users of a system and each has a definition of usability. For example, there are both direct and indirect users of the system. It is important to define what developers, managers and users of the software mean by usability. This characteristic has three sub-characteristics:

- *Understandability*: the effort needed to recognize logical concepts and their applicability.
- *Learnability*: the effort needed to learn the application, for example how often the user manual is consulted.
- *Operability*: the effort for operation and operational control, for example backup and file management.

Efficiency refers to the level of performance and the amount of resources needed to achieve the performance. This characteristic has two sub-characteristics:

- *Time behaviour*: this is related to response and processing times.
- *Resource behaviour*: has to do with the amount of resources needed to perform functions. This sub-characteristic is also concerned with how long the resources are held while performing the functions.

Maintainability refers to the effort needed to make specified modifications. These modifications may include corrections, improvements or adaptation. In general, modifications are caused by changes in the environment and by changes to requirements and functionality. This characteristic has four sub-characteristics:

- *Analysability*: the effort needed for diagnosis or deficiency detection. We wish to detect the causes of failure in this case and to identify parts of the system requiring modification.
- *Changeability*: related to the effort that is needed for modification, fault removal or environmental change.
- *Stability*: the risk of unexpected effect of modification. This is the sub-characteristic that gives managers and project leaders nightmares. Traditional object-oriented software projects tend to suffer from this problem because of their

inherent bottom-up approach. The end-result is a tightly coupled set of object networks that *can* lead to huge maintenance problems.

- *Testability*: the effort that is needed to validate the modified software or the effort that is needed to test it.

Portability refers to the ability of software in a system to be transferred from one environment to another environment. This includes organizational, hardware and software environments. This characteristic has four sub-characteristics:

- *Adaptability*: the opportunity for adaptation of software to different specified environments. This implies that no other actions should be applied or changes made.
- *Installability*: the effort needed to install software in a specified environment.
- *Conformance*: whether software adheres to standards or conventions.
- *Replaceability*: the opportunity and effort of using software in place of other software in the same environment. This sub-characteristic may also include attributes of both installability and adaptability.

We give one example here of the interaction between ISO 9126 and domain architectures. We create a matrix comparing the characteristics and architectures. The entries in the rows and columns tell us that there is a weak (triangle), medium (circle) or strong relationship (filled circle). By this we mean that a given characteristic may or may not be important in a given category. For example, in Figure 4.2 we have placed a 'strong' relationship between the MIS category and Functionality because in MIS applications there is a default requirement for Suitability, Accuracy, Interoperability, Compliance and Security (of course, defaults may be overruled if they are not applicable in a particular situation). This observation is based on (the author's) experience with MIS systems but another reader may have different experiences. You can create and populate your own matrices. However, the advantage of actually filling in the matrix is that it forces us to define the relationships and we can thereafter defend our decisions. It also acts as a so-called 'attention director' and it helps you remain focused. Just deciding to think about it improves your understanding.

ISO 9126 is concerned mainly with product quality and should not be confused with the ISO 9001 and CMM standards that are primarily concerned with process quality. Having a good process does not necessarily mean that your product is good (or vice versa). Second, it is possible to quantify ISO 9126 in the sense that metrics can be selected to rate and assess the quality of a product. A metric in ISO 9126 leads to *rating levels* such as values that are acceptable or unacceptable. This topic is beyond the scope of this book but metrics are well established in the Quality Function Deployment (QFD) technique that is used in the automobile industry (for a good introduction to QFD, see Cohen 1995).

What comes after viewpoints? A viewpoint can be seen as a stakeholder's expectation concerning the system to be delivered. A requirement, on the other hand, is a concrete statement of what the system should do. For example, Security is a viewpoint taken by the system administrators in a computer environment, while a requirement could be that all users must enter a password when they log into a system. In general, we see that viewpoints are less tangible than requirements. We use the techniques in the Inquiry Cycle model (see Appendix 1) to *generate* requirements from viewpoints. In particular, we use the 'how to realize?' and 'what kinds of?' questions to deduce requirements from viewpoints.

Each chapter in Part II discusses stakeholder viewpoints based on ISO 9126.

4.4 DOCUMENTING HIGH-LEVEL ARTEFACTS

This book deals with the structural, functional and behavioural views in software development. We begin with business process modelling and end when we are in a position to document artefacts using UML notation.

When you read the chapters in Parts II and III you will notice that the artefacts are documented in a standard fashion. This documentation is in both textual and visual forms. In fact, a good way to learn how to document is to study the chapters in Parts II and III.

In the following sections we give pointers to several chapters in Part III where the reader can find more information.

4.5 GOALS AND CORE PROCESSES

A good source for these artefacts is Chapter 13 (Elevator Control System). Here we describe two major goals and the core processes that realize them. In general, the description of a goal artefact consists of the following fields:

- Name and ID of goal
- Short description
- Detailed description
- Value to the organization if the goal is realized
- In what sense is the goal strategic?
- Sub-goals
- The related system.

By filling in these fields you are forced to think hard about *why* you are developing a system and what the added value is to the organization.

We discover the business processes by applying the Inquiry Cycle model (Appendix 1), in particular the 'how to' and 'what kinds of' questions.

Having discovered a business process, we wish to eliminate any misunderstanding by 'framing the process' (as described in Sharp and McDermott 2001; incidentally, this book is an excellent introduction to workflow modelling). This means that we describe the process using a number of attributes. These are:

- The name of the process (using the verb–noun format)
- The event that initiates the process (including a description of input to the process)
- The products/services that the process delivers and the customer who benefits from these products and services
- Enumeration of between three and six activities that make up the process
- Actors and stakeholders who play a role in the process
- Related processes.

An optional addition is to include information on how the current process works and how it will be adapted in future releases:

- Assessment of current process performance (the 'As-Is' process)
- Performance objectives of the new process (the 'Should-Be' process).

In this book we describe a business process using the following fields:

- Name and ID of process
- Process category (core, supporting, management)
- Short description
- Detailed description
- Major input and output
- Related goals
- Processes that the current process depends on.

See Figure 4.3 for a meta model.

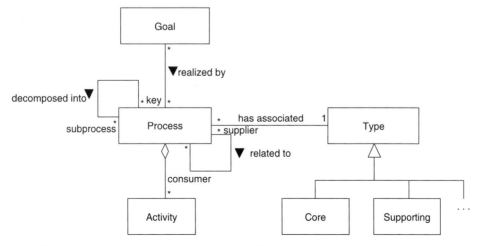

Figure 4.3   Generic model for goals, processes and activities.

4.6 SYSTEM CONTEXT

This is a visual representation of the system under discussion in relation to its satellite systems. This diagram is vital and we must create it as soon as possible in the software lifecycle. Each chapter in Parts II and III has one or more context diagrams.

4.7 STAKEHOLDERS AND VIEWPOINTS

Chapters 13 (Elevator Control System) and 14 (Order Processing System) are good sources for these artefacts.

In general, we describe a stakeholder as a human or non-human entity that directly or indirectly benefits from the fact that we are building a system. In other words, stakeholders can be the external systems that appear in context diagrams. When analysing systems we must take account of the fact that new stakeholders and stakeholder groups may need to be modelled in the future. A special subclass of stakeholders is the class of so-called actors; these are the stakeholders that directly interface with the current system. The Actor concept is standard in UML and has gained wide acceptance. However, we must remember that there are non-actor stakeholders whose requirements must be elicited and analysed, otherwise we will not have a complete system! A good example of a non-actor stakeholder is the law. Some examples of stakeholders are:

- End-users, managers and planners
- Engineers and domain experts
- Business processes and related documentation
- Customers, suppliers and external regulators
- Government regulations
- Physical and mathematical models and laws.

In general, we say that stakeholders are all those entities (human and non-human) that have to do with the processes and activities in the organization's supply and value chains. Furthermore, we model not only the external stakeholder groups but also the 'internal' groups of stakeholders who actually perform activities on behalf of external customers. For example, in an order processing system in a bank, we have stakeholders in the Front Office, Middle Office and Back Office departments (see Section 14.4). They also have requirements and they wish to interact with the current system in a particular way.

In order to manage complexity we group stakeholders into categories. How this is done will depend on the context. We find it useful to partition stakeholders into the following categories (see Sommerville and Sawyer 1997):

- Internal stakeholders (those people who work in the company)
- External stakeholders (external systems in context diagram)
- Domain stakeholders.

Having identified and classified the stakeholders for a system, we need to discover what services they receive from the current system or alternatively what services they offer it. To this end, we introduce the concept of a viewpoint. The use of viewpoints in requirements determination allows us to overcome some of the shortcomings that have been experienced in a number of projects. Viewpoints reflect the fact that there are many different ways of viewing a system. These views correspond to so-called perspectives. Each perspective represents a partial specification that describes what one particular stakeholder group expects from the system. Alternative synonyms for the viewpoints concept are:

- Interest in some aspect of the system
- Information processing entity
- Service recipients
- Formal partial specifications.

We can define viewpoint categories (see Sommerville and Sawyer 1997):

- Interactor viewpoint
- Stakeholder viewpoint
- Domain viewpoint.

An interactor viewpoint corresponds to the people and equipment that directly interact with the current system. In fact, these are external systems that play the roles of clients, servers or collaborators. These are essentially the actor systems in UML. A stakeholder viewpoint has to do with stakeholders that benefit from the system in some way. The benefit may be indirect and this type of viewpoint tends to be forgotten in some requirements determination approaches. Finally, domain stakeholders correspond to enterprise, organizational and domain information. Such viewpoints are applicable to multiple systems and correspond to constraints in many cases. Domain viewpoints lead to non-functional requirements and cannot be assigned to one particular stakeholder. Some examples of constraints are:

- Physical (for example, network performance, propagation time in optical cables)
- Human (e.g. average operator error rate)
- Laws (local, national and international)
- Regulations (e.g. traceable manufacturing process)
- Standards (e.g. the STEP interoperability standard for CAD/CAM systems).

These examples are specific instances of the ISO 9126 characteristics.

Why should we use viewpoints in the first place? For small systems it is probably not necessary to find viewpoints; in such cases, an *ad hoc* use case analysis may be sufficient. However, it is the author's opinion that viewpoints are necessary for enterprise systems if we wish to avoid 'use case explosion,' by which we mean that as a system evolves we are confronted with new use cases that must be integrated with the current system. In short, we use viewpoints for the following reasons:

- They present a view of one part of the system.
- They allow us to collect requirements from different perspectives.
- They aid in the structuring of requirements elicitation and analysis processes.
- They aid in the structuring and loose coupling of requirements descriptions (e.g. devoting one section or chapter to each viewpoint).
- They promote traceability (each viewpoint is associated with some stakeholder and each viewpoint is realized by several requirements).

See Figure 4.4 for a meta model.

4.7.1 Documenting viewpoints

It is important to describe each viewpoint as accurately as possible. We propose a standard template format consisting of the following fields (based on Sommerville and Sawyer 1997):

- The name of the viewpoint
- The focus of the viewpoint
- The associated business concerns and goals
- The corresponding requirements
- The source (where the viewpoint comes from).

We discuss what we mean by 'focus' (the other fields should be fairly obvious). The focus is an explicit statement of the scope of the viewpoint and represents its defining characteristics. No two viewpoints have the same focus but the foci may unfortunately overlap and this leads to inconsistency problems and can be an indication of potential requirements conflicts. Some examples of viewpoint focus are:

- User requirements
- Call charging and communication security imposed by a telecom regulator
- Electrical constraints imposed on system hardware components
- Safe transportation of goods and people (e.g. elevator in a building).

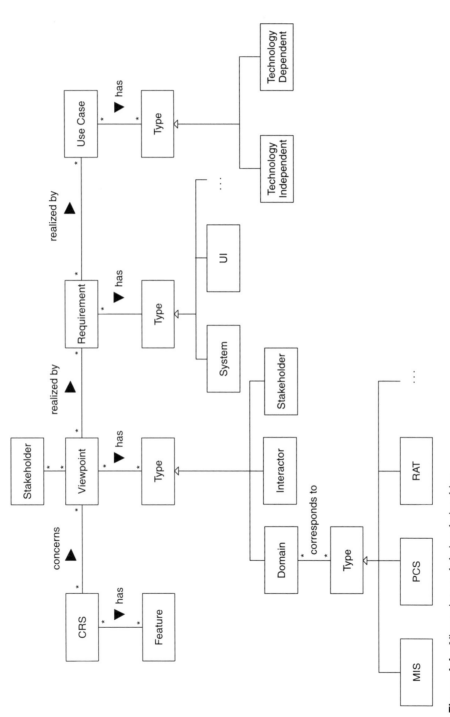

Figure 4.4 Viewpoints and their relationships.

4.8 DOCUMENTING REQUIREMENTS

Describing and documenting system requirements is an important part of the duties of a requirements analyst. In fact, each requirement will be mapped to more concrete entities such as use cases, sequence diagrams and service interfaces during the later stages of the software lifecycle. In this section we give a proposal for documenting requirements. The fields are placeholders that describe what the requirement is, why it is needed, what the risks are, and so on. The fields in the requirements description are:

- Name of the requirement and its unique ID
- Related viewpoints (each requirement is a realization or an 'actualization' of a viewpoint)
- Description of the requirement
- Rationale (why the requirement is needed, its reason for existence)
- Source of the requirement (which stakeholders wish to see the requirement implemented)
- Customer Importance Rating (how important it is for the customer to have this requirement implemented)
- Risk factor (how difficult—technically/politically—it is to introduce the requirement into the organization)
- Quantitative description of the requirement.

The last field (quantitative description) is especially useful for non-functional requirements (NFRs) and constraints. Examples of NFRs are:

- Response time of five seconds
- Efficiency improvement of 10%.

With NFRs you should always be specific; speak in numbers and the bottom line, as it were.

4.9 DEFINING AND DOCUMENTING USE CASES

We now review use cases.

A use case is a description of a single interaction session between a system and its external actor systems. A use case is initiated by an external event and the use case completes when the last event is sent to or received from an external system. It also describes the actions that are executed after the first event triggers and before the last event triggers.

Formalizing things a bit, we propose a template for use case descriptions. The fields in the template are:

- Use case name and ID
- The actors systems that are involved in the use case
- The preconditions
- A description of the use case in terms of the actions to be executed
- The exceptions to the normal sequence of actions
- The postconditions.

We shall see numerous examples of how the template is filled in later chapters. We have added two non-standard fields to the template because they improve trace-ability:

- The related requirement (a requirement is 'realized' by several use cases)
- The other concurrent activities that may be taking place while the use case is executing.

We give many examples of use cases in Part III.

4.10 SUMMARY AND CONCLUSIONS

We have given an overview of how we have documented domain architectures, their instance systems and the related artefacts. We have created a UML meta model for the different artefacts and their relationships in Figures 4.3 and 4.4. These diagrams could be used as input to a software system to manage the artefacts in these diagrams (for example, by analysing and designing the problems as multiple lifecycle models).

APPENDIX 4.1: A CRITICAL LOOK AT USE CASES

We give a short overview of some of the author's experiences with use cases. As often happens in many walks of life, short-term hype and high expectations about a new product or concept tend to be replaced by a more sober view in the medium and long term (remember Internet, .com hype and the Information Superhighway?). Use cases are no exception to this rule, in the author's opinion.

Viewing the world from the perspective of use case diagrams can engender the following work processes and assumptions:

- Actors are usually depicted as humans and stick-like figures (who interact with the system using graphical user interface objects such as dialog boxes). Of course, we can use *stereotypes* in UML to describe actors if the 'stick people' representation is not to your liking.

- Applying use cases by looking at low-level actors means that we can never be sure that all requirements have been discovered.
- The current approach is contrary to the concept of core process and multi-disciplinary workflow. Use case diagrams give no indication of how products and information actually flow.
- There are several non-standard extensions to use cases in the literature in order to model large and volatile systems. Current literature is vague on scaling use cases.
- Use cases are suitable for functional requirements (for example, 'create an order') but are of little use in their current form when we wish to model non-functional requirements, for example reliability, maintainability and usability. Of course, there are techniques for transforming non-functional requirements to functional requirements. For example, you could use the standard questions from the Inquiry Cycle model (see Appendix 1) to generate functional requirements. In particular, the 'how to' and 'what kinds of' questions are particularly useful in this regard.
- Use cases result in bottom-up work practices and habits if we don't watch out. The end-result is a web of tightly coupled classes in a system that becomes more and more difficult to modify and maintain as time goes by.
- Use case diagrams are not scalable and impart little useful information. The author prefers context diagrams because they are well established and in fact are better front-ends to UML than use case diagrams.

Although we are sceptical about the applicability and scalability of use cases in the early stages of the software lifecycle, they do have their uses. However, compared with requirements (which are general and always true), use cases view a system from a very specific and restricted perspective. We see their usefulness during the conceptual and detailed design phases, in particular:

- They are invaluable for software testers who can validate and verify against them.
- They can be mapped to objects and messages when we create UML sequence diagrams during conceptual design (object-oriented analysis).
- They can be used as a communication medium between developers and users/ sponsors if they are documented and presented in a decent way. This last remark implies that the use case should be documented in user terms and not in terms of how the developer is going to implement the use case.

PART II

Domain architectures (meta models)

5 Management Information Systems (MIS)

'The next process is the customer; never send defective parts to those in the following process.'

Kaoru Ishiwaza

5.1 INTRODUCTION AND OBJECTIVES

This chapter discusses applications that we group under the name Management Information Systems (MIS). This is a well-known reference model and has been used since the 1970s. All applications in this class collect low-level data from various sources and then consolidate the data to produce high-level reports and decision-support information.

If we had to state the essential characteristic of MIS we would state the following: the core process in all MIS applications is the production of high-level and accurate information that is presented to a given group of stakeholders.

A word of caution: the word 'management' refers to the general problem of managing information in some physical or simulated world. We do not suggest that the MIS category is applicable only to business or administrative applications. In fact, whether an application is an instance of MIS is determined more by the data itself than why or how the data was produced and which stakeholders are interested in that data. To this end, the examples in this chapter and in this book reflect both industrial and administrative Management Information Systems.

5.2 BACKGROUND AND HISTORY

We discuss MIS systems based on the traditional IT view from the 1970s. This view is the basis for an object-oriented solution in later sections. In general, a management information system (MIS) consists of the following components (see Figure 5.1):

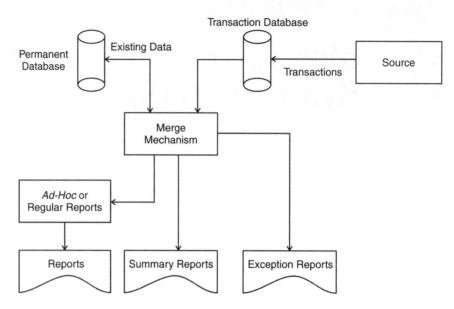

Figure 5.1 The components of a MIS.

- *Permanent Database*: this is the database of master and consolidated records that are updated on a periodic basis.
- *Transaction Database*: the database of 'transient' or transaction records.
- *Merge Mechanism*: a process for merging transaction records with master records. In general, transaction processing consists of matching transaction records against master records and merging, accumulating, replacing or deleting information from the permanent database. In general, we shall need algorithms to help us create master records.
- *Source*: the source containing 'raw' data that is transformed into transaction entities.
- A set of *human−computer interfaces* to enter and modify transaction data. These interfaces also allow users and user groups to create reports. Operational, tactical and strategic user interfaces will be created.

Referring to Figure 5.1 again, we note that the Transaction Database contains records that have been processed from Source. The incoming data from Source may be incomplete, incorrect or not relevant to the current system. This incorrect data is saved in a special error log database and exception reports will be created. The Permanent Database contains historical data and information pertaining to the organization as a whole. Data in this database has been aggregated at different 'levels' in the organization by the application of various merging algorithms. The Permanent Database is similar to a Data Warehouse that contains different kinds of corporate data. This data is usually highly structured and could play the role of source system for Decision Support Systems (DSS) and other data mining applications.

We can classify the data in MIS systems into three main groups, namely operational, tactical and strategic data. Operational data is created from the data entering the system from Source (in Figure 5.1) and is created, validated and modified by Front Office stakeholders (see Section 14.4). Tactical data, on the other hand, refers to data that is of interest to Middle Office stakeholders. Finally, strategic data is created from tactical data by applying aggregation rules and algorithms. This data is of interest to stakeholders such as planners, procurement officers and fund-raising departments.

We can discover requirements and use cases from these processes. In general, the most important business concerns are to maintain master records in the most current state and to retain historical information on transaction lifecycle.

An important activity for requirements and data analysts is to define and document the lifecycle of operational, tactical and strategic data and the relationships between the data. This is a topic to be addressed during requirements elicitation and requirements analysis.

5.3 MOTIVATIONAL EXAMPLES

In order to motivate what a MIS domain architecture is, we give two examples. The first (toy) example illustrates a number of concepts. It also helps the reader to understand MIS systems. The second example is large and complex and gives an indication of the possibilities in general.

We discuss a real-life administrative example in Chapter 11, namely resource tracking with the Manpower Control (MPC) system.

5.3.1 Simple Digital Watch (SDW)

This is a 'toy' example that can be generalized to non-trivial applications. We discuss a model for a digital watch system. When viewed as a black box, SDW receives pulses from an external clock. Pulses arrive every second. The time is displayed in hour:minute format, for example on a light-emitting diode (LED) device. It is possible to change the time by using two special buttons: the A button allows the user to switch modes and the B button increments hours or minutes. It is possible to define the type of watch, for example whether the watch is a 24-hour or a 12-hour watch.

SDW is an example of a MIS category because it displays information in a form that the user can understand. Furthermore, the user can take action based on the output that the SDW produces.

The core process is to display the current time in the current time zone. The time should be accurate. The main activities in the core process are:

- A1: Accept pulses, convert pulses to minutes
- A2: Add a new minute to the current time (using an algorithm)
- A3: Display the new current time.

We paraphrase the core process as follows:

When the SDW is turned on for the first time, the current time is initialized to 00:00 (midnight) and SDW starts accepting pulses (one pulse per second). When 60 pulses have been processed we know that a minute has elapsed. Then the first minute is added to the current time; the new time is 00:01. This time is then displayed on the light-emitting device (LED). The counter that represents the number of accepted pulses is then initialized to zero and the process starts all over again.

There are a number of supporting and management processes in the SDW system:

- Start SDW
- Set the time to a new value
- Change the time zone
- Choose a new display type (analogue instead of digital)
- Define special times and their associated actions (e.g. wake-up call)
- Use a stopwatch facility in SDW
- Shut down SDW
- Choose a 12-hour or 24-hour clock.

The reader might like to describe these processes using text and activity diagrams.

5.3.2 Instrumentation and control systems

This section is quite technical and may be skipped on a first reading. Strangely enough, however, understanding this problem helps us gain insights into other MIS systems. Nonetheless, it is a MIS instance because it has the same context, core process and activities, even though the jargon may be a bit strange for some readers who are not familiar with this specific domain.

The general situation is described as follows: a physical quantity from some device is converted to another form and then displayed on a recording device. We are thus in the domain of instrumentation and in this case we document problems in this domain by a three-block diagram as shown in Figure 5.2. This represents a measuring system. The functional elements are:

- Transducer
- Signal conditioner
- Recorder (or indicator)

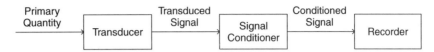

Figure 5.2   Block diagram of a basic measuring system.

Figure 5.3   Representation of a typical transducer.

The transducer is an energy converter. It receives the physical quantity being measured (sometimes called the measurand) and converts it into some other physical variable. In general a transducer can be further decomposed into a sensing element and a conversion or control element. An example is shown in Figure 5.3.

Most recorders have a transducing element as their input followed by some further signal processing. The recorder is the component that provides the results or products of the measurement. The difference between a recorder and a display is that the former produces a permanent record of the signal while the display unit does not.

The reader might like to consider whether this example is really a MIS instance by finding parallels between the entities (activities and objects) in Figure 5.1 and in this section. In this way we can determine whether the MIS category is a good fit for instrumentation and control systems.

5.4 GENERAL APPLICABILITY

The MIS category is applicable in situations where stakeholders are interested in receiving high-level information. This information represents filtered and consolidated data. Based on this data, it is possible to gain insights into how an organization is functioning and to make decisions.

We give a list of some keywords and special terms that arise when discussing MIS systems. As analyst, you should actively listen to customers and other stakeholders because the vocabulary that they use will give you hints on how to develop a system.

- Transaction data, consolidated/aggregated/merged data
- Master records, data warehouse
- Multi-dimensional data (data is seen as a point in N-dimensional space)
- Reporting options (*ad hoc*, periodic, summary, exceptional)
- Scheduled versus used resources
- Data mining and 'drilling' in the multi-dimensional database
- Capacity planning, trending, moving averages
- 'What-if' and sensitivity analysis scenarios.

This list can be used as a check to determine whether stakeholders use the above jargon and vocabulary.

5.5 GOALS, PROCESSES AND ACTIVITIES

The main goals and business concerns in this category are to provide (senior) management and other decision-makers with information concerning the status of resources in some physical or simulated environment. The information should be accurate and usable. The main core process produces this decision information by aggregating low-level, 'noisy' and possibly incorrect data from various sources. The main activities in the core process are:

- A1: Register and validate incoming data from different sources
- A2: Merge data into higher-level information
- A3: Report and present information to decision-makers.

The core process and its activities are shown in a 'combined' activity diagram in Figure 5.4. Each activity (Registration, Merging and Reporting) connects input to

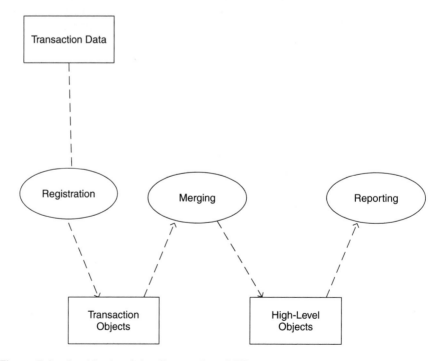

Figure 5.4   Combined activity diagram for a MIS.

output. Each rectangular box is a cohesive unit and contains objects. For the moment it suffices to describe each data type in Figure 5.4 as a one-liner:

- Transaction Data: noisy transaction data from various sources
- Transaction Objects: correct and validated transaction objects
- High-level Objects: merged, aggregated or consolidated data
- Decision-support Data: various presentations of consolidated data.

In general, these entities are documented as networks of classes where the nodes in the networks are classes and the node edges are modelled by association, aggregation and generalization relationships in UML. This is where traditional object-oriented analysis begins life: find the domain classes and application classes and create UML class diagrams using them.

5.6 CONTEXT DIAGRAM AND SYSTEM DECOMPOSITION

The context diagram for a MIS category is shown in Figure 5.5. The Transaction Database is the source of all primary input data. This data must be checked for completeness and against organizational rules (these rules are defined in the Organization system). Basic transaction objects are created from the transaction data. The DSS Systems (Sink) are the recipients of the high-level data and other information. These client systems use this information for capacity planning activities,

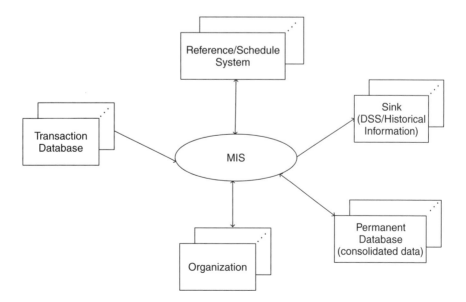

Figure 5.5 MIS environment (context diagram).

goal setting and statistical analyses. The Reference/Schedule System is a collaborator system that contains target (scheduled) values for each kind of transaction data that enters the system. This system advises MIS on what the scheduled values should be (it is usually a RAT instance in its own right because it is interested in resource allocation issues). The Permanent Database contains consolidated data for both actual and scheduled values. We sometimes use the synonym Data Warehouse instead of Permanent Database when it suits us. It contains multi-dimensional data. Finally, the Organization system classifies the data that enters the MIS system. For example, it has data models that describe the functional units and stakeholder groups in an organization and the relationships between them.

System decomposition in MIS is based on the activity diagram for the core process as in Figure 5.4. In this case we discover three main subsystems:

- *Registration*: accept and process transaction data
- *Merging*: create and store high-level data
- *Reporting*: presentation options.

The top-level MIS system is an aggregation containing these three subsystems. We summarize the responsibilities of the subsystems as follows.

The responsibilities of Registration are:

- Determine whether it is allowed to process transaction data
- Process transaction data (from different sources)
- Check for invalid data
- Create a log file of invalid data
- Operational reports.

The responsibilities of Merging are:

- Determine which transaction objects may be merged with the permanent database
- Merge, replace, delete information from the permanent database
- Create a log file of invalid information
- The facility to modify accumulated information (under access control restrictions)
- Reports (for example, medium-term and department-level status reports).

The responsibilities of Reporting are:

- Trending analysis using the Permanent Database (e.g. project post-mortems)
- Contingency planning: early warning of impending disasters or bottlenecks
- Decision-support functionality.

We now describe the information flow between MIS and its satellite systems as shown in Figure 5.5.

1. Accept and create transaction data.
2. Classify transaction data: create transaction objects.
3. Check transaction objects against schedules.
4. Update the permanent database system.
5. Notify interested clients that reporting is possible.
6. Create reports and decision-support information.

Each of the above flows has a sender and a receiver. We are not yet concerned with how or when these activities are realized. This will be discussed in Section 5.8 when we discuss the UML analysis classes.

A good way to visualize the above flow between the systems in the context diagram is by using collaboration and sequence diagrams.

5.7 STAKEHOLDERS, VIEWPOINTS AND REQUIREMENTS

In general, there are three main stakeholder groups. Each group has its own viewpoints and requirements. There is a close relationship between the context diagram and stakeholders because in general we can state that each stakeholder group is represented by a system. The three main stakeholder categories are:

- Operational group
- Tactical group
- Strategic group.

Each group has its own specific duties and activities. The responsibility of the Operational group is to process incoming transaction data. The Tactical group is responsible for defining threshold values and resource usage status. Finally, the Strategic group is responsible for the interpretation of the high-level output from the MIS system and for taking decisions based on that output.

Some specific stakeholders in the above categories are as follows.

- Operational group
  — Front-office data operators
  — Suppliers (where transaction data originates)
  — Customer liaison personnel and contacts
- Tactical group
  — Line managers
  — Department heads
  — 'Medium-term' planners (interested in events in coming weeks)
  — Business rules

- Strategic group
  — 'Long-term' planners, project leaders (interested in events in coming years)
  — Senior management
  — Customers
  — Shareholders.

Each stakeholder group has its own viewpoints. In particular, individual stakeholders in a given group will share the same viewpoints. We use the ISO 9126 characteristics as viewpoint candidates in the MIS category. We cannot say in general whether a given characteristic is important because each specific system is different and stakeholders may or may not find the characteristic important. However, we should examine each characteristic in turn and determine whether it is relevant to a given stakeholder. To this end, we could create an 'importance matrix' with rows representing stakeholders and columns representing the ISO 9126 characteristics (or their sub-characteristics). The matrix entries contain the level of importance of a given characteristic to a given stakeholder; normally, we use the QFD values high, medium or low. We give an example in Figure 5.6. The default values are for guidance only and you may find that they are not applicable in your particular situation. Cells containing no value indicate either that we are not sure whether the characteristic is relevant to a stakeholder or that it is definitely not relevant. In either case, the requirements analyst should clarify why no value was given. By all means, replace or modify the values in Figure 5.6 with your own values if it is appropriate for your specific application! We thus use Figure 5.6 as a guide during requirements analysis.

Having discovered the main viewpoints, we attempt to find the most important requirements and use cases in MIS systems. In general, those viewpoints that are most important for a given stakeholder group will lead to the high-priority requirements and eventually the architecturally important use cases. We can apply the Inquiry Cycle model questions to discover requirements from the viewpoints. Let us take an example from Figure 5.6, the viewpoint 'Reliability' as seen by the Operational group. The main questions and some answers are:

- What does Reliability mean for the Operational group?
  — That no data gets lost
  — That the program does not crash

	Functionality	Reliability	Usability	Efficiency	Maintainability	Portability
Operational	⊘	⊘	⊘	○	△	△
Tactical	○	○	○	△	△	○
Strategic	○	△	⊘	△	△	△

Figure 5.6   Stakeholder viewpoints.

— That we can recover from the consequences of incorrectly entered data (for example, using some kind of rollback operation)
- What kinds of Reliability?
  — Reliability of the MIS system environment in general
  — Reliability of transaction data
  — Reliability of communication with other systems and stakeholders
- How to achieve Reliability?
  — Save and restore procedures
  — Input validation and filtering
  — Standard communication protocols and formats.

Each answer is a potential requirement that should be elaborated by the requirements analyst during Requirements Elicitation. It is possible to discover more requirements by examining all the viewpoints for all stakeholder groups.

5.8 UML CLASSES

We describe the class architecture of MIS systems. The UML class diagram is shown in Figure 5.7. Each subsystem has three layers. We have attempted to standardize the names of the different layers. The most important names to standardize are the

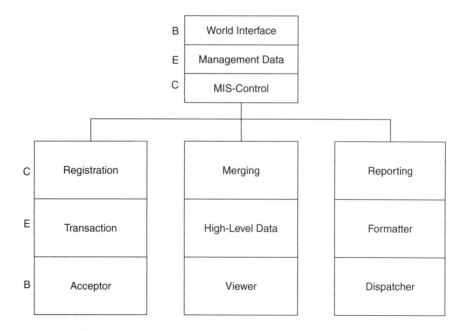

Figure 5.7   UML analysis classes for MIS.

Control and Boundary objects because these are the objects that communicate with other subsystems. We describe each of the layers in Figure 5.7, beginning with the Boundary layer. We distinguish between those Boundary objects that communicate with the server and collaborator systems on the one hand (namely Acceptor, Viewer and Dispatcher) and the Boundary objects in the World Interface layer that communicate with client systems of the current MIS system on the other hand. The responsibilities of the Boundary layers (including their relationships with the external stakeholder systems) are:

- Acceptor
    - Processes and filters incoming transaction data
    - Communicates with Transaction Database, Organization and Reference systems
    - Provides data to Transaction layer
    - Acknowledgements to Transaction Database
- Viewer
    - Provides UI functionality for consolidated lifecycle data
    - Communicates with Transaction Database, Organization and Reference systems (so that data can be consolidated)
- Dispatcher
    - Sends formatted consolidated data to external client systems
    - Some UI functionality to (pre)view consolidated data
- World Interface
    - Sends high-level formatted data to external client systems
    - User and remote interfaces for the presentation of high-level data.

There are four Entity layers in this problem. We distinguish between Entity classes that are specific to a subsystem (Transaction, High-Level Data and Formatter) and those objects in the top-level agent in Figure 5.7. The discovery and documentation of these objects (and the corresponding classes) belongs to the object-oriented analysis phase of the software lifecycle. We discuss this model in more detail in the case of a specific application in Chapter 11, namely the Manpower Control (MPC) system.

5.9 USE CASES

We have shown how to discover requirements in Section 5.7. Another application of the Inquiry Cycle model allows us to deduce use cases for MIS systems. For example, we can apply the 'how to', 'what kinds of' and 'what if' questions. Let us examine two requirements from Section 5.7, namely 'R1: Save and restore procedures' and 'R2: Input validation and filtering'. We recall that these were realizations of the Reliability viewpoint. The first requirement, R1, can be realized by several technology-independent use cases:

- Save transaction data to permanent store
- Restore transaction data from permanent store
- Save incomplete transaction data to permanent store
- Restore incomplete transaction from permanent store.

The second requirement, R2, has the following use case realizations:

- Filter out incomplete transaction data
- Validate transaction data
- Create transaction objects.

We can discover more use cases for all the requirements by applying the standard Inquiry Cycle model questions.

In general, it is possible to discover 'strategic' use cases for a system by asking ourselves how we would realize the core processes in a system. These are the so-called 'architecturally important use cases' (see Jacobson *et al* 1999 where this term is introduced). This form of serendipity is not just restricted to MIS applications but it is a pattern: each core process leads to a number of very important use cases. In the case of MIS, we have seen that the core process has to do with the production of decision-support information and that it has three main activities, namely Registration, Merging and Reporting. A dedicated use case realizes each activity. Furthermore, each use case is decomposed into more manageable and system-bound sub-use cases. For example, the use case 'Register Transaction Data' realizes the Registration activity and has sub-use cases:

- Accept and filter incoming transaction data
- Validate and create basic transaction entities (objects)
- Dispatch and notify clients of transaction entity creation.

These use cases can (and should) be documented using the standard use case template.

5.10 SPECIALIZATIONS OF MIS SYSTEMS

The MIS category models applications that process low-level data and transforms it into high-level decision information. Is it possible to refine the classification to get specializations of MIS? The answer is yes but we are still faced with the problem of how to cluster sets of applications into more specific MIS categories. Our suggestion at the moment of writing is to create MIS sub-categories based on major business domains, for example:

- C1: Telecommunications (e.g. call handling systems)
- C2: Financial Engineering (e.g. sell/hold/buy an option on stock)
- C3: Logistics, Marketing and Sales (e.g. report on sales of products)
- C4: Engineering of all kinds (e.g. Finite Element Method (FEM) and other simulation programs)
- C5: Resource, Project, Risk, Quality and Facility Management environments.

Of course, only parts of the above domains and applications in these domains that model high-level data will be MIS instances. Life is more complex than just hoping that you can cram everything into one system.

Chapter 11 deals with an instance system in the category MIS::C5, namely a system that monitors the resource usage in engineering projects. This is achieved by creating reports that show how used hours fare when compared with the initially scheduled hours.

The next subsection deals with an instance application in the MIS::C4 category. This is a simulation application that calculates noise levels in petrochemical plants and its main goal is to produce high-level decision information for health inspectors and local authorities.

5.10.1 Example: Noise control engineering

We give an example of a (somewhat) technical instance of a MIS category. We do this for two main reasons; first, to show that the MIS type can be applied to industrial and scientific applications, and second, to improve understandability of such applications by associating them with the defining characteristics of the MIS category.

We are interested in developing a software system that models the amount of noise produced in an industrial plant (for example, a chemical plant) consisting of motors, pumps, compressors and other noise-producing equipment. It is important to know what the noise levels will be in order to protect the hearing facility of site workers and those people who live and work in the vicinity of the industrial plant. Temporary loss of hearing sensitivity may occur if people are exposed to intense noise for a few hours. Recovery usually occurs after a sufficiently long rest. Even more seriously, it is possible that those exposed to intense occupational noise during the working day for a matter of years will not be able to recover before the next exposure. Permanent ear damage results and is indicated by dullness of hearing and tinnitus (a kind of high-pitched ringing in the ears).

The system to be built is called the Acoustics Data Lists (ADL) system and the main goal is to ensure the safety of those people who are in close proximity to the industrial plant. In particular, we wish to produce permanent reports and real-time displays depicting noise levels at the plant. The plant is partitioned into a number of units (for example, a boiler room) and each unit consists of specific equipment. This partition allows us to create reports at different levels. For example, we can determine what the noise levels are for the plant as a whole, while it is possible to execute 'what-if' scenarios by calculating the noise contribution of a specific unit in the plant. Speaking mathematically, we wish to calculate the sound power levels (SPL) of each piece of equipment. SPL is a measure of the sound pressure emanating from a source and impinging on the human ear. SPL values are measured in decibels (dB). Noise is caused by sound radiation and emanates from the surface of vibrating machines. The region close to a machine is called the near sound field, while further away from the machine (in the so-called far field) the contributions from the different sources coalesce smoothly; in this case the effect is to produce sound that seems to come from a single source.

Who are the stakeholders in this system? Obviously, the people who work or live in the vicinity of the industrial plant are the most important group. Their main viewpoint is safety and everything must be done to ensure that they do not suffer temporary or permanent ear damage. The other stakeholders are:

- The law/lawyers and doctors: all plants must subscribe to standard noise legislation. Failure to do so results in court cases, litigation tribunals and other legal proceedings.
- Noise engineers: engineers who are able to determine what the SPL levels are in a plant and how to reduce these levels.
- Architects, acoustic consultants and layout planners: specialists who design a plant.

Some important requirements in ADL are:

- SPL reports for plant, units and equipment
- Reduction of noise to a given level
- Prohibition of noise increase without consent
- Standards and certification
- 'What-if' scenarios and their related requirements; for example, what if a new piece of equipment is added to the plant?

We conclude this section with a discussion of the context for ADL. It is a specialization of the context diagram for a general MIS category as already shown in Figure 5.5. We discuss each external stakeholder system in turn. The Transaction Database in this case consists of multiple sound level meters. It consists of a microphone, amplifier and a meter. The microphone converts sound pressure waves into electrical voltage fluctuations that are amplified and that operate the meter. The

Schedule System describes the target noise level values. The Organization System contains the description of the physical entities in ADL, for example a plant consists of units and a unit consists of various pieces of equipment. It also contains information on operating characteristics for each piece of equipment. The Data Warehouse System contains multi-dimensional data pertaining to the system. For example, this system contains historical SPL data on each piece of equipment (for example, near field and far field regions). Finally, the Sink System is responsible for the presentation of SPL data in different formats. Each stakeholder group will have its own presentation requirements.

We have not discussed the precise mathematical details of the algorithms for the calculation of SPLs. These, however, correspond to the merging and conversion algorithms in the MIS category.

We now summarize how the context diagram in Figure 5.5 is specialized for the current problem by looking for the similarities between the ADL and its fitting by a MIS category:

- Transaction Database   ↔ Sound level meters
- Organization   ↔ Operating characteristics of physical equipment
- Permanent Database   ↔ Data for equipment usage
- Reference/Schedule   ↔ Target/acceptable noise levels
- Sink   ↔ SPL presentation information
- Algorithms   ↔ Algorithms that calculate noise levels

We see that fitting this problem to a MIS category is feasible. You can apply a similar form of analogical reasoning to your own applications.

For an introduction to the mathematics of acoustics and noise we refer the reader to Kinsler *et al* (1982) and Smith *et al* (1985).

5.11 USING MIS SYSTEMS WITH OTHER SYSTEMS

It is possible to build large systems by combining MIS instances and instances of other domain categories. This general statement must be made more precise. To this end, we discuss some possible scenarios:

- S1: MIS as a client, server or collaborator of some other system
- S2: Typical relationships between MIS and other domain architecture types
- S3: How viewpoints and requirements lead to new satellite systems.

Scenario S1 is concerned with the issue of linking a MIS system with some other system. We need to know why, when and how this linking takes place. The main reason for the linkage can be ascribed to three main relationships:

1. The MIS is a client of another system and receives its transaction data from it.
2. The MIS is a server system for some other system. For example, the Acoustics Data Lists system that we discussed in Section 5.10.1 is a MIS instance. We could define a new client system (of the PCS type) that 'listens' to ADL for noise levels above a certain threshold value and warns an operator if such a value has been exceeded. The operator can then take action by warning personnel at the plant, for example. Thus, the PCS system is a client of ADL.
3. A MIS system can act as a collaborator or reference system for other systems that need data and information from it. For example, a decision support system could consult a MIS system by tapping in on the consolidated data in the Data Warehouse System.

Scenario S2 has to do with some emerging patterns that arise when modelling large systems. Some general guidelines and patterns can be documented based on the author's current (and incomplete) knowledge. We give some typical examples:

- A PCS system sends data to a MIS system for trending and aggregation
- A MIS system sends 'escalation' data to a PCS system
- A RAT system sends tracking data for a resource or entity to a MIS system
- A MAN system produces transaction data and sends it to a MIS system
- An ACS system is a front-end system to a MIS system (authentication, security)
- MAN, RAT and MIS systems are aggregated to form a lifecycle category.

A good way to see how systems interoperate with a MIS system is to examine the latter system's context diagram. We should then ask ourselves the question: in which domain category does each satellite system in Figure 5.5 belong?

Scenario S3 deals with how viewpoints and requirements can lead to new satellite systems. Let us take an example to show what we mean. Suppose that senior management has the viewpoint 'Security' (in particular, the security of data and programs). To this end, they wish all access to the MIS system to be secure. Some users have read and write access to transaction data (the front office), others can view consolidated data (but may not modify it) while others (the 'super users') have full access to all data in the MIS system. Then, this viewpoint forces us to create one or more front-end ACS systems that users must log into before they can use the data and programs in the MIS system. In general, we use the ISO 9126 quality characteristics as good candidates for viewpoints and we give some indications on how new satellite systems emerge as soon as we demand that a MIS system should 'support' a given viewpoint. This viewpoint will generate new requirements. Some general rules *in the context of MIS* are:

- Functionality
  — Accurate algorithms for data consolidation

- — Ability of MIS system to interoperate with other systems
- — Front-end security systems to MIS system
- Reliability
  - — Recoverability from system crashes
  - — Ensuring that all consolidated data is stored and made persistent
  - — Fault-tolerant transaction processing; transaction rollback
- Efficiency
  - — New systems to monitor core processes
  - — Efficient algorithms
  - — Efficient data mining procedures and access to multi-dimensional data
  - — Throughput and performance measures
- Usability
  - — External systems have easy access to the MIS systems
  - — On-line help systems and repositories
  - — Ontologies (domain vocabularies) and knowledge bases
- Maintainability
  - — Ability to adapt to new customer requirements
  - — Ability to adapt to new types of data (operational, tactical and strategic)
- Portability
  - — Adapting the MIS system for new customers (e.g. monitoring disk space instead of used hours)
  - — Adapting the MIS system so that it works under Linux (as well as Windows).

The topics and issues in this section could form the basis for a more detailed discussion on how systems are formed, how they evolve and how new user requirements affect the stability of such systems.

5.12 SUMMARY AND CONCLUSIONS

We have discussed a class of applications that describes how low-level data is combined to produce meaningful decision-support information. This is for the benefit of those stakeholders who must make decisions concerning the progress in some business endeavour. The main focus is on producing high-level reports and presentations that show how a given plan or schedule is actually progressing; basically, MIS systems answer the question 'how well are we doing?'. It is hard to conceive of a problem domain (whether industrial or administrative) where MIS systems are not needed. Management Information Systems are ubiquitous.

A quick and efficient way to check whether your current application is an instance of MIS is if you can align your context diagrams and core processing with Figures 5.1, 5.4 and 5.5. In this way you can check your assumptions.

6 Process Control Systems (PCS)

'We have tried to demonstrate by these examples that it is almost always incorrect to begin the decomposition of a system into modules on the basis of a flowchart. We propose instead that one begins with a list of difficult design decisions or design decisions which are likely to change. Each module is then designed to hide such decisions from the others.'

David Parnas

6.1 INTRODUCTION AND OBJECTIVES

This chapter examines a class of applications that we group in the category of Process Control Systems (PCS). Such systems monitor and control the values of certain variables. Application areas include engineering and industrial control systems, control systems in the human body, management control, and modelling financial derivative products. The name of the category should not suggest that it is only applicable to technical applications.

This chapter describes the essential dimensions of process control systems. First, we give some examples to motivate the PCS category and we note that PCS is applicable not only to industrial systems but to any situation (real or virtual) where certain processes need to be monitored and controlled. Second, we discuss process control systems from the well-established viewpoint described in the engineering literature. Finally, we map this body of knowledge to a domain architecture.

This chapter develops a domain architecture that closely approximates the domain of process control applications. We shall show how to capture the essential elements in these applications by structural and behavioural models. We separate concerns by partitioning such problems into more manageable and simpler sub-problems. In particular, we decompose these into three major subject areas; first, the Delivery agent that is responsible for providing services; then, the Regulator agent that senses changes in the environment; and finally, the Control agent that is responsible for all interaction with humans and operators. We hide difficult and volatile design decisions in these agents and we ensure that the agents communicate via narrow interfaces. This approach is in keeping with the 'information hiding' principle: hide difficult design decisions in well-defined subsystems.

6.2 BACKGROUND AND HISTORY

Process control systems have been around for a long time. Many automated industrial systems implement some kind of process control mechanism. In the software process arena, we mention the early work of Hatley and Pirbhai (1988). This is a method for analysing real-time systems using structured analysis techniques. This has been successful in a number of projects but it lacks an Information Model, thus making it difficult to apply in a number of cases. The present author was influenced by the method in the early days of the object paradigm because many of his customers were making the paradigm shift from structured analysis to object technology (we give a short overview of the Hatley–Pirbhai method in Appendix 3 and how it has influenced the author's thinking). To this end, it was important to compare the two approaches in order to make the transition to objects easier. In fact, the Home Heating System (HHS) problem that we analyse in Chapter 12 was the first proof-of-concept application that the author used to show how the two approaches compare. The HHS problem is one of the problems in Hatley and Pirbhai (1988), although in the author's opinion it is not worked out in enough detail to be useful to the developer. The HHS problem is analysed in Chapter 12 according to the Datasim Development Process (DDP) and its solution can be used as a model for other applications in the same domain.

Thinking and talking about HHS and other applications in the same category eventually led us to discover a common theme running through them. In particular, we succeeded in constructing a generic model that subsumed HHS and other process control applications. Finally, we managed to construct a generic PAC model for process control applications after having studied the discussion of the PAC model (see Appendix 2 for an introduction to PAC).

6.3 MOTIVATIONAL EXAMPLES

We discuss three model problems to motivate process control systems. All three examples are concerned with monitoring the values of certain variables, for example water level, asset price, room temperature and so on. The values are scheduled or constrained in some way and to this end we speak of *actual* and *scheduled* values (we use codes AV and SV, respectively). Some examples of constraints are:

- AV should not be larger (smaller) than SV
- AV must be larger (smaller) than SV

- AV lies in an SV range, that is sv_low $\Leftarrow$ av $\Leftarrow$ sv_high
- AV must be a value in some SV sequence {sv1, sv2, ...}
- Some combination of the above constraints.

Once an actual value has broken its threshold value we are forced to take action in order to address this disturbance. To this end, we define actuators in the systems that are activated to bring the system back into equilibrium. Some examples of actuators are:

- Motors that produce warm water when the temperature in a room reaches a low value
- Turn off a pump when the water level in a tank reaches a high limit
- Turn on a pump when the water level reaches a low limit
- Inform the portfolio manager when a financial option ceases to have any value.

We discuss these examples in the next three subsections.

6.3.1 Simple water level control

This example is taken from Leveson (1995), pages 346–350. Let us consider a program to monitor and control the water levels in a tank, as shown in Figure 6.1. The water levels are called High (U) and Low (L). The objective is to ensure that the actual water level is always in the closed range [L, U]. The values L and U are called *setpoints* and they are configurable. The actual water level is measured by one or more sensors or other measuring devices. The tank is also coupled to pumps that drain water from the tank and that inject water into the tank.

In order to describe the workings of this model we document it using a statechart (see Harel and Politi 2000, Rumbaugh 1999). To this end, we view the tank as being in one of three mutually exclusive states at any one moment in time:

- LowLevel: the actual water level is below L
- HighLevel: the actual water level is beyond U
- OKLevel: the actual water level is in the range [L, U].

There are a number of major events that cause the tank to transition from one state to another state:

- A low reading occurs
- A high reading occurs
- Reading at setpoint I (level drops from HighLevel to OKLevel)
- Reading at setpoint II (level rises from LowLevel to OKLevel).

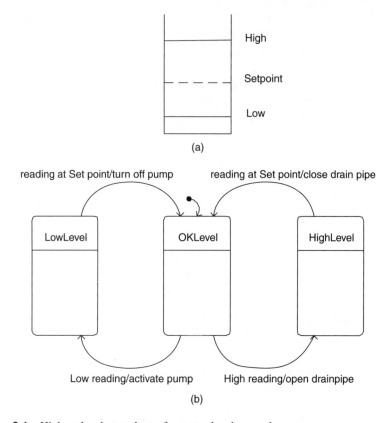

Figure 6.1 Highest-level statechart of a water level control.

Each of these events triggers a response. For example, if a low reading occurs
we must activate the pump so that it starts injecting water into the tank. The
responses are officially called actions and can be seen in Figure 6.1 because they
are closely associated with their corresponding transitions. The basic syntax is
<transition>/<action> in general as documented in the standard UML documen-
tation (see Rumbaugh 1999).

6.3.2 Bioreactor

This is similar to the previous example in the sense that we are modelling parameters
that have to do with a tank. In the current case we are interested in monitoring and
controlling the temperature of the liquid in the tank. The temperature should be
in a certain range [L, U] at all times. All setpoint values must be saved to disk
(flash memory in this case) if the operator changes them. Furthermore, if the actual
temperature (the so-called *process value*) changes and if the new value is above

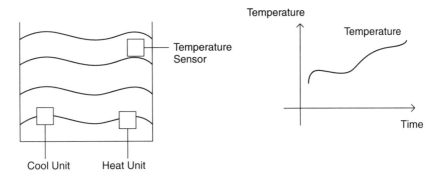

Figure 6.2   Model for bioreactor system.

or below the reference value, an actuator (cooling unit or heating unit) will be activated to restore equilibrium (see Figure 6.2). In general, real bioreactor systems model multi-parameter environments. Typical parameters are water level, oxygen concentration, pH level, flow rate and so on.

6.3.3 Barrier options

An option is a so-called financial derivative (see Hull 1993). There are two kinds of option. In the first, a *call* option gives the holder the right to buy the underlying asset by a certain date for a certain price. For example, an asset could be a share. A *put* option gives the holder the right to sell the underlying asset by a certain date for a certain price. The price in the contract is called the strike price or exercise price that we denote by X. The date in the contract is known as the expiry date, maturity or exercise date. American options can be exercised at any time up to maturity while European options can only be exercised at maturity.

There are two sides to every option contract. First, there is the investor who has taken the long position, by which we mean that he or she has bought the option. On the other hand we have the investor who has taken the short position, that is the person who has sold or written the contract. The writer of the option receives cash up-front but has potential liabilities later. To this end, we define the payoff as the amount of money to be made at maturity. In principle, the payoff is between zero and plus infinity for the long position while it is potentially minus infinity for the short position. This means that the writer is exposed.

The above option types are called plain or vanilla options. This is in contrast to so-called exotic options where the payoff is somewhat more complicated. Exotic options are designed to suit particular needs in the market. For example, barrier options are options where the payoff depends on whether the underlying asset's price reaches a certain level during a certain period of time before the expiry date (Haug 1998). Barrier options are the most popular of the exotic options. There are two kinds of barrier that are defined as a particular value of the underlying asset (whose value we denote by H):

- *In barrier*: this is reached when the asset price S hits the barrier H before maturity. In other words, if S never hits H before maturity then the payout is zero.
- *Out barrier*: this is similar to a plain option except that the option is knocked out or becomes worthless if the asset price S hits the barrier H before expiration.

A schematic representation of barrier options is given in Figure 6.3. Figure 6.3(c) is an example of a so-called double barrier option. This is an option that is knocked in or out if the underlying asset touches a lower boundary L or upper boundary U, prior to maturity.

Why do we consider the study of barrier options as falling under a process control category? We use this model because we are interested in exceptional situations (the so-called knock-out and knock-in events) and we are interested in tracking the value of the underlying asset price from the current time to the maturity time T (which is some time into the future). In general we are not interested in knowing the asset values if they remain within certain bounds. It is only when a barrier is reached that we need to carry out certain actions. To this end, we are really only interested in

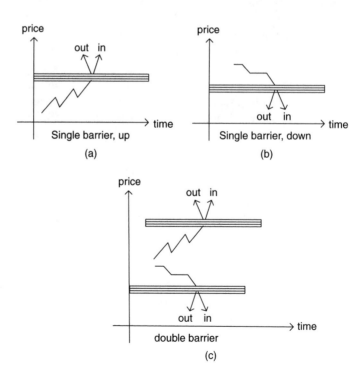

Figure 6.3 Options and barriers.

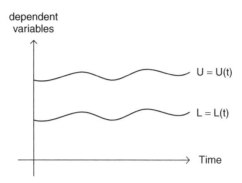

Figure 6.4 Time-dependent setpoint values.

exceptional data, whereas Management Information Systems (MIS) are interested in all kinds of data.

A second reason for choosing this example is to show that the realm of process control systems is not limited just to physical systems such as home heating systems and avionics control systems, but that instances of PCS arise in any world where 'actualized' data drifts too far away from 'scheduled' data. For example, we hope that asset price does not reach a barrier value, but if it does we must take action.

A remark: the three examples just given were based on constant values for U and L. In other words, we assumed that the values of U and L do not change with respect to time (they are called time-independent). This is a major simplification; in general U and L are actually functions of time, $U = U(t)$ and $L = L(t)$. In fact, these functions may even be discontinuous. A generic graph of these functions is given in Figure 6.4.

6.4 REFERENCE MODELS FOR PROCESS CONTROL SYSTEMS

This section is a technical introduction to the essentials of process control systems. We introduce the most important terms and concepts. Thus, this section can be seen as an overview of process control for those readers who are new to the subject.

6.4.1 Basic components and variables

A process control system consists of a set of components that work together to achieve a common objective or purpose. In this case we can identify four major types of components:

- Process
- Sensors

- Actuators
- Controller.

Before we discuss each of these components in more detail, we need to introduce the types of information or data in process control systems. In general, all variables are called process variables. Several specific kinds of process variable can be distinguished:

- Manipulated variables (reference values)
- Controlled variables (actual values)
- Input and output variables
- Setpoints.

A manipulated variable is one whose value may be changed by the controller. This is an analogue or digital device used to implement the so-called control function. This control function helps ensure that the system goals are achieved even though disturbances take place in the system. A controlled variable is a process variable that the system is intended to control. An input variable is a process variable that measures an input to the process. A special kind of input variable is the input to the system itself, while a special kind of output variable is the output from the system. Finally, a setpoint is the desired value for a controlled variable.

Having defined the types of variables in a process control system we are now in a position to discuss each of its components in more detail. The general setting is shown in Figure 6.5. The process is responsible for converting input materials (of various kinds) to products with specific properties by performing operations on the inputs and on intermediate products (see Shaw and Garlan 1996). The behaviour of the process is monitored through the controlled variables and controlled by the manipulated variables. In some cases it is possible to define a mathematical function that describes the process, but in general the process is highly non-linear and other techniques must be used to define the process. Typically, we employ linear and quadratic optimization techniques, fuzzy logic and generic algorithms techniques. Sensors monitor the actual behaviour of the process by measuring the controlled variables. Examples of sensors and their controlled variables are:

- A thermometer that measures the current temperature in a solvent in a bioreactor
- A temperature sensor that measures the current temperature in a room
- A barometric altimeter that measures aircraft altitude.

Actuators are devices that are used to manipulate the behaviour of the process. Actuators physically execute commands in order to change the manipulated variables. Examples of actuators and their corresponding manipulated variables are:

- A valve that controls the flow of fluid
- A physical unit that delivers hot or cold air.

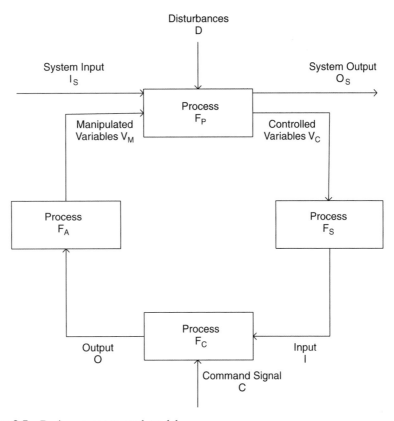

Figure 6.5 Basic process control model.

As already mentioned, the controller is an analogue or digital device that is used to implement the control function. The process is influenced by internal conditions, through the manipulated variables and by disturbances that are not subject to adjustment and control by the controller.

The general control problem (see Leveson and Heimdahl 1994) is to adjust the manipulated variables in order to achieve the system goals despite disturbances.

We summarize each of the above components and the relationships with variables by introducing some mathematical notation. We adopt the following symbols (as shown in Figure 6.5):

- I_S: input to the system
- O_S: output from the system
- D: disturbances
- t: time variable
- V_C: controlled variable
- V_M: manipulated variable

- I: output from the sensor (or input to the controller)
- O: output from the controller (or input to the actuators)
- C: commands to the controller.

The goal in a process control system is to maintain a particular relationship or function over time (t) between the system input (I_S) and system output (O_S) in the face of disturbances (D). We describe the process by the so-called process function that is defined by the mapping whose input is the vector (V_M, I_S, D, t) and whose output is (O_S, V_C). The other functions and their output are now described:

- Sensor function: (V_C, t) → I
- Actuator function: (O, t)   → V_M
- Controller function: (I, C, t) → O

One of the objectives in this chapter is to approximate the domain model in this chapter by the PCS domain architecture type.

6.4.2 Control engineering fundamentals

Many engineering and industrial systems include aspects of control systems at some point. This is the domain of control engineering and it can be broadly defined as being concerned with ensuring that systems behave in a desired way. This section may be skipped on a first reading without much loss in continuity.

We discuss the mechanics of how the process is actually realized. There are a number of possibilities, some of which we discuss (see, for example, Shaw and Garlan 1996, Pallu de la Barriere 1967):

- Open-loop system
- Closed-loop system
- Feedback control system
- Feedforward control system.

An open-loop system is one in which information about process variables is not used to adjust the system. There is one major entry point and one major exit point. A closed-loop system is one in which information about process variables is used to manipulate other process variables in order to compensate for variations in process variables and operating conditions. A feedback control system measures a controlled variable and this result is used to manipulate one or more other process variables. Finally, a feedforward control system has the property that some process variables are measured and anticipated disturbances are compensated for. However, the system does not wait for changes in the control variables to be visible.

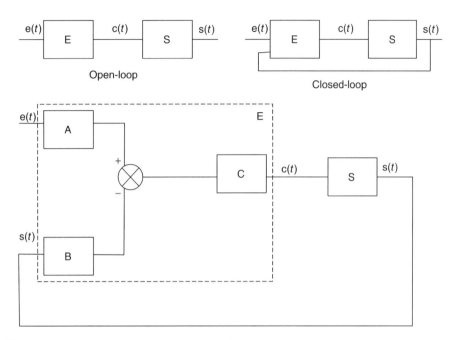

Figure 6.6 Types of control in process model.

Referring to Figure 6.6, we see that the system S has input denoted by $c(t)$ in all cases and output denoted by $s(t)$. Let us assume for the moment that we insert an 'upstream' system E whose output is $c(t)$ and suppose that $e(t)$ is a given quantity. We wish the system E to calculate or determine $c(t)$ so that $s(t)$ is as close as possible to $e(t)$ in some sense. For the open-loop case there is only one entry $e(t)$ to E. In the case of a closed-loop system, however, we see that E has inputs $e(t)$ and $s(t)$. In this latter case we say that it constitutes a servo system. In both cases E is called a control system and the quantity $c(t)$ is called the control.

A special case of a closed-loop system is that of an error-correction system as shown graphically in the third case in Figure 6.6. Consider the situation where two systems A and B have respective inputs $e(t)$ and $s(t)$. We compare their outputs by a so-called differential system and the difference is used as input to a third system C whose output is given by the function $c(t)$. Again, $c(t)$ is input to system S. We say that A is called the anticipation system, C is called the compensation system and B is called the feedback system.

A good example of a feedforward control system is to be found in the neural network literature (see Hecht-Nielson 1990). We give an example of a so-called linear associator. This is a system whose input is an n-dimensional vector **x**. The output is a vector **z** that is derived from the input vector by the formula

$$z = Wx$$

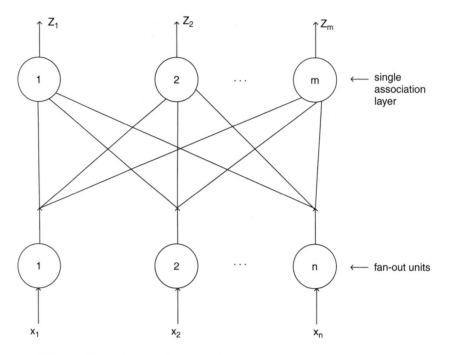

Figure 6.7 Feedforward associative network.

where $\mathbf{W}$ is an $m \times n$ weight matrix. Thus, each component of the vector $\mathbf{z}$ is a linear combination of the $\mathbf{x}$ input signals and the output vector is created in a single feedforward pass. This is shown in Figure 6.7.

Summarizing, feedback control uses information about the current state of the process in order to generate corrective actions; the process develops some undesired characteristics that must be corrected. Feedforward control, on the other hand, attempts to anticipate undesired changes in the process and then issues commands to prevent them. We shall see in this and later chapters how the above concepts are mapped to a domain architecture in which all the requirements have been realized. In this way we hope to align the software solution as closely as possible with the entities and requirements from the problem domain.

6.5 GENERAL APPLICABILITY

In general, we apply the PCS category in situations where we are interested in monitoring exceptional and possibly undesirable situations. We could say that 'no news is good news'; when some variable reaches a limit we must take corrective action. We give a list of some keywords and special terms that arise when discussing PCS systems. As analyst, you should actively listen to customers and other stakeholders because the vocabulary that they use will give hints on how to develop a system:

- Actuators, sensors, control panels
- Monitoring and control applications
- Monitored and control variables
- Setpoint values, process values
- Safety systems
- High reliability, availability and performance
- State machines
- Watchdog systems (themselves instances of the PCS category)
- Real-time and historical data; 'out-of-bounds' data
- Trending and capacity planning
- Security systems: monitoring unexpected and unusual behaviour
- Safety; alerts and alert procedures.

The PCS category is appropriate in organizations in the process control and embedded software worlds, for example. In a real enterprise application we should expect to discover several PCS instances that monitor and control various aspects of the application.

The categories PCS and MIS are not the same but they are closely related. MIS systems are concerned with comparing actual and scheduled values of a given variable irrespective of their values, whereas PCS systems are essentially only interested in situations where the actual values 'drift' too far away from the scheduled values. Furthermore, PCS systems can model real-time behaviour of single objects while MIS systems model past and present behaviour of clustered objects. Once the threshold value has been reached in PCS systems we must take corrective action by activating actuators. In general, the scheduled values needed in PCS systems are under the control of one or more RAT instance systems while the actual values could be created in MAN instances, for example.

6.6 GOALS, PROCESSES AND ACTIVITIES

We have seen that the goal of a process control system is to maintain a particular relationship or function over time between the input to the system and the output from the system in the face of disturbances in the process. These relationships involve fundamental chemical, thermal, mechanical, aerodynamic or other laws (Leveson and Heimdahl 1994). For example, in a Home Heating System the goal is to produce a feeling of well-being as experienced by the inhabitants of a house; the room temperature (and other parameters such as humidity) should not be too high or too low, but just right.

The distinction between goals and core processes can be confusing for software developers, especially for those who work in real-time and embedded environments. IT is important to discriminate between 'what', 'how' and 'when'. The goals in PCS systems correspond to 'what' (for example, keep the temperature at the right level) while the core process corresponds to 'how' (for example, burn fossil fuel). Finally, the 'when' issues correspond to events such as sensors sensing that the values of certain variables have changed. In order to avoid confusion we advocate the following steps in the analysis process:

- Determine the goals (what and why)
- Determine the core processes (how)
- Determine the events in the system (when; these will be modelled as use cases).

Having cleared up these misunderstandings, we now discuss the core processes in PCS systems. In general, core process P1 consists of three (essentially concurrent) activities:

- P1.1: Activate and start actuators
- P1.2: Monitor the status in the system: is there equilibrium?
- P1.3: Present the status to clients.

We shall see a concrete example of this in Chapter 12 where we analyse the Home Heating System (HHS).

6.7 CONTEXT DIAGRAM AND SYSTEM DECOMPOSITION

The generic context diagram for the PCS category is shown in Figure 6.8. The SUD and the stakeholder systems must cooperate to realize the goals, namely to ensure that a certain condition is valid at all times. The stakeholder systems in PCS systems are:

- *Environment (sensors)*: These systems monitor the actual behaviour of the process by measuring the controlled variables. Examples of sensors are thermometers, barometers and real-time data feeds.
- *Actuators*: These systems manipulate the behaviour of the process. The actuators physically execute commands issued by the controller in order to change the manipulated variables. Examples of actuators are valves, humans (who can modify the manipulated variables via a dialog box, for example), furnaces, solar panel and mass flow controllers.
- *Sink*: The ultimate recipients of status information concerning the process.

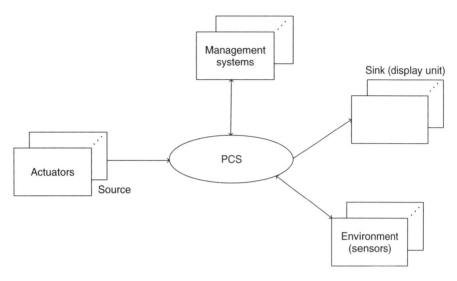

Figure 6.8 PCS environment.

- *MIS*: Management systems that monitor the current PCS system in some way. These are clients of PCS. Some responsibilities of these systems are:
  — Downloading setpoint and configuration data to PCS
  — Uploading real-time from PCS for historical and trending analysis
  — Monitoring exceptional and unusual behaviour in PCS and its hardware-based external systems.

We notice that the controller entity from the process control reference model is not present in Figure 6.8. We do not model it explicitly in this case, but tacitly assume that it is implemented in the SUD itself. This may be a restriction in practice and it may be necessary to include a new stakeholder system that delivers controller functionality.

6.7.1 Decomposition strategies

In order to decompose a system into loosely coupled subsystems we must determine what the primary input is. There are two candidate solutions and scenarios in general:

- Type 1: The input requests from users, operators and the environment
- Type 2: The raw materials input.

We must determine which input is primary and which type is secondary. Having determined the primary input and knowing what the system output is, we must determine how the former is transformed to the latter. This is achieved in the usual way by transforming the input to output in a series of steps and delegating the responsibilities to a number of subsystems. We can document the workflow using UML activity diagrams.

6.7.1.1 Workflow decomposition model

In the case of PCS applications that use raw materials as primary input we identify three subsystems as shown in Figure 6.9. First, Delivery is responsible for processing raw materials and transforming them into internal materials that are then distributed by Regulator. Regulator produces half-products that are subsequently packaged and presented to the appropriate stakeholder actors. Notice the names that we have chosen and the reasons why they have been chosen: Delivery is responsible for the transformation of raw materials (this is why it contains actuators), Regulator is responsible for the process and represents the 'brains' of the system (this is why it contains sensors that monitor changes in the environment), while Control contains operator panels that allow human actors to determine what the system is doing and when to start and stop it. In short, Delivery is responsible for operational activities (what has to be done), Regulator is responsible for tactical activities (how and why something has to be done) and Control is responsible for strategic activities (when something has to be done). We have already noted that primary input is through Delivery while secondary input is through Control and sometimes through Regulator.

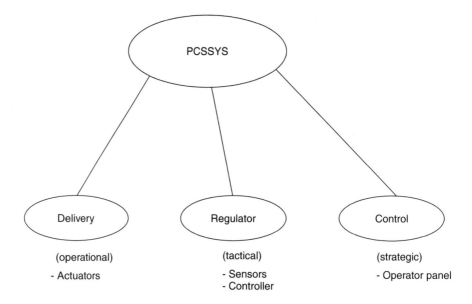

Figure 6.9   Initial system decomposition.

6.7.1.2 A 'tracking' decomposition model

The second choice for PCS applications is to model them as RAT systems as shown in Figure 6.10. In this case the primary input is a customer request and the output is the status of that request (for example, status can take the form of a finished product). The flow of information is more important in this case than raw material flow, which is why the model in Figure 6.10 is slightly different from the model in Figure 6.9 on a number of counts:

- The names and responsibilities of the subsystems
- The satellite systems communicating with the current system.

The model in Figure 6.10 is based on the way in which the customer request 'travels' in the system. First, subsystem Registration processes and validates the customer request in order to classify it. This classification problem is the responsibility of KnowledgeBase. Once the request has been checked and validated it is then admitted to the Assignment subsystem whose responsibility is to allocate physical resources that are needed to realize the customer request. The Assignment subsystem knows about the status of a request at all times and this fact can be dispatched to Presentation. We note that Assignment communicates with the satellite system ResourceAllocator whose responsibility is to allocate physical resources.

Summarizing, discovering subsystems by using a process or tracking model is acceptable as long as the responsibilities of each subsystem are well defined and if

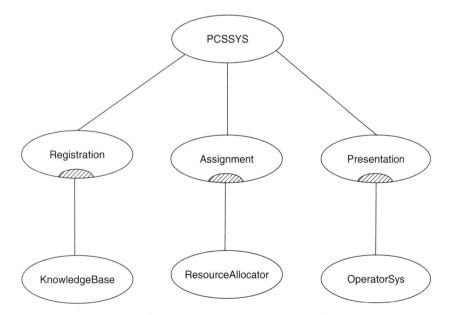

Figure 6.10 System decomposition based on RAT paradigm.

they hide difficult design decisions. However, you should choose the category that best fits the vocabulary and jargon of your current project.

6.7.1.3 Detailed decomposition and layering

Once the main subsystems have been identified (as in Figures 6.9 and 6.10) we must determine how each subsystem produces output from input. In this section we achieve this by three generic activities:

- Read and check input
- Create entities of interest
- Dispatch and notify.

Each subsystem is levelled into three layers and each layer is given the responsibility for one of the above activities. Reading and checking of external information is realized by so-called Boundary layers or objects as shown in Figure 6.11. The entities that contain the data of interest in the given subsystem live in the Entity layer while notification and dispatching to other subsystems is achieved in the Control layer. The general situation is shown in Figure 6.12 corresponding to an elaboration of the model in Figure 6.9. Notice that the subsystem names in Figure 6.9 have now been mapped to the control layer names in the elaborated model. The Boundary layer entities such as Actuators, Sensors and Panel are the components that communicate with external actors. The Entity layer objects are more difficult to find but in general they contain the static and dynamic data of interest in the system.

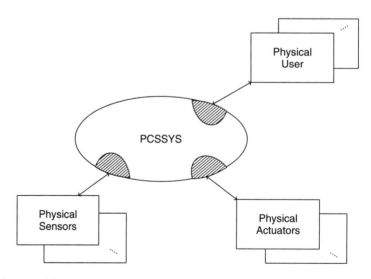

Figure 6.11 Initial context diagram.

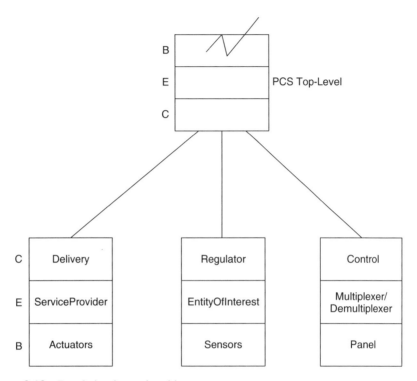

Figure 6.12   Populating layers by objects.

Referring to Figure 6.12, we note the following:

- ServiceProvider has knowledge of capacity in the subsystem. Capacity is closely related to load. Load is defined as the rate at which the system requests a particular service while capacity refers to the ability to handle the rate. We distinguish between two types of capacity. The rate at which sensors produce data and send it to the system is called the input capacity, while output capacity is defined as the rate at which actuators can accept and react to data from the system. We note that ServiceProvider is aware of both input and output capacity. Output overload occurs if sensors generate inputs at a faster rate than the output environments can 'absorb' process inputs (see Leveson 1995). We model load and capacity in UML by creating classes and class relationships.
- EntityOfInterest: the entity whose behaviour we wish to monitor and control. For example, in the Home Heating System (Chapter 12) this would be the Room abstraction (we wish the temperature to stay within given limits).
- Multiplexer/Demultiplexer: this layer is responsible for the translation and formatting of commands in both directions (operator actions translated to internal commands and translation of internal messages to display options on the operator panel).

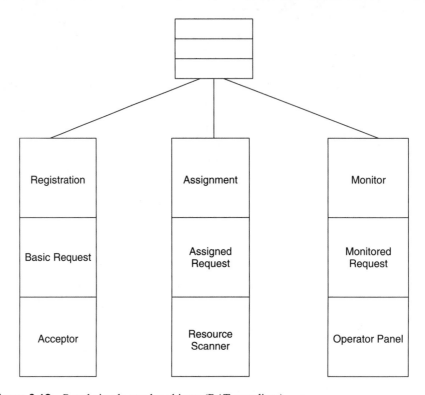

Figure 6.13   Populating layers by objects (RAT paradigm).

We now discuss system levelling in the case where we have chosen to model the problem using customer requests as primary input as already seen in Figure 6.10. In other words, we model the problem as a Resource Allocation and Tracking (RAT) instance system to determine how good the fit to reality is. The basic objective is to track the movements of a request in the system. The basic model is shown in Figure 6.13. Again, the control objects are 'free' because of the subsystem names in Figure 6.10, while the boundary objects can be discovered from Figure 6.10 by examining the external actor system. The entity layers are populated by a Request entity in different phases of its life.

6.8 STAKEHOLDERS, VIEWPOINTS AND REQUIREMENTS

The main stakeholders are found from the context diagram. They are:

- Actuators
- Sensors

- Operator
- Management.

Each of these groups has its own viewpoints and perspectives. Reliability at all levels (hardware, data) is important because PCS systems are usually found in 'difficult' environments where certain non-functional requirements are important. In particular, safety is an important attribute in many cases (see Leveson 1995). For the operators, Usability is essential. Many developers may be dismayed by the fact that Functionality and Efficiency may not be important for many applications in the process control domain.

Process control and real-time applications are special in the sense that they have special requirements. These have to do with safety and reliability issues because process control applications that break down or malfunction can cause serious economic and/or human injury. Before we introduce the main requirements for Process Control Systems we need to introduce a number of definitions. Most of the discussion in this section is based on the comprehensive and well-documented information in Leveson 1995 (in particular Chapter 15 of that book). We discuss the main requirements associated with process control applications. The reader may use them as a baseline for his or her own applications. We discuss several requirements. These could be relevant to specific PCS applications.

6.8.1 Input and output variable completeness

The inputs and outputs correspond to the information that sensors provide to the system (the controlled variables) and the commands that the system provides to the actuators (to change the manipulated variables), respectively. It is vital that these variables and commands are rigorously defined in the requirements document.

Some major rules concerning input and output variables are:

1. All information from the sensors should be used somewhere in the specification.
2. Legal output values that are never produced should be checked for potential specification incompleteness.

This requirement has to do mainly with Conformance and Compliance in ISO 9126.

6.8.2 Robustness criteria

A robust system is one that detects and responds in an appropriate manner to violations to the assumption that all parts of the system are functioning in a certain way. For robustness to be true, the events that trigger state change must satisfy the following conditions (see again Leveson 1995):

1. Every state must have a transition defined for each possible input.
2. The logical OR of the conditions on every transition out of any state must form a tautology. This means that one and only one transition is 'fired' or is actually active when the conditions on all transitions are evaluated.
3. Every state must have a software transition defined in case there is no input for a given period of time (a timeout).

These conditions deserve some explanation. Condition 1 states that there is a one-to-one correspondence between transitions and their corresponding inputs. Condition 2 refers to a tautology and this is by definition a logically complete expression. To take an example, suppose that t1, t2 and t3 are three transitions out of a certain state. Then the tautology states that one and only one of the transitions is triggered based on some external event. Condition 3 states that it is not possible to remain in a state for longer than a given period of time.

We now introduce the concept of robust data structures. In order to motivate this concept we first define reliability and redundancy. Reliability is defined as the probability that a piece of equipment or component will perform its intended function satisfactorily for a prescribed time and under stipulated environmental conditions. Redundancy, on the other hand, involves deliberate duplication to improve reliability. A robust data structure uses redundancy in the structure or data to allow reconstruction if the data structure is corrupted.

This requirement has to do mainly with Reliability in ISO 9126 and is particularly relevant to the Delivery (new actuators) and Regulator (setpoint integrity) agents.

6.8.3 Timing

Timing problems are often a cause of run-time errors. There are two main timing assumptions that are essential in the requirements specifications of triggers, namely timing intervals and capacity (load).

As far as timing intervals are concerned, a timing specification should be associated with each event. In general we note the following rule:

All inputs must be fully bounded in time and the proper behaviour specified in case the limits are violated or an expected input does not arrive.

In general we must define time limits on external events (that is events originating from outside actor systems). The first limit is a lower bound on the time of arrival and the second limit is an upper bound on the interval in which the input is to be accepted. Of course, the exceptions to these constraints must also be documented. The exceptions are:

- Inputs that arrive outside the time interval
- Non-existence of an input during a given time interval.

In other words, the robustness criteria will ensure that behaviour is specified in case the time limits are violated.

It is possible to partition the system state space into two mutually exclusive states, namely normal and overloaded. The required response to an input will be different in each state and both cases must be specified.

Overloading is caused not so much by human operators or slow system components but more often by malfunctions that cause spurious, excessive inputs. Robustness demands that we specify how to handle excessive inputs and that we specify a load limit for such inputs as a means of detecting possible external malfunctions. The general rule is:

A minimum and maximum load assumption must be specified for every interrupt-signalled event whose arrival rate is not dominated (limited) by another type of event.

If interrupts cannot be disabled on a given port then we run the risk that we will run out of CPU resources. The follow-on rule is:

The response to excessive inputs (violations of load assumptions) must be specified.

The main requirements for dealing with overload are (see Leveson 1995):

1. Requirements to give a warning message.
2. Requirements to generate outputs to tell external systems to 'slow down'.
3. Requirements to lock out interrupt signals for the overloaded channels.
4. Requirements to produce outputs that have either reduced accuracy or reduced response time. In general, these are requirements that allow the system to continue to cope with the higher load.
5. Requirements that allow the system to work in degraded mode (e.g. reduce the functionality of the software) or shut the system down.

These requirements can be mapped to use cases and designed using patterns (GOF 1995, POSA 1996).

We can conclude with the following general rule:

If the desired response to an overload condition is performance degradation then the specified degradation should be graceful and operators should be informed.

It is important to specify the conditions under which a system returns to normal processing mode after it has entered a degraded state. It is also important that the system does not attempt to return to normal mode too quickly.

This requirement has to do mainly with Efficiency in ISO 9126 and is particularly relevant to the Delivery (the load on actuators) and Regulator (the load on algorithms and sensors) agents.

6.8.4 Human–Computer Interface (HCI) criteria

HCI requirements specifications should include the following attention points:

1. Specification of the events to be queued.
2. Specification of the type and number of queues to be provided, for example alert queues and routine queues.
3. Ordering scheme within a given queue, for example based on priority, time or arrival.
4. Operator notification mechanism for items that are inserted into a queue.
5. Operator review and disposal of commands for queue entries.
6. Deletion of entries in a queue.

These requirements should be realized by the system under consideration. This is usually done in the design phase of the software lifecycle.

The requirements in this subsection have to do mainly with Usability and Efficiency in ISO 9126 and are particularly relevant to the Control agent (this contains the operator's panel).

6.8.5 State completeness

This requirement corresponds to the high-level partition of the system into two disjoint modes, namely normal and non-normal processing modes. We include some rules:

1. The system and software must start in a safe state.
2. All system and local variables must be properly initialized upon start-up.

There are two kinds of start-up. The first kind is when the system is initially started after a complete process shutdown. The second kind is when the system has been started after it has been temporarily off-line but the process has continued under manual control. Of course, the system clock, system and local variables must be initialized.

Another important requirement is how long the system should wait until the first event arrives. Furthermore, there should be some finite limit on how long the system waits for input before it tries alternative strategies, for example alerting an operator.

Finally, normal-processing states should be divided into substates (as can be modelled by statecharts). We conclude with the rule:

There must be a response specified for the arrival of an input in any state, including indeterminate states.

We shall see how the requirements in this subsection are realized by statecharts in Chapter 12.

The requirements in this subsection have to do mainly with Functionality in ISO 9126 and are relevant to all subsystems.

6.8.6 Data age requirement

This requirement has to do with how long data remains valid. In other words, we speak about data obsolescence. It is vital that control decisions are based on the data from the current state of the system and not on obsolete information. For example, even if nothing happens in a system and even if the program is idle, it is still possible that the real world in which the program is embedded may not be still.

In general we demand that input and output be bounded in time. The basic rule is:

All inputs used in specifying output events must be properly limited in the time for which they can be used (data age). Output commands that may not be able to be executed immediately must be limited in the time for which they are valid.

Data age requirements may be applicable to human–computer interface action sequences, for example how a given operator action remains valid.

6.9 UML CLASSES

The initial system decomposition for the PCS category is shown in Figure 6.9. First of all, the four agents and their responsibilities are as follows.

- *Delivery*: produces actuator output to redress disturbances in the process; this is the operational system.
- *Regulator*: monitors the environment and determines whether actuators must be activated; this is the tactical system. This system contains sensors and local actuators.
- *Control*: presents the process status here. This system is termed strategic because all major input and output decisions take place here.
- *PCS Top-level*: the façade interface system to external client systems. This systems sends information to, and receives information from, high-level client systems.

Each agent is further decomposed into layers as in Figure 6.12. The Boundary layers communicate with the corresponding physical units in the external stakeholder systems, while the Control layers are motivated (as always) from the activities in the core process. The Entity layer deserves some attention now. In the Delivery agent, it is called Service Provider and this is a virtual machine (decision-hiding in the Parnas (1972) sense) to the physical actuators. It knows the service capacity that it can deliver to the process and it knows the status of pending requests. The entity layer in the Regulator agent contains the entities that we are actually modelling, for example:

- Rooms (in a home heating system)
- Medium (in a bioreactor)
- Barrier option (in a portfolio management system)
- Aircraft (aircraft avoidance system, see Leveson and Heimdahl 1994).

Finally, the entity layer in the Control agent contains 'formatter' objects that are in fact two-way converters between internal data and commands and external data and commands.

6.10 USE CASES

Many process control applications share the same requirements. In order to make things concrete, we draw up a list of the most important use cases in a system. A use case is an interaction session between the system and its actors. We need criteria that help us partition system behaviour into independent use cases. One possible strategy is to partition time into three time domains and we determine the appropriate use cases in each domain:

- Start-up (the power-up option)
- Steady-state
- Shutdown.

The start-up mode is concerned with getting the system up and running and contains the following main use cases:

- U0.1: Start system and wait for physical units to respond
- U0.2: Download configuration information and data
- U0.3: Enter normal or degraded operating modes.

Some special use cases and variations in this area are:

- Start system after a failure (variation on U0.1)
- Enter emergency mode (variation on U0.3)
- Enter rescue mode (variation on U0.3).

Emergency mode is entered when a vital physical unit fails to function. Rescue mode is entered when some piece of hardware fails and the system simulates its behaviour in software.

Once the system is up and running we are in a position to examine the so-called steady state use cases. These are concerned with the interactions between the system and the different stakeholders, such as:

- Users and operators
- Customers
- Suppliers
- Other systems (for example, Watchdog systems).

We list the main use cases associated with these stakeholders:

- U1.1: Enter semi-manual mode
- U1.2: Change system's configuration data in some way
- U1.3: Environmental disturbance takes place
- U1.4: Send information to Customers
- U1.5: Receive raw materials from Suppliers
- U1.6: Communicate with external systems.

Of course, these use cases represent a very small subset of all the use cases in real-life Process Control Systems. Finally, we wish to describe what happens when the system shuts down:

- U2.1: Shutdown under normal circumstances
- U2.2: Emergency shutdown.

These use cases are to be found in all process control applications and they can be used by the reader as basic building blocks for his or her own applications. For example, we shall describe and document the use cases for the Home Heating System (HHS) in Chapter 12 based on this generic use case set.

There are many ways of discovering use cases in PCS applications:

- Serendipity and *ad hoc* approaches (chance discovery)
- Event–response lists as in structured analysis and traditional OO approaches
- By investigating how SUD interacts with its external stakeholder systems.

The first two options are used quite a lot and unfortunately lead to unmanageable systems. The third option is more structured and this is the technique that we use in Chapter 12 to discover and document use cases from the Home Heating System problem. In general, the last approach is not incorrect as such but we wish to subsume it under a more general paradigm. To this end, we use some ideas from agent theory (see Wooldridge 2002) to help us generate (as it were) a reasonably complete set of use cases for this category. Incidentally, there is no reason why we could not apply the ideas to the other categories in this book! In general, agents are autonomous, active objects with the ability to negotiate, cooperate and react to the environment. Agents have the following capabilities:

- *Reactivity*: Agents can sense their environment and respond in a timely fashion to changes that occur in it in order to satisfy their design objectives.
- *Proactiveness*: Agents are able to exhibit goal-directed behaviour by *taking the initiative* in order to satisfy their design objectives.
- *Social ability*: Agents are capable of interacting with other agents (and possibly humans) in order to satisfy their design objectives.

We could get the impression that agent technology is a somewhat richer and deeper paradigm than that based on objects. In fact, this would be a valid conclusion. The reason that we introduce agents here is that we apply agent communication protocols to help us find a large number of use cases, possibly a larger set than is possible with the object paradigm and use case technology. In particular, we discuss some so-called *performatives* that describe how agents interact. We give a list of some of them (for more, see the website www.fipa.org, the Foundation for Intelligent Physical Agents):

- *Call for Proposal* (*cfp*): This performative initiates negotiation between agents. An action must be carried out in this case. For example, the SUD could send a broadcast message to its external stakeholder systems (that is, physical units) to activate them in order to bring the SUD into standby mode.
- *Proposal*: This performative allows an agent to make a proposal to another agent, for example in response to a previous cfp message that was previously sent out. An example in a PCS environment is when actuators propose to supply the SUD with services when needed.
- *Request*: A fundamental performative that allows an agent to request another agent to perform some action. For example, the SUD could ask an actuator to provide heat, or the operator system could ask the sensors for the current temperature readings.
- *Inform*: A basic mechanism for communicating information. The content of the performative is a statement and the idea is that the sender wants the receiver to believe something. For example, a sensor could inform a room that the current temperature has changed.
- *Confirm*: Allows the sender of the message to confirm the truth of the content to the recipient where, before sending the message, the sender believes that the recipient is unsure about the truth or otherwise of the content. For example, we may introduce a new sensor to measure humidity in a room and we may wish to check whether a room knows what humidity is in the first place.

- *Subscribe*: The sender wants to be notified whenever something relating to the system changes. For example, the SUD may be interested in knowing when sensor readings change.

Having determined the useful protocols in PCS systems, we could use the questions in the Inquiry Cycle model to generate new use cases.

6.11 SPECIALIZATIONS OF PCS SYSTEMS

The PCS category can be applied to many types of problem, not just industrial applications. There is no unique way of clustering these systems because there are so many dimensions along which we can classify:

- *Time*: hard real-time (microseconds response), soft (seconds response)
- *Domain*: discrete and continuous process control, embedded systems, financial and business applications
- *Data that is monitored*: real-time, medium-term and historical data.

A full discussion is beyond the scope of this book. To the best of my knowledge, it is an open problem at the moment of writing.

6.11.1 Multi-level architectures

Real-life manufacturing and process control applications consist of many systems. Thus, the context diagram in Figure 6.8 needs to be extended in some way in order to accommodate the requirements from different stakeholders. To this end, we need to develop systems that interface with the current process control system. One possible configuration is shown in Figure 6.14. In this case we identify a number of systems:

- *PCS*: the process control system under discussion (the SUD).
- *Watchdog*: this system receives messages from PCS on a periodic or some other basis. If a service occurs too late or out of sequence, the watchdog takes corrective action such as reset, shutdown, alarming or some other elaborate error recovery mechanism (Douglass 1998). Watchdogs can be implemented in either hardware or software. An example of a watchdog is one that is woken up periodically and that performs Built-In Test (BIT) suites, for example CRC checks on the executable code. This system can be modelled as a process-control system.
- *MIS*: management information systems that receive transaction information from PCS. The different kinds of transaction data are used as input for trending, statistics gathering, cost control and material usage.

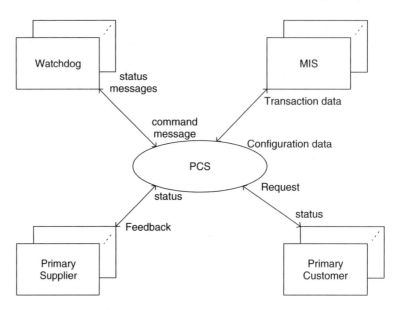

Figure 6.14   Multi-level Process Control System.

- *Primary Suppliers*: the systems that represent the source of all raw materials input to PCS.
- *Primary Customers*: the systems that receive the products or services from PCS.

6.12 USING PCS SYSTEMS WITH OTHER SYSTEMS

PCS systems can be described as the 'policemen' systems in the domain architecture galaxy. In this sense they can be viewed as clients of other systems. In particular, they monitor critical attributes in other systems, for example:

- Scheduled and actual values in management systems (MIS systems)
- Monitor breaches in service level agreements (RAT systems)
- Breaches in security; security violations (ACS systems)
- Errors in manufacturing processes (MAN systems).

Furthermore, a PCS system could itself be server to other systems, for example:

- Multiple PCS instance systems that send data to a MIS system
- A PCS instance that is a client of another PCS instance (for example, 'watchdog watching another watchdog')
- A RAT instance that tracks errors and events in a PCS instance.

There are many applications where the process control model can be successfully applied. In fact, any application that needs to monitor the difference between reference and actual data is a candidate. Thus, the PCS model finds applications in the following diverse domains:

- Industrial process control
- Manufacturing (MAN category)
- Management Information Systems (MIS category)
- Resource Allocation and Tracking systems (RAT category)
- Process simulation of real-life environments (see Garrido 1998).

Various possible topological relationships are defined between a PCS application and one of the above types. The first possibility is that the PCS system communicates with another satellite system of a given type. Some examples can be seen from Figure 6.14:

- Transaction data is sent from PCS to a MIS system
- Finished products are sent to Customers system (this could be a MAN category)
- 'Keep-alive' messages are sent to a Watchdog system.

The second possibility is that the PCS application is itself a satellite system associated with another system. Examples are:

- Monitoring resource usage overrun in an engineering project (see Chapter 11)
- Monitoring 'out-of-band' behaviour of shares on the stock exchange
- Monitoring escalated calls in a help desk application (see Section 7.3.1).

Figure 6.14 gives an example; the Watchdog system is of PCS type and monitors certain critical attributes of the 'base' PCS system.

6.13 SUMMARY AND CONCLUSIONS

This chapter introduced the features common to Process Control Systems. In particular, we introduced the most important entities and concepts in this domain and we then mapped these into the so-called process control (PCS) category. We also discussed the main requirements that are associated with such systems and we drew up a list of useful requirements and use cases for analysts when embarking on such applications. We paid some attention to non-functional requirements and the class architecture in PCS systems.

This chapter drew heavily from various sources and adapted the information in those sources to domain architectures for process control applications. The critical sections that help us determine whether a system is a PCS instance are Sections 6.5 and 6.8. The context diagram in Figure 6.8 is also a vital artefact to consult.

APPENDIX 6.1: MESSAGE PATTERNS IN PROCESS CONTROL SYSTEMS

We conclude this chapter with a discussion of the types of messages that are exchanged between a PCS system and its satellite systems (in fact, the discussion and conclusions are also applicable to other domain categories). This is an important aspect of process control systems, because we are interested in determining whether congestion problems are occurring or whether the hardware has died or is not functioning according to its normal operational pattern. Furthermore, we can define arrival patterns. There are different ways to describe congestion, for example in terms of the queueing time of messages from other satellite systems or in terms of the free and busy periods in the PCS system itself. In order to predict one or more of these quantities we must specify the following attributes:

- *The arrival pattern*: the average rate of arrival of messages and the statistical pattern of the arrivals.
- *The service mechanism*: this has to do with when service is available, how many messages can be serviced at a time and how long the service takes. The latter aspect is modelled by a statistical distribution of service time.
- *The queue discipline*: this is the method by which a message is selected for service out of all those awaiting service. For example, the simplest queue discipline consists of serving customers in order of arrival. This is also called FIFO (first-in, first-out) service regime.

The main patterns that we discuss are as follows.

- *Completely random arrivals*: In this case the arrivals are completely random. Random messages may have an average rate that represents the computed average frequency. In general, the arrival of a message does not affect the probability of the arrival of the next message. The Poisson statistical distribution usually models random messages.
- *Regular or periodic arrivals*: Periodic messages are characterized by a period with which the messages arrive and by so-called jitter that is defined as the variation around the period with which messages actually arrive. The uniform random process models this variation.
- *General independent arrivals*: This arrival pattern is a generalization of the previous two patterns. In this case the intervals between the arrivals of successive messages are random variables.

- *Regular arrivals with unpunctuality*: This is the case in which messages should arrive at equally spaced intervals but are unpunctual. If the degree of unpunctuality is small compared with the arrival interval then its effect is unimportant. However, if the dispersion is large, the system behaves as a completely random one.
- *Aggregated arrivals*: This is the case in which messages arrive in groups of varying sizes.
- *Complex deterministic arrivals*: In the above cases we assumed that the irregularity in arrivals is statistical in character and is described as a random variable. In some cases, however, this irregularity is produced by a complex recurring pattern. An example is in a semi-automatic machine that requires unloading every 10 minutes, reloading with new raw materials every 5 minutes and general adjustment every 6 minutes (see Cox 1974).
- *Discrete-time arrivals*: In this case the irregular pattern of arrivals is represented by a series in which arrivals can occur only at a discrete set of time instants. This case is closely related to the aggregated arrivals case. The arrival instants are equally spaced and the number of arrivals per instant is 0 or 1.

Non-stationary arrival patterns

The above arrival patterns are called stationary because the probability structure does not change with time. In some cases, however, the structure does change and this leads to so-called non-stationary arrival patterns. A good example is that of a telephone exchange in which the arrival pattern is completely random at a rate that varies smoothly with the time of day.

- *Arrivals correlated with other aspects of the system*: In this case the rate of arrival of messages is correlated with other properties of the system, for example the number of messages awaiting service. Another example is the case of a queue at a supermarket in which customers may be either deterred or attracted by the presence of a long queue of other customers. Another example is in an industrial process where the arrival of new messages may be cut off as soon as the number of unserved messages reaches a critical value.
- *Arrivals in a continuous flow*: We have assumed until now that messages arrive as discrete entities and that their arrival takes place at well-defined (albeit random in some cases) instants in time. In this case, however, we model message arrivals as a continuous flow. An example is the arrival of fluid in a storage system. The arrival is described by a continuous time-series obtained by plotting rate against time.

Having discussed the specifics of message arrival, we now discuss how messages are processed. This is called the service mechanism. The three defining attributes of such a mechanism are:

- Service time
- Capacity of system
- Availability of the service.

The service time is defined as the time that is needed to serve or process a message. In most cases we assume that the service times of the different messages are independent random variables with the same probability distribution. In some other more complicated cases the messages may be of different types.

The capacity of the system is defined as the number of customers that can be served at any one time. For example, the capacity of a one-server queue is 1 while the capacity of an m-server queue is m.

We now discuss some statistical models that describe service time:

- Constant service time
- Exponential service time.

In the first case we assume that the service time is constant. This model works well in some cases (for example, problems with irregular arrival patterns) but it is an ideal situation. The second model is described by an exponential probability density function. For example, this function models the duration of telephone calls well: here we have a large number of customers requiring fairly short service while a small number of customers will require longer service.

Relevant background information on the above topics is to be found in Garrido (1998), Saaty (1961) and Cox (1974). Having detailed knowledge about message arrival and service time can help us understand performance, congestion and other non-functional issues associated with the analysis of Process Control Systems.

7 Resource Allocation and Tracking (RAT) systems

*'**Communicator:** a personal communication device contained within the insignia badge worn by Starfleet personnel. Communicators also emit a signal that can be used to locate the person wearing the badge. The feature provides a Starship's transporter system with the means for determining exact coordinates, which are necessary for transporting personnel from one location to another.'*

7.1 INTRODUCTION AND OBJECTIVES

We introduce a class of applications that occur in many business, financial and industrial domains. In this case we model the flow of information, objects or other entities from the moment these entities enter the system to the moment that they are no longer needed. The word 'Tracking' is in the title because we wish to locate the entities at all times. The word 'Allocation' is used because resources are needed if we wish to move entities from one place to another.

Applications in the RAT category abound both in the real world and in the OO literature. Some specific applications include:

- Warehouse Management System (WMS, Jacobson *et al* 1993)
- ECO Tank Loading System (Coleman *et al* 1994, Duffy 1995)
- Elevator Control System (Yourdon and Argila 1996).

There are many more. These applications have been analysed in the past using the implicit assumption that one should look for the objects in the systems using CRC card techniques, for example. Our approach is to determine the core processes, map them to subsystems and 'populate' each subsystem with objects by using a Layers or PAC pattern, for example.

This book analyses two RAT instances in detail, namely the Order Realization System (Chapter 14) and Elevator Control System (Chapter 13).

7.2 BACKGROUND AND HISTORY

The RAT category models workflow or supply chain applications (Sharp and McDermott 2001, Gattorna and Walters 1996). In general, these systems are well understood and much has been written about them. It is hard to think of any human endeavour where such systems are not needed. Some examples where the RAT model plays an important role are:

- Distribution of physical goods from one location to another location
- Insurance and banking applications (for example, loan processing)
- Tracking of instrumentation information (for example, signals from satellites)
- Tracking of the information flow in organizations
- Transportation systems (for example, Starfleet personnel)
- Integrated logistics systems.

All workflow applications have a number of common characteristics. First, they are concerned with the registration of information and with tracking that information in physical or simulated environments. Second, it is possible to determine the status of information while it is in the environment and which stakeholders are responsible for performing activities pertaining to that information. Finally, information may be removed from the system.

One of the best ways to learn what RAT entails is to study one of its instances in greater detail.

7.3 MOTIVATIONAL EXAMPLES

Our first example of a RAT instance is a Help Desk System (HDS). The core process in this case is to resolve customer problems within a given period of time and to inform the customer of the resolution status. The main activities are:

1. To register and classify the customer request and create a call entity and assign a priority to it.
2. To assign the call to a specialist or group of specialists who should resolve and close the call within a given time period.
3. To report on the status.

Thus, the most important questions for the customer are who is working on my problem and how long will it now take to resolve the problem? Calls that are not resolved on time should be escalated to the Service Level Manager (SLM) system that will then take corrective action. The basic context diagram is shown in Figure 7.1. We now discuss how to resolve a problem by discussing the core

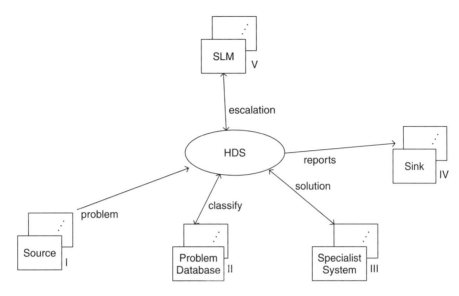

Figure 7.1   Context for Help Desk System.

process in relation to the systems in Figure 7.1 (we denote the systems by Roman numerals because they are easier to read than text):

1. HDS processes request data from system I.
2. The request data is verified against system II.
3. Once data has been verified, we create a basic call object.
4. The call object is assigned to a specialist resource in system III.
5. The status of the assigned call is dispatched to external systems IV.
6. Optionally, service level management systems V are informed of the request.

We speak of a contract ('resolve the problem within a certain period of time') and this is why system V is needed. In particular, Service Level Agreements (SLAs) are defined in this system.

   We now give two specific instances of the RAT category. The first problem describes a traditional help desk environment and it was this problem that helped the author formalize the RAT model. The second example is more technical and describes a model that tracks the tooling and trimming of computer chips.

7.3.1 Help Desk System (HDS)

We now discuss a special case of the Help Desk System discussed at the beginning of this section. To this end, the public transport authority in a medium-sized European city wishes to improve its processes and it has decided to develop a new Help Desk

System (HDS). The core process in HDS is to solve user problems. Each problem should be assigned to a specialist or group of specialists who resolve the problem as soon as possible and then report back to the customer or their contact person. The new system should improve service levels, both within the main office in the centre of the city and in the local transport offices.

The most important stakeholder groups that are involved with the new system and their relationships are shown as a concept map in Figure 7.2. This map displays the major stakeholder groups as ellipses and the structural relationships between them as edges. We see that there are three major stakeholder categories:

- *Users*: the stakeholders (for example, end-users) who work with the computer systems. Each office has one representative called the application manager (APM) who is responsible for promoting the interests of the different user groups. In particular, the application manager is responsible for registering problems with the Helpdesk. The Helpdesk is responsible for further processing of these problems. The Helpdesk also provides feedback to the application manager.
- *Service Groups*: those stakeholders that interact with the Helpdesk. The three main groups are Helpdesk, Product Specialist (PS) and Computer Facilities (CF). The PS group is responsible for the solution of a customer problem. It may call on other groups to help it solve a problem.
- *Service Level Groups*: the stakeholders who are responsible for service level agreements, management and security. First, Service Level Management (SLM) is responsible for the creation and maintenance of contracts with user groups. The Security Manager (SM) is a role that can be played by a person or group of persons and its responsibility is to ensure the integrity of data and programs at all times. 'Integrity' includes issues such as privacy, access to historical information and disaster plans.

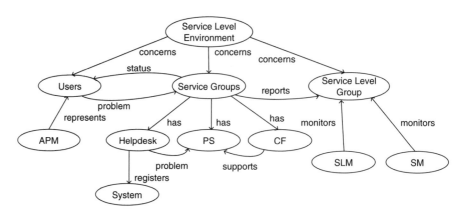

Figure 7.2 Concept map for Help Desk System.

There are also *Service Level Rules*: handbooks and standard procedures that describe each application. They contain the following sections:

- Reliability issues (availability, planning and organization)
- Budgeting (estimation, maintenance costs)
- Support (Helpdesk, Product Specialist and Computer Facilities)
- Version control (production, acceptance and development versions of the software)
- Security and access control policies
- Application replacement and disaster plans.

Notice that Service Level Rules are not human stakeholders! These tend to be forgotten in some object-oriented projects.

Agreements between customers and service groups are documented in Service Level Agreements (SLAs). In particular, the SLA must contain information on what to do in the following extreme situations: the services of the computer centre are no longer available; an application can no longer access its database; and the computer that hosts an application is malfunctioning.

In order to satisfy the above requirements we propose the initial context diagram as shown in Figure 7.2. Here we see that HDS cooperates with a number of satellite systems. These systems realize the core process that describes how a problem is first registered and then solved. The main satellite systems and their responsibilities are as follows:

- *Source*: the system where problems originate.
- *Problem database*: a knowledge base containing historical information on problems, types of problem, source of problems and how to solve these problems.
- *SLM*: the system that contains information concerning service level agreements between customers and service level management groups.
- *Specialist system*: contains information about the specialists who resolve and solve problems and what their availability is. This system is an instance of the RAT category and its main responsibility is to ensure that calls and problems are assigned to specialists.
- *Sink*: the ultimate client systems.

7.3.2 Discrete manufacturing

We describe a class of problems that we group under the name 'discrete manufacturing'. This general term refers to those applications that are concerned with the loading of discrete items and objects, processing them in some way and finally removing them from the system by an offloading mechanism. We thus see that this is a useful and important sub-category of RAT because many business and industrial organizations must develop software systems for problems in this category. Specific examples in the literature and in real-life applications are:

- Package router control problem (see Jackson 2001)
- Elevator control system (Yourdon and Argila 1996)
- Warehouse management system (Jacobson *et al* 1993)
- Egg-sorting machines
- Semiconductor chip tooling machines (the example in this section)
- The Communicator device in Star Trek.

These applications have a number of common features. We model them as RAT systems because we are interested in tracking the status of objects in time and space. By 'time' we mean that it must be possible to state how long production will last and by 'space' we mean that we must know where an item or object is.

We motivate the *discrete manufacturing sub-category* by describing one of its instances, namely a semiconductor tooling problem. In particular, we describe the man–machine interface (MMI) aspects of this problem. This means that we are not tracking the physical hardware objects as such but rather the representation of those objects in a graphical user interface environment. A short description of the problem (we call it MMISYS) is as follows:

Pallets containing (half-product) semiconductor chips are loaded into the machine. The chips are taken from the pallets and sent to a tooling machine where they are tested, trimmed and formed. Finally, the finished products are offloaded and placed in special containers to be subsequently transported to other systems.

We show the context diagram for MMISYS in Figure 7.3. The Loader systems are responsible for loading the pallets that contain the chips while the OffLoader systems are responsible for removing the chips once they have been tooled. The PressUnit systems are responsible for the actual tooling and testing of the chips. These three external stakeholder systems are essential for the proper functioning of MMISYS. There are two more systems that also have a role to play. First, the Tracker system is an instance of a Process Control System (PCS) and is a kind of 'watchdog' system that monitors and controls abnormal behaviour. Second, the Host system is an instance of MIS and is responsible for the configuration of MMISYS and the creation of management reports. The Host is usually a bridge to some Enterprise Resource Planning (ERP) package.

We see a clear 'load/process/offload' metaphor in this example. Many applications are in fact specific cases of this metaphor and once we realize this our life as analyst becomes much easier. For example, the well-known elevator or lift control system (Yourdon and Argila 1996) could be compared with MMISYS. There are many similarities to be explored. In particular, we could adopt the naive view that an elevator control system is the same as MMISYS and then explore the consequences of this assumption. We give some parallels between the two systems:

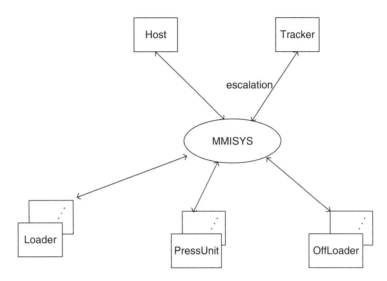

Figure 7.3   MMISYS context diagram.

- People are 'loaded' into an elevator (Loader)
- People are transported to a destination (by the equivalent of PressUnit)
- People leave the lift when it arrives at its destination (OffLoader)
- Security management is watching for faults (Tracker system)
- Usage statistics gathering (Host system).

Once we have convinced ourselves of the general similarities between the two systems, we can then start the task of 'transferring' our knowledge of MMISYS to help us with an analysis of the new 'target' system (in this case the Elevator Control System).

7.4 GENERAL APPLICABILITY

The RAT category is useful for applications where there are clear transportation and tracking patterns. We give a list of some keywords and special terms that arise when discussing RAT systems. As analyst, you should actively listen to customers and other stakeholders because the vocabulary that they use will give hints on how to develop a system:

- People, places, things, time
- Transportation of goods and information
- Help desk features: customers and service providers
- Status of requests at all times (in space and time, as it were)

- Who is working on the request?
- Where is the request?
- When should the request be resolved or closed?

This list can be used as a check to determine whether stakeholders use the above jargon and vocabulary. We are usually interested in a single request or a tightly coupled cluster of requests when using the RAT model. Grouping loosely coupled groups of requests is a matter for MIS systems.

7.5 GOALS, PROCESSES AND ACTIVITIES

The main goal of each RAT instance is to track an entity. The core process P1 is responsible for the production of status information concerning the 'whereabouts' (in the broadest sense of the word) of objects from the moment they enter the system to when they leave it. The input can take many forms but must contain information pertaining to the following attributes:

- The sender of the request
- The kind of request (so that the internal stakeholders know what to do with it)
- Other relevant attributes (for example, constraints and annotations).

The main activities in P1 are:

- P1.1: Registration (this produces an internal Request entity)
- P1.2: Assignment (allocates resources to fulfil the request)
- P1.3: Presentation (dispatches request status information to subscribed clients).

Summarizing, the major information entities in the RAT category are:

- Request data: raw data from various sources
- Request: basic entity that must be tracked in the system
- Assigned request: information concerning actions to be taken on the request
- Status information: presentation to authorized stakeholders of relevant information concerning request status.

These entities are modelled as UML class diagrams. This aspect will be examined in Section 7.8.

7.6 CONTEXT DIAGRAM AND SYSTEM DECOMPOSITION

In general, a context diagram should contain all the systems that realize all core, supporting and management processes in a system. In the case of the RAT category,

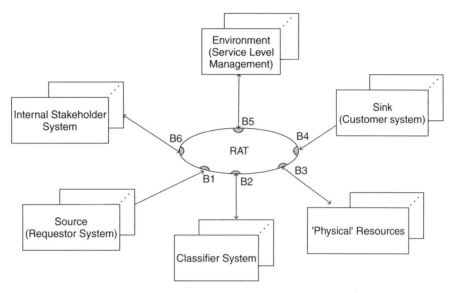

Figure 7.4 RAT context environment.

we are interested in tracking the journey of a request from the moment it enters the system to when it leaves it (or when it is not needed). To this end, we depict the generic context diagram for the RAT category in Figure 7.4. The main satellite systems and their responsibilities are as follows:

- *Requestor Systems* (*Source*): the systems containing all basic request information. This information can be in various formats and has various arrival rates. For example, information arrival can be deterministic (at specified times) or stochastic (random). See the Appendix to Chapter 6 for a discussion of message patterns.
- *Customer Systems* (*Sink*): the systems that benefit from the RAT system. In particular, these are the systems that receive strategic information concerning the status of the request. Such information should be available to these recipients at all times.
- *Classifier Systems*: the systems that determine the category of an incoming request. These systems are adaptive knowledge bases and they contain historical information about the kinds of requests that entered the system in the past and which request categories are known to, and accepted by, the system.
- *Service Level* (*Environment*): the management systems (usually of MIS and PCS type) that monitor and control RAT. The number of systems and their responsibilities is infinite in general, but we can give certain guidelines:
  — Historical information about all orders in RAT (both present and past)
  — Systems that track exceptional situations and predict impending capacity problems (over-capacity and under-capacity)

— Systems that monitor service levels and 'quality of service' aspects in the system
— Systems for cost, information and control flow in RAT.

- *Physical Resource Systems*: the systems that are responsible for the lifecycle of the physical resources that are needed to execute the request. These may be RAT systems in their own right. For example, they may track the flow of physical resources, while the SUD is also a RAT system that tracks the information concerning the request that the ultimate clients see. In this way we see a form of patterning that we term 'multi-levelled' RAT systems.
- *Internal Stakeholder Systems*: a special group of systems. These systems are optional. For example, we could create three internal stakeholder systems, one for each major group in the organization:
  — Front Office: the ability to create and modify requests
  — Middle Office: assigning resources to requests
  — Back Office: grouping orders into clusters; notifying client systems of order status.

We now decompose the SUD into its subsystems. They are called Registration, Assignment and Presentation. Their responsibilities are:

- Registration
  — Accept request data from different sources
  — Create and validate basic request objects
  — Notify other systems of request creation status
- Assignment
  — Allocate resources that 'realize' the request
  — Schedule the request using different policies and strategies
  — Notify other systems of request allocation status
- Presentation
  — Format request status information
  — Gather and group requests for further dispatching
  — Notify interested clients of new formatted information.

7.7 STAKEHOLDERS, VIEWPOINTS AND REQUIREMENTS

It is possible to discover the main stakeholder groups in a RAT category by examining the context diagram in Figure 7.4. These are:

- *Requestors*: systems that send requests to RAT
- *Sink*: systems that receive status information
- *Classifiers*: systems that filter, classify and categorize requests
- *Physical Resources*: systems that allocate resources to resolve the request

- *Internal Stakeholders*: persons and functional units that are involved with the request in some way
- *Environment*: client and collaborator systems that monitor and control RAT in some way.

Each stakeholder group has its own specific viewpoints. The 'default' and possibly most important viewpoints are Reliability and Efficiency. Of course, the other ISO 9126 characteristics may be important in specific RAT instances.

It is interesting to examine the sub-characteristic Time Efficiency in more detail. In particular, we examine time in more detail by asking the question 'what kinds of time?'. In the case of workflow systems the answer is as follows (see Sharp and McDermott 2001):

- *Cycle time*: the total elapsed time, measured from the moment when a request enters the system to when it leaves it. This is the time measure that is most obvious to the customer.
- *Work time*: the time that the activities that execute the requests are worked on. In practice, activities are sometimes idle or waiting for other activities to finish and for this reason cycle time and work time are not the same.
- *Time worked*: concerned with the actual hours of work expanded on the request. Sometimes more than one person is working on a request at one time. Thus, time worked is not the same as work time!
- *Idle time*: refers to when an activity or process is not doing anything (it is waiting).
- *Transit time*: the time spent in transit between activities or steps. For example, work or goods may be moved from one location to another location. The movement does not add any value to the workflow.
- *Queue time*: the time that a request is waiting on a critical resource; the request is ready for processing but it is waiting for resources from another activity to reach it.
- *Setup time*: the time required for a resource to switch from one type of task to another.

Depending on the application, you may need to monitor some or all of these times. In particular, scheduled values (upper limits and lower limits) need to be defined. Other dimensions could be space (the location of requests in some physical or simulated world) and who is responsible for requests.

7.8 UML CLASSES

The PAC model for RAT is shown in Figure 7.5. The Control and Entity layers have been found from the corresponding system responsibilities while the Entity layers

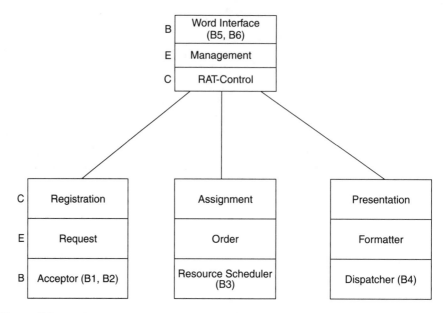

Figure 7.5   PAC model in RAT domain architecture.

are found from the activity diagrams in the core process. Finally, the Boundary layers deserve some attention. The objects and partitions in these layers are found from the context diagram in Figure 7.4. The rationale for placing boundary objects in a given subsystem is as follows:

- The subsystem Registration communicates with the external stakeholder systems Source and Classifier (hence the presence of the Boundary objects B1 and B2).
- The subsystem Assignment communicates with the external stakeholder system PhysicalResource (hence the presence of the Boundary object B3). In some cases this subsystem may communicate with the Classifier system (object B2).
- The subsystem Presentation communicates with the external stakeholder system Sink (hence the presence of the Boundary objects B4).

An interesting design/analysis decision is to determine where to place the Boundary objects B5 and B6 that communicate with the Internal Stakeholder systems and the Environment systems. In Figure 7.5 we place these in the top-level subsystem (in the Boundary layer) because these systems have access to the RAT system as a whole and not just to its subsystems. This is a direct application of information hiding techniques: a client has a limited number of access points to server systems.

7.9 USE CASES

The most important use cases are deduced from the core processes in RAT. One particularly important use case is the one that describes the tracking of a request in the system. This is an enterprise-wide use case and we call it:

- U1: Process request data from A–Z.

A summary of the main actions in this use case now follows. These are described as a collaboration diagram as shown in Figure 7.6:

- Read request data
- Check validity of data (classify)
- Create basic request object
- Notify other systems of new request object
- Assign resources for request
- Notify other systems of assignment (collaborator systems, tactical)
- Prepare for dispatching of request status
- Notify other systems of new status (client/customer systems, strategic).

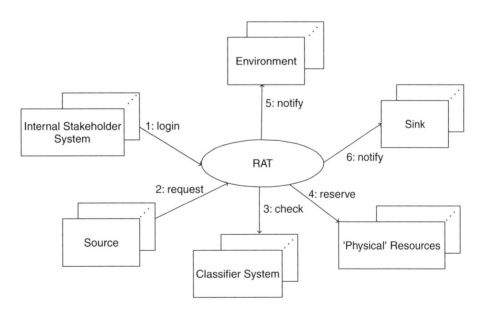

Figure 7.6 Computational model in RAT.

In order to make things more tractable, we partition U1 into three smaller use cases as follows:

- U1.1: Create basic request entities
- U1.2: Assign and schedule resources for a request entity
- U1.3: Present information on request status.

We do not document these use cases according to the standard template; however, in Chapters 13 (Elevator Control System) and 14 (Order Processing System) we give several examples of how to document use cases in RAT instances.

We describe the scope of the use cases by describing their preconditions and postconditions. Furthermore, we associate each use case with one specific subsystem in Figure 7.5.

- U1.1 (associated with subsystem Registration)
  Preconditions: System operational and accepting requests
  Postconditions: Basic request object created and waiting for further processing
- U1.2 (associated with subsystem Assignment)
  Preconditions: System operational and there are requests to be processed
  Postconditions: Request object assigned and waiting for further processing
- U1.3 (associated with subsystem Presentation)
  Preconditions: System operational and it is time to notify clients of request status
  Postconditions: Request status has been dispatched and is waiting for further processing.

The collaboration diagram that describes the flow in these use cases is shown in Figure 7.6.

7.10 SPECIALIZATIONS OF RAT SYSTEMS

We classify RAT systems as follows:

- Call handling systems (concerned with information tracking and customer requests)
- Transportation systems (tracking of physical goods in an environment)
- Discrete and continuous batch systems (chip trimming, plastics production).

We discuss three instances of the RAT category in this book. First, in Chapter 13 we analyse the Elevator Control System (ELS) that models the transportation of passengers in an elevator. This is a technical RAT system. Second, Chapter 14 analyses a business problem called Order Processing System (OPS). Finally, in Chapter 16 we analyse a Lifecycle model for a plastics manufacturing system. One of its subsystems is an instance of RAT and this subsystem tracks the flow of molten plastic on its way to becoming plastic film.

7.11 USING RAT SYSTEMS WITH OTHER SYSTEMS

Once an entity has been created (in a MAN category, for example), it can be tracked using a RAT category. In this sense we can say that a RAT category is a client of some MAN category. Furthermore, since RAT systems track single entities or groups of entities we need to have some ways of reporting on the status of tracked entities. To this end, we see that RAT systems can deliver 'transaction data' to MIS systems for further processing.

Finally, many systems can be modelled as 'multi-levelled' RAT systems. To take an example, let us consider the case of a large investment bank. There are various levels of tracking as can be seen in Figure 7.7. At the 'lowest' level we are interested in tracking changes in market variables such as share prices, volatility, short-term interest rates and other events such as international crises, fluctuations in oil prices and so on. In financial terms, we can say that this layer contains basic market realities. At the second level, we have a number of trading systems. Traders trade in financial instruments such as options, bonds, shares and swaps. These instruments are bought, sold and consolidated into portfolios. Changes in market variables will cause the portfolios in the trading systems to be adjusted. At the next level, we have the Value At Risk (VAR) systems, risk sensitivity analysis and hedging analysis applications (see Dowd 1998); these are responsible for determining how exposed a certain portfolio is and what risks a trader is taking. VAR can be defined as the maximum likely loss of a trader's portfolios. Finally, all VAR systems should report to a Regulator system that tracks the absolute risk in an organization. The systems in

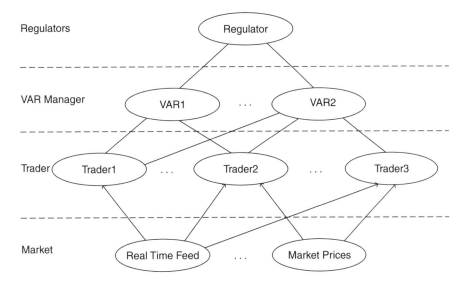

Figure 7.7 Multi-levelled RAT system.

Figure 7.7 are essentially RAT instances. Each system operates on its own specific request types.

The layered systems in Figure 7.7 are interdependent. The systems in the market layer provide data to the Trader layer. Finally, the VAR layer uses the information and data provided by the lower layers. This layer will be populated by various management and decision support systems.

Finally, a special RAT system is one that registers major events in other systems.

7.12 SUMMARY AND CONCLUSIONS

We have analysed a class of problems that are related to workflow and supply chain metaphors. We use the term RAT (Resource Allocation and Tracking) to describe those applications that register requests from outside sources, assign resources to resolve request and inform interested client systems of the status. The main activities in the core processes are request registration, resource assignment and presentation of request status. The RAT category is probably the most important and most ubiquitous of all the domain categories that we discuss in this book. RAT instances are subsystems in larger real-life systems.

A good way to determine whether your current problem can be fitted by the RAT category is to examine the Help Desk System in this chapter and look for the similarities.

8 Manufacturing (MAN) systems

'The holodeck uses two main computer subsystems, the holographic imagery subsystem and the matter-conversion subsystem, to create remarkably sophisticated simulation programs.'

8.1 INTRODUCTION AND OBJECTIVES

This chapter introduces a class of applications that have one thing in common: they all create products or services from basic raw materials. It does not matter whether the products are physical or represent information *about* other entities. In general, all manufacturing applications process raw materials and convert them to half-products. These half-products are then converted and formatted to suit individual stakeholder needs. The end-result is a product delivered to them.

Many applications create objects and entities and the MAN category describes this process. Some possible worlds where the model is applicable are:

- Natural or artificial
- Real or conceptual (virtual)
- Static or dynamic
- Deterministic or stochastic (probabilistic)
- Control (cybernetic) or non-control
- Rigid or flexible.

There are several issues that we address when analysing MAN instances. First, the type and format of raw data that enters the system (the input) as well as the type and format of the data that the system produces (the output) need to be documented. Furthermore, we must describe the type and format of the internal objects and half-products. Second, the algorithms that convert internal objects to finished products are usually complex, difficult and time-consuming to realize. Finally, the role of the manufacturing system in a larger context needs to be examined. This is because manufacturing systems deliver goods and services to other systems (for example, management, tracking or process control systems). The interfaces and the corresponding data standards that arise due to the interaction between the manufacturing systems and its satellites need to be defined.

8.2 BACKGROUND AND HISTORY

In this section we discuss the essentials of manufacturing processes. The term 'manufacture' appeared in 1622 as a translation from the Latin *manu factum* (made by hand). The emphasis was on making tangible things. The definition has been extended to include manufacturing, construction and public utility generation.

There are three major flows in any manufacturing process (see Hitomi 1996):

1. Flow of materials (material flow): the conversion of raw materials into products. This is sometimes called technical production.
2. Flow of information (information flow): the planning and control of production.
3. Flow of cost (cost flow): the economics of production.

Associated with each flow are processes, activities and stakeholder groups. The conceptual schema for a manufacturing process is shown in Figure 8.1. The material

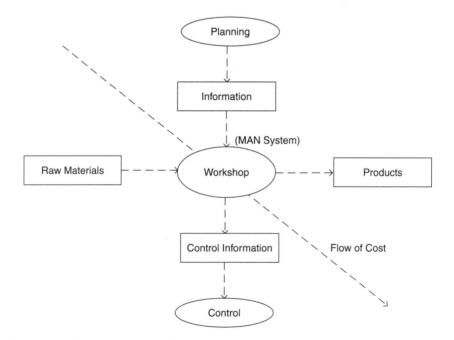

Figure 8.1 Flows in manufacturing processes.

flow has to do with the utilization of resources of production (such as money, materials, manpower and information) in order to produce the product. This flow represents a core process (it connects input to output) and the corresponding activities are:

- Procurement (receives raw materials from suppliers)
- Production (produces products from an inventory of raw materials)
- Distribution (distributes commodities to the market)
- Sales (sell commodities to consumers).

This is a standard generic model and it can be specialized to many specific domain and applications.

The information flow represents the management function in the manufacturing process and models the planning and control functions. It is a market-based process in the sense that it must grasp the market needs and reflect those needs in the production process (Hitomi 1996). Planning is defined as the selection of a future course of action and is realized by activities that produce products in a workshop. The information flow is the driving force in the production process.

The cost flow is concerned with how the production process adds value at each stage of that process. Costs are involved in each activity of the production process.

A common approach to system design is the so-called hierarchical method. The essence of this method is to vertically arrange and integrate subsystems, each of which is responsible for tactical planning and control, whereas there is one highest-level system that is responsible for strategic planning. We show these relationships in Figure 8.2. The highest-level subsystem makes strategic decisions that

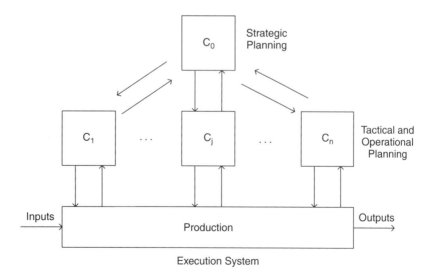

Figure 8.2 Combining manufacturing and management systems.

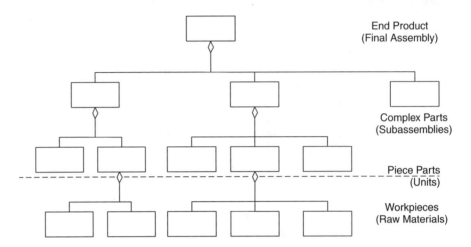

Figure 8.3   Hierarchical product structure.

restrict the operations of the lower-level subsystems. These subsystems report to the highest-level subsystem. The relationship with domain architecture is clear: each subsystem can be analysed as a MAN category, for example.

In general, the created products are quite complex and are typically aggregates or composite entities. In some cases the finished product consists of a number of complex parts. Each complex part consists of piece parts (or units). Finally, a unit is built from workpieces. A workpiece is essentially a raw material. The structure of a finished product is shown in Figure 8.3 as a UML class diagram (in fact, a three-level aggregate object).

8.3 MOTIVATIONAL EXAMPLES

We introduce and motivate three examples to help the reader gain insight into the manufacturing model and why it is important in software development.

8.3.1 Compiler theory

A good example of a manufacturing model can be found in the area of software compilers. A compiler is a program that accepts a source file and produces a target program that then runs in a given computer environment. The first commercial compilers were built in the early 1950s. Some well-known examples are the compilers for Fortran and Cobol. It has been estimated that the first Fortran compiler took almost 40 man-years to write, whereas nowadays university undergraduate students are able to write a compiler in the space of a few months.

The reason for this increase in productivity is that compiler theory is now well developed.

A compiler takes a source program as input and produces as output an equivalent sequence of machine instructions (Aho and Ullman 1977). Because this is a complex process, compiler builders partition the compilation process into a number of activities, or phases as they are called. A phase is the same as an activity in UML because it takes as input one representation of the source program and produces as output another representation. The activity diagram for the compilation process is shown in Figure 8.4. The main activities are:

- *Lexical analysis*: the phase (also called the scanner) that is responsible for separating characters in the source program and grouping them. These groups are called tokens and they usually represent keywords. The output is thus a stream or tree of tokens.
- *Syntax analysis*: the syntax analyser (or parser) groups tokens into syntactic structures called expressions. These expressions are then combined to form statements. The output from the parser is a so-called parse tree.
- *Intermediate code generator*: creates a stream of simple structures. It is possible to produce many kinds of intermediate code. This code can be seen as a kind of machine-independent assembly code (or p-code) because it does not specify the registers for each operation.
- *Optimization*: this phase optimizes the intermediate code so that it runs faster or uses less space and memory. It produces the same output as the intermediate code generator but the code runs faster, for example.

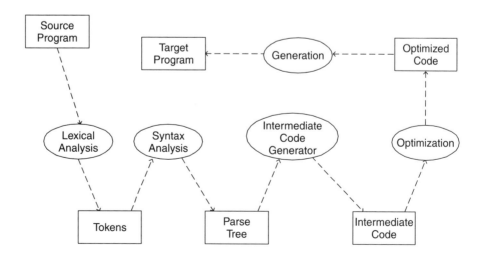

Figure 8.4   Phases of a compiler.

- *Generator*: this is the phase that produces the final object code that will run on the target machine. We decide on memory locations for data and we select the registers in which each computation is to be done.

There are two other issues that we must deal with that are not depicted in Figure 8.4. First, symbol table management or bookkeeping keeps track of the names used by the program and records information about each name. Second, we need to support error handling. This is invoked whenever a flaw is detected in the source program. Both error handling and symbol table management interact with all phases of the compiler. Figure 8.4 suggests that the process is sequential and it is indeed possible to implement a compiler as a batch sequential program. However, modern compilers employ an improved architectural style called a central shared representation (Shaw and Garlan 1996).

The compiler analogy is very useful and we can use it as a baseline architecture for many kinds of dataflow applications. The added value of using compiler theory as a model for our applications is that it serves as a general metaphor in many situations where data in one format is transformed to data in some other format. Examples are:

- Encoding and decoding of information
- Binding data in GUI dialog boxes with the corresponding data in relational database tables
- Formatting data and displaying it on various output media
- 'Import' and 'export' routines from and to external programs (for example, Excel)
- Creating software objects in an object-oriented language (GOF 1995).

8.3.2 Graphics applications

We introduce and document a simplified model for an interactive application that processes information from an ASCII file and produces a display on some output medium. We give the current toy problem a name—we call it Business Graphics System (BGS)—and we view this problem as a specialization of the compiler problem in Section 8.3.1.

The goal is to process an ASCII input file containing numeric data and transform it so that the generated information can be presented on the user's screen using the GDI (Graphics Device Interface) driver. It must be possible to display both pie charts and line diagrams (by 'toggling' between each choice using radio buttons, for example). The context diagram, system decomposition and logical PAC model for BGS are shown in Figure 8.5. The source data is situated in a 'disk' actor system and in this version we assume that the ASCII file contain CSV (comma-separated variable) data in array form; for example, the array data (100, 200, 100) will produce a pie chart with three slices (one slice is 180 degrees while the other two slices

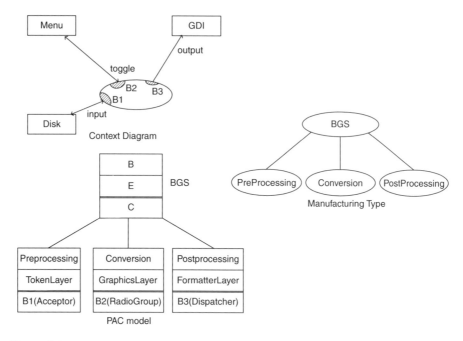

Figure 8.5 Business Graphics System (BGS).

represent 90 degrees). The products of BGS are sent to GDI driver software (GDI is a set of application programming interfaces (API) that allows programmers to create device-independent applications in a Windows environment). Furthermore, the Menu actor system allows us to toggle between different display representations such as line graphs, bar charts and pie charts. The core process is to display data and we realize it by three major activities:

- Preprocessing (produce a parse tree from the source data)
- Conversion (map the parse tree to device-independent graphics objects)
- Postprocessing (create device-dependent displays from the device-independent graphics).

We have chosen the names 'Pre/PostProcessing' for historical and personal reasons. Many manufacturing applications such as Finite Element Methods (FEM) and Computer Aided Design and Manufacturing (CAD/CAM) use the same terminology.

Since BGS is a specialization of a compiler program, we can ask ourselves what the parse tree (internal objects) and optimized code (half-products) are. For the case in which the source data contains CSV data we conclude that the internal data objects are entities such as arrays, lists and other recursive collections. The half-products consist of recursive representations of the charts that will be displayed in GDI. These half-products can be described as 'device-independent graphics objects'

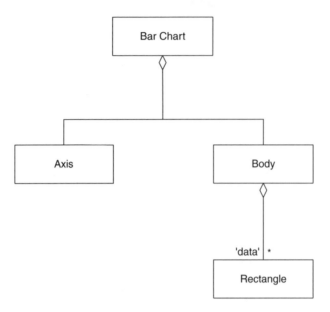

Figure 8.6 'Half product' in BGS.

and they should be modelled as UML class diagrams. For example, a bar chart is shown as a UML class diagram in Figure 8.6. A bar chart consists essentially of an axis and a list of data that is represented as rectangles. Finally, it is the responsibility of the PostProcessing subsystem to accept a bar chart in 'neutral' form, format it and then display it on the appropriate output medium.

We have included the sequence diagrams that depict how to realize these activities in Figures 8.7, 8.8 and 8.9. The diagrams help to motivate the information flow in the system at a conceptual level.

8.3.3 Human memory models

The following example is taken from cognitive psychology. To this end, we discuss a model for human memory that is based on the so-called information process paradigm. The reason that we see this problem as a MAN instance is that there is a clear process of converting one kind of information (namely real-world perceptions) into a permanent record of these perceptions (long-term memory). The mind is classified as a set of processes that store and process information about the individual and the world that she or he inhabits (Lee and Pranja 1995, Gross and McIlveen 1995). There are several attention points that we need to address:

- *Encoding*: the process of taking information about the world and converting it to memory

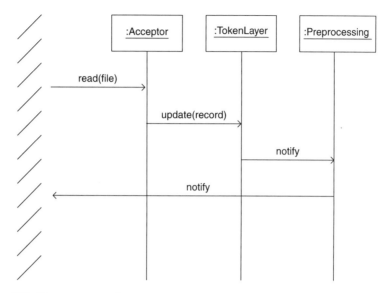

Figure 8.7   Process source data.

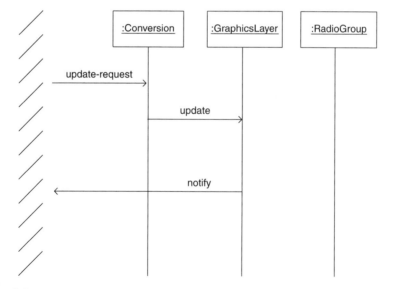

Figure 8.8   Create new graphics objects.

- *Storage*: the way in which information is represented in the brain
- *Retrieval*: how information is made available to people.

The memory information processing model is shown in Figure 8.10. This is a highly simplified model but it is useful because it captures some important features

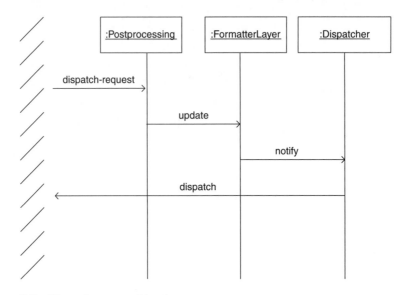

Figure 8.9   Dispatch new graphics data.

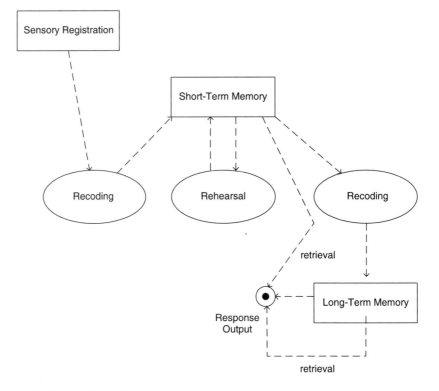

Figure 8.10   Modal model of memory.

of memory. The Sensory Registration holds information that has just entered the cognitive system. Examples are sounds and images. This is information that is in a 'raw state' and it usually consists of electrical signals. These signals are then converted into complex patterns and objects in the brain. The short-term memory (STM) store can typically hold seven chunks of information and represents information that is forgotten within 6–10 seconds (see Miller 1956). However, a process called *rehearsal* can extend the lifetime of information. This is the process of repeating the contents of the short-term store repeatedly in one's head. The long-term memory (LTM) store represents a large storehouse of information in which memories are stored in a relatively permanent way. There seems to be no limit to the amount of information that can be stored in LTM. There are two kinds of organizations in LTM. First, personal or episodic information is stored in chronological order. Events are linked to when and where they occurred. Second, factual or semantic information is stored in semantic categories. Each category contains concepts with similar or associated meanings and these are stored together in the LTM. Human memory models could be used as a useful metaphor for software-based information processing systems, especially shared-memory models.

8.4 GENERAL APPLICABILITY

The MAN category is applicable when there is a clear case of tangible (or intangible) products and services being produced from raw materials. This category models both physical and virtual worlds and we must view 'manufacturing' in the broadest sense of the word. For example, an insurance company could apply the model to 'manufacture' insurance policies and portfolio contracts.

We give a list of some keywords and special terms that arise when discussing MAN systems. As analyst, you should actively listen to customers and other stakeholders because the vocabulary that they use will give hints on how to develop a system.

- Raw materials, stock control, inventory
- Half-products, bill of materials
- Finished products and services
- Resources and objects that are needed for other systems
- Information, product and cost flows.

The workflow models in this category suggest a sequence of activities, with each activity producing added value to the next activities in the 'value chain'. In general, the format and representation mismatch between raw materials and finished product is harmonized by these activities.

8.5 GOALS, PROCESSES AND ACTIVITIES

In general we state that the major goal of MAN systems is to produce products, services or information that is used by other client and collaborator systems. The input
to the core process is raw data having a defined format and the output represents
products that are used by client systems. The activities are:

- *PreProcessing*: accept and validate raw data (produces internal objects)
- *Conversion*: create half-products from internal objects
- *PostProcessing*: manufacture products and services to satisfy customer needs.

8.6 CONTEXT DIAGRAM AND SYSTEM DECOMPOSITION

The context diagram for the MAN category is shown in Figure 8.11. Together
with its satellite systems, a manufacturing application can achieve its goals, namely
produce products and/or services from raw materials. There are five major satellite types:

- *Source*: where the raw materials come from
- *Token System*: classifies and validates incoming raw materials
- *Resources*: contains resources that are needed in order to manufacture the product
- *Management*: systems that monitor and control the manufacturing process
- *Sink*: the ultimate recipients of the finished products.

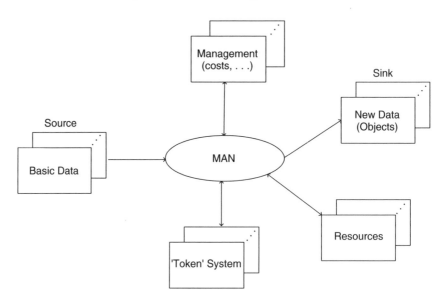

Figure 8.11   MAN environment.

The Source systems may be external legacy systems and different input format types will be supported by the manufacturing system. Of course, it is important that knowledge of these formats does not percolate throughout the system if we wish to avoid a maintenance nightmare. Again, different output formats are possible. The Resources systems hold all resources and spare parts that are needed to support the main manufacturing process. We note that the Management systems in the context diagram may belong to the MIS or PCS categories. In the first case the manufacturing system sends transaction data to the MIS systems for consolidation and reporting, while in the second case the PCS systems receive high-level interrupts and other 'push' alerts via their sensor interfaces and are thus the 'watchdog' or control systems for the manufacturing system. Finally, the Token systems are responsible for the creation of basic building blocks from the raw materials and for validating these raw materials.

We describe the information flow between the current manufacturing system and its actor systems while referring to Figure 8.11:

1. The raw materials are processed.
2. The information in the raw materials is classified and validated.
3. Resources are allocated (this is sometimes called stock control).
4. Management systems (e.g. costs, planning) are informed of the status of the manufacturing process.
5. Sink systems are notified of the status of the final product.

A MAN system is decomposed into three loosely-coupled subsystems: first, the Preprocessing subsystem accepts raw materials and produces internal building blocks and parts; second, the Conversion subsystem produces half-products from the internal objects; and finally the PostProcessing subsystem creates finished products and services.

8.7 STAKEHOLDERS, VIEWPOINTS AND REQUIREMENTS

We give a short description of the main stakeholders that are involved in MAN systems, how they view these systems and what their major viewpoints and requirements are.

8.7.1 Stakeholders and viewpoints

The main stakeholders are:

- *Customers*: client systems that receive the products and services
- *Suppliers*: systems that provide the SUD with raw materials
- *Management*: systems that monitor and control the flow in the MAN system

- *Quality control*: systems that check and validate raw data and Supplier quality
- *Stock control*: resource pools from which the MAN system acquires resources.

Each group has its own special business concerns and viewpoints. These will drive the requirements determination process. Some examples of viewpoints that we based on ISO 9126 are:

- Customers
  - Suitability of product
  - Accuracy of product
  - Usability of product
- Suppliers
  - Reliability
  - Interoperability
  - Stability
- Management
  - Efficiency of manufacturing process
  - Security
  - Reliability of manufacturing process
- Quality control
  - Suitability and accuracy of raw materials
  - Training of manufacturing personnel
  - Conformance and compliance standards
- Stock control
  - Resource efficiency (just-in-time stock)
  - Time efficiency
  - Interoperability with other systems.

It is important for the requirements analyst to determine how the stakeholders view the system. Consciously or unconsciously, a stakeholder has expectations about what kind of system she or he would like to have. It is the analyst's job to make these expectations explicit and to describe them as requirements and use case. For example, we can map these viewpoints to requirements and then to use cases using the Inquiry Cycle model.

Failing to discover the most important viewpoints in the system will lead us to a system that does not satisfy the needs of certain stakeholder groups.

8.7.2 Requirements

Recall that the goal of MAN systems is to produce products, services and information for other client systems. We can qualify this statement by insisting that the product should satisfy certain functional and non-functional requirements. Some examples are:

- *Accuracy*: The system should produce correct and expected products.
- *Security*: It should not be possible to compromise the integrity of the data or products.
- *Interoperability*: The system can receive data from Source systems and send data to Sink systems by the use of predefined standards and protocols, for example XML.
- *Fault-tolerance*: high up-time and low MTBF (mean time between failure).
- *Recoverability*: rollback and the ability to recover from disasters.
- *Time efficiency*: The system should create the products as effectively and as efficiently as possible.
- *Resource efficiency*: The system should create products with the least amount of waste and with optimal use of available resources.
- *Usability*: The system should be easy to understand, learn and operate.
- *Analysability*: The system should have the ability to execute diagnostic procedures that pinpoint bottlenecks in the manufacturing process.
- *Stability*: Local changes to the system structure or functionality have local impact.
- *Portability*: The system should be able to modify the manufacturing process to suit new hardware, customer and software configurations.

The list can be used as input to discussions between the requirements analyst (RA) and the customers of the system. The RA can apply the Inquiry Cycle model (see Appendix 1) to discover requirements and use cases for specific MAN instances. Let us take an example: resource efficiency. We ask the question 'What kinds of resource efficiency?'. Possible answers are 'raw material efficiency', 'human efficiency' and 'machine efficiency'. These newly-discovered requirements are made very tangible by asking 'how to' questions. For example, we could ask the question 'How to realize machine efficiency?'. Answers will allow us to define procedures and use cases that realize this requirement.

The Inquiry Cycle model questions can be applied to the other ISO 9126 characteristics.

8.8 UML CLASSES

This section describes the PAC model for the MAN category. The architecture is shown in Figure 8.12 and we already know that the system has been decomposed into operational, tactical and strategic subsystems, namely PreProcessing, Conversion and PostProcessing. These subsystems are then mapped to a PAC model. The introduction of objects in the entity and boundary layers will tell us how to realize the responsibilities of each subsystem. Each layer is populated by a network

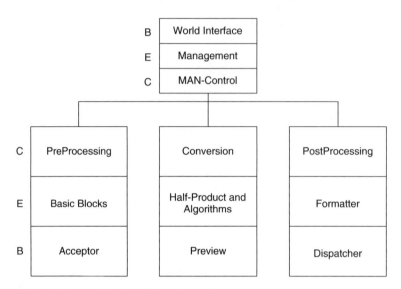

Figure 8.12 PAC model in MAN domain architecture.

or graph of objects. UML class diagrams document this network. The classes are discovered by elaborating the use cases for the particular MAN instance.

We paraphrase how the objects and object layers in Figure 8.12 realize the core process in a MAN category: 'The Acceptor reads, interprets and validates the data from the Source system. Then basic internal objects are created and other systems are notified of this event. The Conversion is requested (for example, through Preview) to convert the newly created internal objects into half-products. Finally, these half-products are formatted and edited to suit the needs of external client systems. The Dispatcher layer is responsible for communication with these clients.'

8.9 USE CASES

It is impossible to document all use cases for a MAN category because each MAN instance is context dependent. However, it is possible to give general guidelines and list those use cases that are common to all MAN instances. These use cases are the realizations of core, supporting and management processes. Of course, the core process is what the customer is interested in: 'produce a product from raw materials'. The corresponding use case U1 describes how this is to be achieved. Its sub-use cases are:

- U1.1: Create basic building blocks (subsystem PreProcessing)
- U1.2: Produce half-products (subsystem Conversion)
- U1.3: Package, manufacture and dispatch product (subsystem PostProcessing).

By examining the context diagram in Figure 8.11 and by documenting the sub-use cases we are able to discover a number of actions in each use case:

- U1.1.1: Read data from Source system
- U1.1.2: Check, validate and create internal objects
- U1.1.3: Notify other systems.

- U1.2.1: Process conversion request
- U1.2.2: Execute conversion algorithm
- U1.2.3: Notify other systems.

- U1.3.1: Start dispatching request
- U1.3.2: Format and transform internal representation
- U1.3.3: Notify and dispatch.

In general, use case U1.2.2 is complex and time-consuming because it is here that we must develop algorithms that convert internal data to half-product data. Furthermore, even more difficult is the problem of ensuring that these algorithms satisfy non-functional requirements such as Reliability, Efficiency and Portability. Project managers beware! The realization of use case U1.2.2 can consume much of the project budget.

Each of the above-mentioned use cases has variants and exceptions which in turn lead to new use cases. This is an attention point when you analyse applications in the MAN category.

Finally, management systems monitor the performance of MAN applications (see Figure 8.11 again) and will have their own set of use cases. For example, we can create a MIS satellite system that monitors the costs in the MAN system. Most of these have to do with normal and exceptional reporting concerning the processes in MAN. For this reason, it is a good idea to view these systems as instances of MIS and PCS categories. The resulting interaction between the current systems and its satellites is a rich source of use cases.

8.10 SPECIALIZATIONS OF MAN SYSTEMS

The MAN category is not restricted to physical production and manufacturing systems. In fact, anything that is created from simpler 'materials' and adds value to some stakeholder group can be viewed as an instance of the MAN category.

A rough classification of MAN applications is:

- Manufacturing of tangible and physical products
- Simulation of real-life situations (CAD/CAM, graphics and visualization)
- Manufacturing of service-related products.

Domain-specific examples can be given but they tend to be very complex and not relevant to some readers. For example, a system to create financial derivative objects (such as options, swaps and portfolios) may not be very interesting to a mechanical engineer. The conceptual distance between the two application types may be too great, even though there are many similarities between the two applications.

8.11 USING MAN SYSTEMS WITH OTHER SYSTEMS

We note that the Management systems in the context diagram (see Figure 8.11) can belong to the MIS and PCS categories. In the first case the manufacturing systems send transaction data to the MIS systems for consolidation and reporting, while in the second case the PCS systems receive high-level interrupts and other 'push' alerts via their sensor interfaces.

It is possible to build large systems by combining MAN instances and instances of other domain categories. To this end, we discuss some possible scenarios:

- S1: MAN as a client, server or collaborator of some other system
- S2: Typical relationships between MAN and other domain architecture types
- S3: How viewpoints and requirements lead to new satellite systems.

Instances of the MAN category typically play the role of sources (servers) to other systems. These objects 'enter' other systems. For example, a common pattern is when a system consists of a number of subsystems, one of which is a MAN system. We see this in Lifecycle models, for example; these consist of MAN, RAT and MIS system. The MAN system creates the basic objects that are then tracked by the RAT system. Of course, it is then possible to create reports for groups of objects in the MIS system.

8.12 SUMMARY AND CONCLUSIONS

We have discussed a class of applications that we group under the name of the Manufacturing (MAN) category. The major process in all instances of this category is to create products and services from raw materials. It is possible to use this model in many software projects and its applicability is not limited to 'strict' manufacturing systems (although it is of use here as well). In fact, objects need to be created in many applications and the MAN category model should be used as a baseline model. A good way to learn MAN systems is to study how compilers are built or how CAD/CAM systems are designed. After all, much of the early research and emerging object products had to do with graphics applications.

Instances of MAN systems are used by other systems. This is because products from MAN systems are tracked, monitored and controlled by instances of other domain categories.

The most critical question to ask is: does my system involve the manufacture of entities that are used by other systems? If the answer is yes, you can be fairly sure that you can model the system as an instance of MAN systems. Otherwise, you should continue with your investigations.

9 Access Control Systems (ACS)

'To learn meaningfully, individuals must choose to relate new knowledge to relevant concepts and propositions they already know.'

Joseph Novak

9.1 INTRODUCTION AND OBJECTIVES

In this chapter we describe applications that are concerned with the problem of accessing entities, objects and resources using well-defined access policies and procedures. Many real-life systems and applications are concerned with this kind of problem and to this end we establish a general framework for all existing and future systems in this category. In particular, we benchmark the well-known Reference Monitor model that was devised to model security and access control policies in mainframe and minicomputer systems.

There are many situations where the ACS category can be found. Usually, it is a satellite system of some other system but it is important enough to be studied in its own right. We give some well-known examples of this category:

- Drink vending machines
- Automated teller machines
- Gambling machines
- The Reference Monitor model in operating system theory
- Systems that model access to entities (in the widest sense of the word)
- Interactively accessing database information
- Security systems in general.

In fact, the Reference Monitor model will be used as the motivator for ACS.

9.2 BACKGROUND AND HISTORY

Access control systems are very common. As we shall see, standard reference models were developed in the 1960s that describe how to analyse and design secure computer systems.

We show how to construct a general model. This model will subsume many specific examples and test cases that we encounter in textbooks and real-life applications.

9.3 MOTIVATIONAL EXAMPLES

We give a non-trivial example in this section. This is the famous Reference Monitor model that describes secure computer systems. The model is almost 50 years old and we also discuss how it has evolved to accommodate developments since its inception.

9.3.1 The Reference Monitor model

The background for the category in this section is research that was carried out in the 1960s on how to achieve security in multi-user computer systems. Initial attempts were chaotic and development work was aimed at finding all the things that could go wrong with the system's security and then attempting to resolve these problems one at a time. Researchers soon realized that the best way to solve these problems was to create a basic model for a secure computer system. To this end, the so-called Reference Monitor model was born and it has been used with success in several operating systems, for example VAX/VMS from Digital Equipment Corporation (DEC). (Incidentally, the author was a system manager at a large oil and gas company during the 1980s and this is where he gained hands-on experience in this area.) For more information on this model, see DEC (1988). We describe a computer system in terms of a number of generic entities as shown in Figure 9.1 and the relationships between them. The main actor systems are Subjects, Objects, Authorization Database, Audit Trail and Reference Monitor Mechanism. We now describe each actor and its role in the model.

- *Subjects*: These are active entities that gain access to information on behalf of people. When a user logs in to VMS, the user provides a user name and password. The password serves as an authentication that is known only to the user and to VMS. Once a process has been created, VMS assigns a so-called User Identification Code (or UIC) and this corresponds to the name of the user who created the process. Furthermore, the UIC identifies the user's membership in a

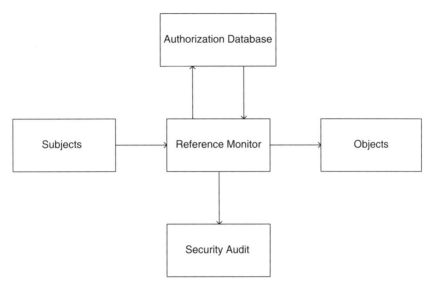

Figure 9.1   Reference Monitor diagram.

group. This group could correspond to the user's department, project or function, for example.

- *Objects*: Objects are passive repositories of information and they must be protected in VMS:
  — Files
  — Directories
  — Logical names
  — Disk volumes
  — Network objects
  — Mailboxes
  — Queues.

  VMS protects these objects from unauthorized access and provides several mechanisms for their controlled sharing.

- *Authorization Database*: Each subject's authorization credentials that are needed to gain access to an object are stored in an authorization database. Different objects are shared with different levels of access and are subject to a so-called UIC-based protection. This type of protection specifies whether access to an object is allowed or denied depending on the subject that is attempting to access it. For example, access can be defined in terms of the owner of the object, in terms of the other members in the same UIC group as the owner, or in terms of all users in all groups. For example, we could define protection levels in such a way that all users in the same UIC group have read and execute access to an object while users outside the group have no access whatsoever. It is possible to augment

UIC-based protection by sharing objects using access control lists (ACLs). An ACL describes which users or groups of users are allowed or denied access to objects in the VMS system.

- *Audit Trail* (*also known as Security Audit*): It should be possible to audit classes of events. It is important to monitor events such as successful and unsuccessful attempts to gain access to sensitive objects. For example, a terminal can be designated as a security alarm console where all auditable alarms are displayed. The audit trail mechanism allows security managers to record many kinds of events.
- *Reference Monitor Mechanism*: This mechanism enforces security rules and should satisfy the following requirements:
  — It mediates every attempt by a subject to gain access to an object.
  — It provides a tamperproof database and audit trail that are fully protected from unauthorized access.
  — It should be small, simple and well structured, thus promoting its effectiveness in enforcing security requirements.

The main responsibilities of the Reference Monitor mechanism are authorization of subjects, granting subjects access to objects according to the database requirements (called authentication) and recording events in the audit trail (if the audit trail feature is enabled). We note that it is possible in VMS to grant a user the authority to modify or subvert the Reference Monitor mechanism. For example, a process with the BYPASS privilege can gain access to any object in VMS without having to refer to the authorization database.

Each user in the system has a unique UIC assigned to it by the system manager. A UIC in alphanumeric format consists of a user name and optionally a group name, for example:

[member]
[group, member]

It is also possible to specify a UIC in numeric format, for example [100, 3] which specifies user 3 in group 100. The UIC is translated to a 32-bit numeric key that is kept in a so-called *system rights database*.

We define protection levels for an object by using the command language in VMS. For example, the following code defines access to file 'myfile.dat':

```
SET PROTECTION = (OWN: RWED, GROUP: RE, WORLD: R) myfile.dat
```

This statement says that the owner has read, write, execute and delete privileges for 'myfile.dat' while the group in which the owner belongs has read and execute privileges. Finally, all other users (the world) have read privilege only.

ACLs consist of access control list entries (ACEs) that grant or deny access to a particular system object. Each ACE specifies a user or group of users and the type of access permitted. The authorization database is often represented as an *access matrix* and this lists subjects as rows and objects as columns (the matrix is often a *sparse matrix*, that is one that has few non-null entries). Each matrix entry represents the access that one subject has to one object. An example of such a matrix is given in Figure 9.2. The asterisk '*' is used to denote access to the object; different kinds of access are possible, such as READ, WRITE and EXECUTE. Blank entries state that there is no access to the object from the given subject.

If we break up an access matrix by rows we arrive at a so-called *capability-based system*. This means that each subject carries a list of the objects that it can access. It is of course also possible to break up the matrix by columns and in this case we get a listing of all the subjects for each object. This is called an *authority-based system*. Each column describes who has access to a given object.

Objects	U	V	W	x
Subjects				
A	*			*
B			*	
C		*		

Figure 9.2　Example of an access matrix.

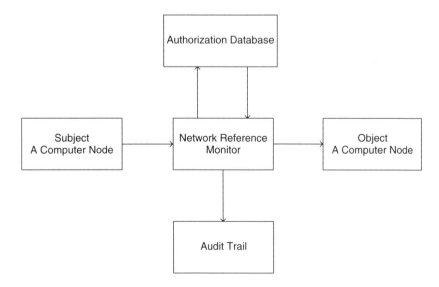

Figure 9.3　Reference Monitor in a network.

Finally, Figure 9.3 represents the Reference Monitor in a network. In this case subjects and objects are in different address spaces. This makes security issues all the more difficult. This subject is outside the scope of the current book. For more on designing such systems, please consult POSA (1996) and Schmidt *et al* (2000).

9.4 GENERAL APPLICABILITY

The ACS category is useful when we wish to protect other systems from unauthorized access. It is typically a front-end 'proxy' to other systems. We give a list of some keywords and special terms that arise when analysing ACS systems. As analyst, you should actively listen to customers and other stakeholders because the vocabulary that they use will give hints on how to develop a system:

- Customer access to certain resources in certain ways
- Authorization issues (who is authorized to do what)
- Authentication (check customer credentials when he or she tries to access resources)
- Security levels
- Normal users and 'super' users
- Audit trails
- Security viewpoint (in ISO 9126)
- Availability (a kind of Reliability in ISO 9126).

This list can be used as a check to determine whether stakeholders use the above jargon and vocabulary. They will give hints regarding the applicability of the ACS model to your current application.

9.5 GOALS, PROCESSES AND ACTIVITIES

The main goal of this category is customer service because all instances of the category have to do with providing access to valuable resources. In order to convince ourselves of this fact, just think of the different kinds of ACS systems:

- All kinds of product vending machines
- Automated teller machines (ATM)
- All kinds of systems that access databases using batch and interactive interfaces
- Gambling machines (for example, 'one-arm bandits' and fruit machines)
- Local (batch, interactive) and remote access to software and hardware objects in a computer network.

There may be several associated sub-goals such as security, availability (of product and resources), reliability and usability. The most important stakeholder in an ACS category is the beneficiary of the products and services that the system delivers. Thus, we are not far wrong if we state that the core process is responsible for the delivery of products based on some kind of customer request:

The Core Process (P1) in ACS is responsible for the delivery of products and services to authorized customers.

The main activities in this process are:

- P1.1: Process customer request
- P1.2: Check customer credentials and product availability
- P1.3: Commit customer request.

Activity P1.1 produces an internal representation of a customer request that is checked by P1.2 (in fact, this is a kind of *proxy*). If the customer credentials are good and if the product is available, P1.2 sends a commit request to P1.3. Finally, P1.3 is responsible for delivering the products to the customer.

It is interesting and useful to think of the activities in P1 as follows: P1.1 is responsible for *strategic* issues such as interfacing with the customer, P1.2 is responsible for *tactical* issues such as checking product availability and customer credentials, while P1.3 is responsible for *operational* issues such as actions that have to do with product availability status and the actual delivery of products. These categories will be explored in an example when we introduce and analyse the Drink Vending Machine (DVM) in Chapter 15.

9.6 CONTEXT DIAGRAM AND SYSTEM DECOMPOSITION

The context diagram for ACS is based on the Reference Monitor model and we show it in Figure 9.4. We include the generic boundary objects for completeness, as we will need them when we create the corresponding PAC model. The main stakeholder systems are:

- *ACS*: the system to be modelled
- *Source*: the system where customer requests originate
- *Authentication system*: Checks customer credentials
- *Resource system*: the physical location of products and services
- *Sink*: the ultimate client systems
- *MIS*: various management systems (for example, Audit Trail systems).

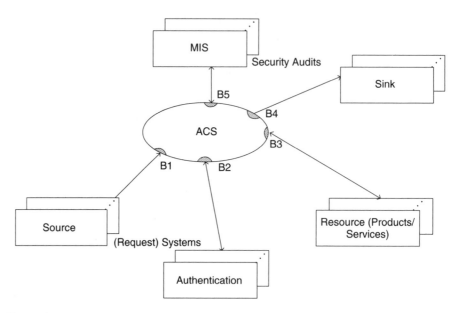

Figure 9.4 Context diagram for Access Control System.

Each instance of ACS will have a different interpretation of these responsibilities. To take an example, in the case of a gambling machine (fruit machine) in a casino, we interpret these responsibilities as follows:

- *ACS*: the system that models the gambling machine
- *Source*: the buttons on the front panel of the gambling machine
- *Authentication system*: the coin unit
- *Resource*: the product is the number of points that you can win
- *Sink*: alarm bells, flashing lights that indicate that you have won the jackpot
- *MIS*: audits of customer behaviour and other resource monitoring information.

We now decompose ACS into its constituent subsystems. This is based on the core process and its activities as seen in Section 9.5. The main subsystems are:

- *Source*: responsible for product lifecycle (operational)
- *Transaction Centre*: responsible for customer and product validation (tactical)
- *Interface*: responsible for interactions with the customer.

9.7 STAKEHOLDERS, VIEWPOINTS AND REQUIREMENTS

As can be seen from Figure 9.4, each system falls under the responsibility of a stakeholder or group of stakeholders. We discuss these as humans in this case:

- *Customers*: responsible for using the ACS system, entering commands and being informed of the status of a transaction. A customer can play the roles of selector (selecting a product) or receiver (receiving the products or goods).
- *System administration/access mangers*: determine which customers have access to which products and services. These managers are responsible for the life of the authorization database.
- *Product systems*: the systems that receive commands from the ACS system.
- *Various management groups*, for example *category managers* (who are interested in knowing how well a product is selling), security managers and legislative bodies.

As with MIS systems, we could partition stakeholders into operational, tactical and strategic groups.

We now discuss the viewpoints taken by each stakeholder group. Customers are usually interested in Functionality, especially Accuracy and Suitability. System administrators and managers are interested in Security and Compliance. Finally, category and product managers are interested in Reliability (no down-time), Efficiency (time and resource efficiency) and Availability (a kind of Reliability)

9.8 UML CLASSES

The PAC model for the ACS category is shown in Figure 9.5. This picture is self-documenting, especially if we view it from the perspective of the context diagram (which determines the location of the Boundary objects) and the activity diagram for the core process (which determines the location of the Control objects). The most important Entity layer is Session as it is here that transactions are born, updated and committed.

9.9 USE CASES

The high priority and most critical use cases are deduced from the corresponding core processes. For each process we are able to discover a large number of use cases that realize it. The requirements analyst should be able to discover these use cases by using the questions from the Inquiry Cycle model.

The main use case is the realization of the core process P1 that we discussed in Section 9.5. We call it U1 'Execute customer request' and it has the following sub-use cases:

- U1.1: Process customer request
- U1.2: Check customer credentials and product availability
- U1.3: Commit customer request.

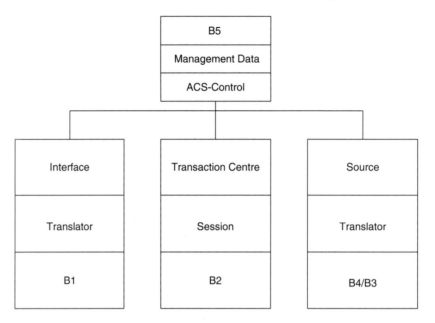

Figure 9.5 PAC model for ACS.

It is possible to document U1 and its sub-use cases using the standard template mechanism. We leave this as an exercise; however, we show the most important details:

- U1: Execute customer request
  Precondition: Product system idle, operational and accepting requests
  Description:
  — U1.1: Process customer request
  — U1.2: Check customer credentials and product availability
  — U1.3: Commit customer request
  Postcondition: Product delivered and product system reverts to idle mode
- U1.1: Process customer request
  Precondition: Product system idle, operational and accepting requests
  Description:
  — Read customer request data
  — Check and validate request data; create basic request
  — Notify ACS that a new pending request has arrived
  Postcondition: System waiting for request to be committed
- U1.2: Check customer credentials and product availability
  Precondition: System waiting for request to be committed
  Description:
  — Check customer credentials
  — Check product availability

— Send request to Resource (product) system

Postcondition: Request commitment pending

- U1.3: Commit customer request

Precondition: Request commitment pending

Description:

— Execute request

— Commit and close transaction

— Notify client systems of transaction status

Postcondition: Product delivered and product system reverts to idle mode.

9.10 SPECIALIZATIONS OF ACS

We discuss two specific specializations of the ACS category. The first example concerns the development of security models for distributed applications and the second example discusses how the well-known design pattern called Proxy (GOF 1995, POSA 1996, Schmidt *et al* 2000) can be subsumed under the ACS category.

9.10.1 Security models for Web-based applications

An interesting extension to the Reference Monitor model is to define security models for Web-based applications (see Joshi *et al* 2001). As always, the goal is to protect information systems from unauthorized access. In particular, we can list the main sub-goals:

- Confidentiality (secrecy)
- Integrity
- Availability
- Accountability
- Assurance.

Our interest in this section is in describing several models that address the access control requirements of distributed systems:

- Direct access control (DAC)
- Mandatory access control (MAC)
- Role-based access control (RBAC).

The first two models are traditional while the latter model is new. We now discuss each model in some detail.

- *DAC*: All subjects and objects are defined in much the same way as in the Reference Monitor model. Subjects that are owners of objects may grant or revoke access rights on those objects to other subjects. DAC policies are the most widely used in Web applications. The disadvantage is that they do not provide good security. An extension to DAC is the Dynamically Typed Access Control (DTAC) model in which no distinction is made between subjects and objects. DTAC is suitable for dynamic environments where the roles of subject and object change on a regular basis. The approach in DTAC is to group entities into types, thus making administration easier.
- *MAC*: All subjects and objects are classified based on predefined sensitivity levels. A goal of MAC is to control information flow so that confidentiality and security of information can be ensured. This property is absent in DAC. For example, it is not possible for low-integrity information to flow to high-integrity objects. In general, we are interested in multi-level classifications of information that are enforced by a service provider. This provider distinguishes among users and the type of information being accessed.
- *RBAC*: This is a generalization of traditional models and is based on role modelling. A role represents organizational responsibilities and functions and is defined independently of the physical subjects which play that role. The role-based model directly supports arbitrary, organization-specific security policies. Security administration is simplified because the number of roles is usually much less than the number of subjects in an organization. The UML diagram in Figure 9.6 shows the relationship between Subject, Roles and Objects. We see that it is possible for a subject to dynamically switch roles. The advantages of RBAC are:
  — Flexibility
  — Policy neutrality
  — Good support for security management and administration
  — A natural mechanism for addressing the security issues associated the execution of tasks and workflows
  — Ease of deployment over the Internet.

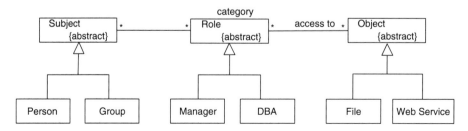

Figure 9.6   UML model for role-based access policies.

9.10.2 Access control during design: the Proxy pattern

We now discuss a special case of an ACS category that occurs during the design and implementation phases of the software lifecycle. This is the so-called Proxy pattern. The Proxy pattern makes the clients of a component communicate with a representative rather than the original component itself (GOF 1995, POSA 1996). There are many reasons for the introduction of this ambassador or 'go-between'. In general, the proxy is used to shield the client in some way from the original component. We first discuss how to implement a simple variant of the Proxy pattern in an object-oriented language (GOF 1995) and we then discuss several extensions that are needed for large systems (POSA 1996). To start, let us assume that a class called `MySource` implements a certain service called `service_request()`. We allow clients the possibility to call this function indirectly. To this end, we create a new class `Proxy` that has a reference to `MySource` and implements the function `service_request()`. Both classes are subclassed from an abstract class `Source` that declares `service_request()` as an abstract function (as in Java) or as a pure virtual function (as in C++). The UML class diagram is shown in Figure 9.7. The client accesses the `Proxy` class and this class then forwards the request to the original component as shown in the sequence diagram in Figure 9.8. We note that a `preprocess()` function is executed before the request is forwarded and a `postprocess()` function is executed after the request has been forwarded. The reader will notice that we have included a timing constraint in the sequence diagram in Figure 9.8 and this is needed in cases when the original component `MySource` is not responding or has crashed.

Buschmann has identified a number of proxies that can be used in conjunction with other systems. We are interested in using these proxies with domain categories and their instances. In all cases we speak of a client system C that wishes to access

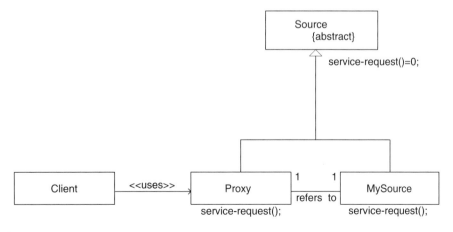

Figure 9.7 Proxy class structure.

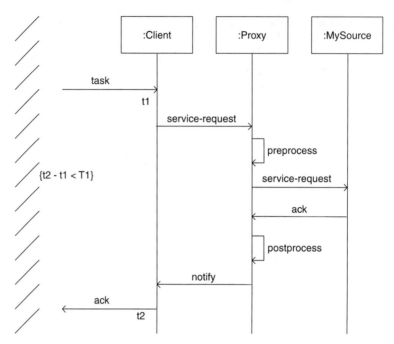

Figure 9.8   Sequence diagram for proxy pattern.

the services of some other system S. We introduce an instance of an ACS between the two systems. Requests from system C to S are intercepted by the ACS system. The ACS system decides what is to be done with the request. There are various kinds of proxies depending on what the software requirements are:

- *Remote proxy*: Clients or remote components are shielded from the idiosyncrasies of network addresses and interprocess communication (IPC) protocols, such as sockets. The proxy encapsulates and maintains the physical location of the original component. There are three options concerning the address space of client and original component:
  — Client and original are in the same address space
  — Client and original are in different address spaces in the same machine
  — Client and original are in different address spaces in different machines.
  For the first case we do not need a proxy as such but we could use the Gamma proxy as shown in Figures 9.7 and 9.8. For communication between components in different machines we need to define information such as machine ID, port ID (or process number) and an object ID.
- *Protection proxy*: This proxy protects the original component from unauthorized access. To this end, the proxy must check the access rights of each client by some kind of authentication process.

- *Cache proxy*: This is a component that is able to hold temporary data in some special data area. Of course, we must develop a strategy to model the lifecycle of this temporary data, that is its creation, access to it, its refresh policy and the policy for destroying the data (after a certain time-out period). In particular, we must pay attention to the following issues (POSA 1996):
  - *What* object creates the cache data and *how* is the cache data created?
  - How to free up space for new entries (develop a strategy)?
  - 'Cache invalidation': how to update distributed cache data when the original component changes (ensuring that data is up-to-date)?
- *Synchronization proxy*: This controls multiple simultaneous client access to an object. It is possible to control the number of clients that access the original component by defining semaphores or mutexes; furthermore, we can distinguish between read and write actions. For example, we can construct a proxy for single write and multiple reads.
- *Counting proxy*: This is a technique for automatic deletion of objects when they are no longer needed. It is sometimes called *reference counting*. This technique is to be found in Microsoft's COM/DCOM technology, for example.
- *Virtual proxy* (*lazy construction*): This is used when a client wishes to access objects from secondary storage, for example a hard disk. The client does not know whether the data is in main storage or in secondary storage. The data is loaded from the hard disk when first accessed; it is then loaded into memory after which time it is no longer necessary to use the data from the hard disk.
- *Firewall proxy*: This is a proxy that is needed in a secure network environment. A firewall machine is placed between the system to be accessed and potential clients. This is sometimes called *a proxy server*.

We conclude this section with some remarks on the Proxy pattern:

1. We have subsumed design-level proxies under the ACS category. Each type of proxy is an instance of the ACS category and it can be analysed just like any other system.
2. It is an easy task to model single and mixed-mode proxies using the PAC model. For example, we could create a proxy that is both caching and remote.
3. The rationale for using this proxy. Our thesis is that the appropriate proxy is a realization of one or more ISO 9126 characteristics. See Figure 9.9. For example, all proxies protect the original component from direct access and hence they promote Security (note that Security is a sub-characteristic of Functionality!).
4. Our approach subsumes other patterns that use proxy, for example the Forwarder–Receiver pattern (see POSA 1996). In general this pattern allows two systems on different machines to communicate with each other, not directly but through so-called forwarders and receivers that are essentially instances of the ACS category. See Figure 9.10 for a sketch.

	Functionality	Reliability	Efficiency	Usability	Portability	Maintainability
Remote	△			◕	○	
Protection	◕	◕		○		
Cache	○		◕	○		
Synchronization	○	◕		○	○	
Counting	○	◕		◕		
Virtual	○		◕	○	○	
Firewall	◕	◕		○		

◕ Strong

○ Medium

△ Weak

Figure 9.9 Proxy type and quality characteristics.

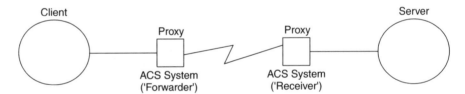

Figure 9.10 High-level view of the Forwarder–Receiver pattern.

9.11 USING ACS WITH OTHER SYSTEMS

The ACS category is used mainly as a 'buffer' system between client and server systems. Its main function is to screen and filter information and data. It is a common model in many application areas.

10 Lifecycle and composite models

'*riverrun, past Eve and Adam's, from swerve of shore to bend of bay, brings us by a commodious vicus of recirculation back to Howth Castle and Environs.*'

James Joyce *Finnegans Wake*

'*When tackling a problem, try to decompose it into simpler sub-problems.*'

George Polya

10.1 INTRODUCTION AND OBJECTIVES

Real applications are more complex than the five basic types that we have discussed in the previous chapters. In fact, most applications will be composed from a number of these basic types. In particular, we focus in this chapter on one special case; we call it the Lifecycle Model (LCM) and it consists of manufacturing (MAN), tracking (RAT) and management (MIS) parts.

We recall that we discussed the 'big five' building block categories:

- MAN (manufacture products/services/goods from raw materials)
- RAT (track products/objects in space and time)
- MIS (produce high-level information from low-level transaction data)
- PCS (monitor and control exceptional situations in some real or artificial world)
- ACS (control and restrict access to objects or information).

We give a provisional definition of what LCM is:

A lifecycle category models an entity from the moment it is created to when it is no longer needed or used in a system.

In fact, the Lifecycle category is an aggregation of MAN, RAT and MIS categories. First, the MAN category creates objects from raw materials, then the RAT category assigns these to resources and the MIS category produces reports that describe how the objects behave and function in the multi-dimensional world in which they live.

Lifecycle models abound in all phases of the business and software lifecycles. Business people speak in terms of product and customer lifecycles and designers talk about C++ object lifecycle patterns (see GOF 1995). There are many similarities. Furthermore, the concept of lifecycle models is particularly strong in the retail industry and in marketing circles. Our interest in this chapter is to show how to model the lifecycle of *any* entity by using the Lifecycle category.

10.2 BACKGROUND AND HISTORY

One motivation for the Lifecycle category comes from the retail industry (Gattorna and Walters 1996). In this domain we are interested in product lifecycle models. There are four major phases or stages in the life of a product:

- Product introduction
- Product growth
- Product maturity
- Product decline.

During product introduction the product is available to innovator groups that will account for the success or failure of the product. Costs are not unimportant but they are viewed less rigorously than in later phases of the product lifecycle. The growth stage is characterized by the introduction of distribution channels as demand grows. Availability and delivery reliability are important during this stage in order to ensure sustained growth. As the maturity stage is reached, sales volumes are high and competition is intense. Furthermore, new means of maintaining margins must be investigated. For example, third-party distribution service companies may be seconded, thus maintaining cost-effectiveness. During the decline stage both product and distribution characteristics are rationalized. Customers usually become highly price sensitive and this means that margins may be seriously affected unless the logistics activity is reviewed.

10.3 MOTIVATIONAL EXAMPLE: THE RENT-A-MACHINE SYSTEM

We now give an example of a lifecycle model. This is a discussion of a problem in the retail (non-food) domain and we show how high-level and 'patchy' customer requirements are integrated into a lifecycle system. Once this model has been constructed we will be in a position to improve our understanding of the problem and to help the customer focus on the essential issues (in this case the core processes). In this particular case we have seen that some stakeholders tend to concentrate on exceptions and secondary requirements while losing sight of the main workflow.

A large garden centre on the outskirts of the city sells and rents machines (such as lawn mowers, saws and other hardware). It has been decided to automate the rental activities in the centre. The system is called RAM (Rent-a-machine system). To this end, the requirements analyst has carried out a number of interviews with domain experts and customers. To make a long story short, it has been determined that the main goal is to provide customer service. The core process is to accept customer requests (for example, a customer may wish to rent a lawn mower and an electric saw during the first week of July). Reports, invoices and other management information must be produced. Figure 10.1 is the product manager's impression of the workflow in the system and a chart that shows the reporting functionality that is to be produced. We paraphrase the core process as follows:

The objective is to rent a machine, use it for a given number of days or weeks and then return it to the garden centre. To this end, the customer usually reserves the machine by telephone or by Internet. Then the customer travels to the garden centre to pick up the machine. A contract is drawn up (including an insurance policy). The customer returns the machine when it is no longer needed. It is inspected for any possible damage. The contract is signed off.

We develop a lifecycle model for this problem. There are three major processes:

- P1: Create (basic) Reservation object (Manufacturing system)
- P2: Create (committed) Contract object (Tracking system)
- P3: Create Machine usage (transaction) object (MIS system).

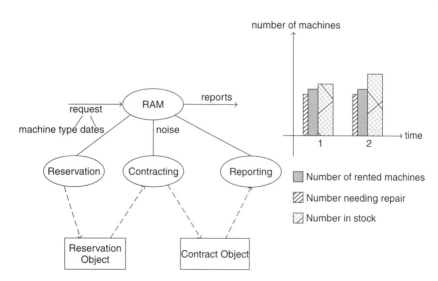

Figure 10.1 The product manager's impression of the workflow after first meeting with the customer.

The input for P1 is customer request data (type of machine and when customer wishes to rent the machine); the output from P1 is a basic reservation that is also input for P2. Process P2 then determines whether it is possible to rent the machine and, if successful, draws up a contract (including insurance policy, terms of use and operating manual). The customer collects the machine that he or she then uses for a given period of time.

The input for P3 takes place when the customer returns the machine. The input is validated and the machine is checked to determine whether it has been used according to the contract in process P2. For example, the machine may have been damaged while in use by the customer. A report is made and the deal is closed. The data is placed in the DataWarehouse.

The processes P1, P2 and P3 are realized by three domain categories of a given type, namely P1 is realized by a MAN category, P2 by a RAT category and P3 by a MIS category. The context diagrams for these systems are given in Figures 10.2, 10.3 and 10.4 and are in fact the *instantiations* of the corresponding context diagrams for the MAN, RAT and MIS categories as discussed in earlier chapters.

The high-level activities in process P1 are:

- P1.1: Create basic **request** object (type of machine only)
- P1.2: Reserve the machine for a period of time (in machine database)
- P1.3: Create **reservation object** and notify interested parties.

The high-level activities in process P2 are:

- P2.1: Create **basic contract** object
- P2.2: Physically assign the machine to the contract (it's a deal!)
- P2.3: Notify interested parties of new **assigned contract** object.

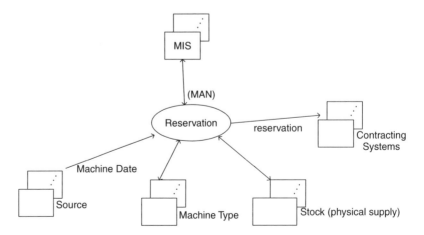

Figure 10.2   Context diagram: manufacture of reservation objects.

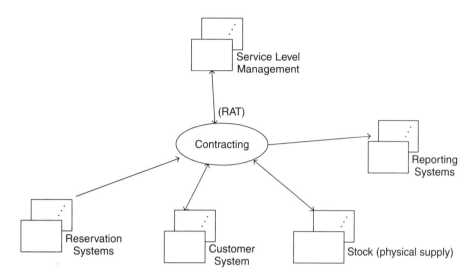

Figure 10.3 Context diagram: creating a contract.

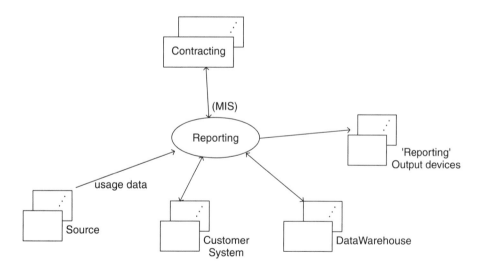

Figure 10.4 Context diagram: closing the contract.

The high-level activities in process P3 are:

- P3.1: Create **basic transaction** object (when customer brings back machine)
- P3.2: Calculate and merge the data (compare used and scheduled resource usage)
- P3.3: Create a **report** (including extra costs, damage reports, etc.).

Let's have a look at the use cases for process P1:

- U1.1: Create basic **request** object (type of machine only)
- U1.2: Reserve the machine for a period of time (in machine database)
- U1.3: Create **reservation object** and notify interested parties.

It is a good idea if the requirements analyst documents these use cases using the standard template document structure. The task is made easier because the customer has provided the requirements analyst with a list of requirements and features. These are essentially actions in the corresponding use case description. To show what we mean we give the list of features for process P2 (Create Contract):

- F1: When collecting a machine, find the corresponding reservation object.
- F2: Create a unique contract number.
- F3: Check whether there are special things to be noted (machine damaged in some way).
- F4: Other possible accessories to be rented as well (for example, protective goggles).
- F5: It is possible to insure the machine.
- F6: It may be necessary to place a down payment.
- F7: Create contract and calculate amount due.
- F8: Payment type (credit card, cash, cheque) and discount schemes.
- F9: Print the contract.
- F10: Print the manual and 'how to use' guidelines.

Many customers think in terms of features. There are many dangers in this *point-to-point* way of thinking, the main one being that we run the risk that features and not requirements will be implemented in this system. It is the job of the requirements analyst to assimilate them into use cases. In the initial stages, we should concentrate on those use cases and features that have to do directly with the most important processes in the system.

10.4 GENERAL APPLICABILITY

The Lifecycle Model (LCM) is suitable for systems that model entities for their entire life. The basic scenarios are always the same: create an entity, assign resources to it, track it in time and space and produce long-term and historical decision-support information on individual entities and groups of related entities. Most organizations will need several LCM systems. This is because product development is a multi-layered process in general; complex products are built from simpler products and each product is potentially the end-result of a LCM system. A simplified example

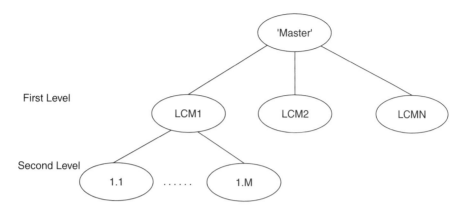

Figure 10.5 Multi-levelled LCM system.

is shown in Figure 10.5. In this case, the Master system controls and monitors a number of first-level lifecycle systems, each of which may be coupled to second-level and possibly 'simpler' lifecycle systems. Such a topology is to be found in production companies such as the automotive and process industries.

We give a list of some keywords and special terms that arise when discussing LCM systems. As analyst, you should actively listen to customers and other stakeholders because the vocabulary that they use will give hints on how to develop a system.

- The full product lifecycle from A to Z
- Use when you feel that your problem is a combination of the 'big five' categories
- Use when operational (manufacturing), tactical (tracking and distribution) and strategic (long-term management) viewpoints play a role.

The final remark deserves comment. Let us suppose that you have developed a system that tracks the status of individual orders in a furniture factory (this will be a RAT instance) and let us suppose that the system is up and running. As always happens with good software, management now wants to have reporting functionality and links to popular programs such as Excel. In many cases the knee-jerk reaction is to reanimate the system source code, add new member functions to the Entity classes, add new Boundary classes and carry out other duties in order to satisfy the new requirements. The end-result is spaghetti! What we should have done was to leave the tracking system intact, add a new satellite system (of the MIS category) and define the interfaces and client–server relationships between the RAT and MIS systems. This is achieved by another round of requirements analysis. The advantage is that we still end up with a maintainable system that adheres to loose coupling and strong cohesion principles. Furthermore, we arrive at a configuration in which each system has clearly defined and standardized interfaces with other systems.

An important dimension in Lifecycle models is time. It is important at the outset to determine when life starts and when life ends, so to speak. For example, what do we do when an order in an Order Processing System has been closed? There are various answers depending on the requirements, for example:

- Physically remove the order from the system.
- Archive and store the order for a number of years.
- 'Reanimate' old orders at some later date.

Each option must be examined and a thorough analysis will lead to new viewpoints, use cases and satellite systems.

10.5 GOALS, PROCESSES AND ACTIVITIES

In general we can state that the goal of a Lifecycle category is to have full knowledge of an entity. The activity diagram for the LCM category is shown in Figure 10.6. The primary input is a request for a new product or entity. The primary output is decision-support information concerning the product. There are three main sub-processes, each of which corresponds to a basic domain category. It is important to determine what the internal products and half-products are.

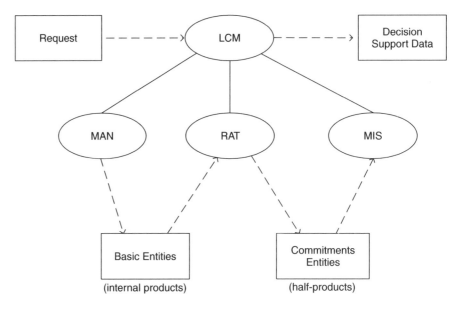

Figure 10.6   Activity diagram for Lifecycle Model (LCM).

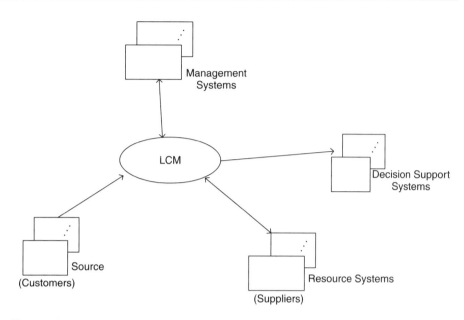

Figure 10.7   Context diagram for Lifecycle Model (LCM).

10.6 CONTEXT DIAGRAM AND SYSTEM DECOMPOSITION

The simplified context diagram for this category is shown in Figure 10.7. We have shown the main satellite systems. The two most important systems are Source and Decision Support, which are the systems where basic requests come from and where decision-support information is sent to, respectively. The Resource Systems are where suppliers' raw materials and other resources are stored. Finally, Management Systems is a general name for those client systems that represent various stakeholders such as the Law, Regulations, Planning, Service Level Management and Quality Management. Each specific instance of LCM will have its own set.

10.7 STAKEHOLDERS, VIEWPOINTS AND REQUIREMENTS

This is a short section because much of what can be said is deduced from the fact that LCM's stakeholders are the union of the stakeholders from the corresponding MAN, RAT and MIS systems. In particular, functional and non-functional requirements need to be specified. The main bottlenecks have to do with the interfaces between MAN and RAT systems on the one hand, and the interfaces between RAT and MIS systems on the other hand. We give some guidelines and hints; a full list is beyond the scope of this chapter and the ISO 9126 characteristics should be examined when you embark on a real-world project.

- *Interoperability*: We must define a suitable ontology or language that each sub-system understands. For example, the structure and semantics of products must be known to each subsystem in LCM.
- *Reliability*: Product information, resources and product status information must be available at all times.
- *Efficiency*: Efficient and effective throughput in the system is important. This includes performance measurement (for example, the total order cycle time for an order in an order processing lifecycle system).
- *Usability*: How easy is it for stakeholders to learn the system and how easy is it for them to communicate with other stakeholders?
- *Portability*: Is it possible to adapt the system to new kinds of products, requirements and stakeholder groups?
- *Maintainability*: How stable is the system when new modifications are introduced? How long does it take before the system becomes unmaintainable? Does a minor modification take three days or three weeks to implement?

10.8 UML CLASSES

Since LCM is composed of three simpler categories we can describe its UML structure as in Figure 10.8. (We do not show the UML analysis classes for the

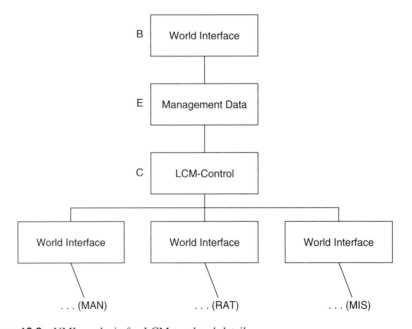

Figure 10.8 UML analysis for LCM top-level detail.

sub-categories because they have been described in other chapters.) We see that the LCM can cooperate with its own client systems via its World Interface while it is itself a client of MAN, RAT and MIS. We see, however, that the Control layer in LCM communicates with the Boundary layers of its components. We could build a PAC model for the LCM category whereby only Boundary layers communicate with each other but we have not yet examined all consequences of this approach. It is important to remember that Figure 10.8 is a *logical model* and that it may be modified during the design and implementation phases of the software lifecycle. The structure in the solution domain does not necessarily have to be the same as the structure in the problem domain.

10.9 USE CASES

It is very easy to find the most important use cases by examining the core processes. We define them as follows:

- U1: Create Basic Objects
- U2: Create Committed Objects
- U3: Provide decision-support data.

Each of these should be documented in the usual fashion. However, we do specify here the preconditions and postconditions of each use case because they partition the functionality nicely and they represent milestones in the system. For U1 these conditions are:

- Pre: Manufacturing system is operational and accepting requests.
- Post: Basic object has been created and is waiting for further processing.

For U2 the conditions are:

- Pre: Tracking system is operational and accepting assignment requests.
- Post: Basic objects have been assigned ('committed objects').

Finally, the conditions for U3 are:

- Pre: Management system is operational and accepting usage data.
- Post: Usage data has been consolidated and reporting is possible.

This is a boon for analysts; we now know the scope of each use case. The rest is a question of filling in the details. But be warned: there is still a lot of work to do! The good news is that you have a better idea of the scope of that work.

10.10 SPECIALIZATIONS OF LCM

The motivation for the Lifecycle category in this chapter came from the oil, gas and process industries where the concept of product and project lifecycles has been standardized and institutionalized. There are clearly defined phases for product feasibility, product initialization, monitoring and ending the life of a product. In fact, the management system that we present in Chapter 11 (the Manpower Control (MPC) System) is part of a large lifecycle project in the process industry.

Lifecycle models are found in well-established disciplines such as the retail industry, process industry and banking. Here we speak about the lifecycle of orders, products, customers and raw materials.

The software industry is peculiarly lacking in high-level lifecycle models. A notable exception can be found in the patterns movement where much thought has gone into developing models to help developers create flexible and reusable software systems. Much more work needs to be done. The Lifecycle model can be applied to almost any concept or entity that you can think about! The main questions to ask are:

- How, when and where are the entities created?
- What happens to the entities after they are created?
- How do we monitor these entities?
- When and how do the entities 'disappear' from the system?

10.11 USING LCM SYSTEMS WITH OTHER SYSTEMS

An LCM is related to other systems in several ways that are described by the following scenarios:

- S1: It is a client of another system
- S2: It is a server of another system
- S3: It collaborates with one or more other systems.

Scenario S1 is quite common, seeing the importance of LCM. In particular, it is a client of its MAN, RAT and MIS subsystems. On the other hand, scenario S2 describes the situation in which LCM supports other systems. For example, referring to Figure 10.5 we see that the 'Master' system is a client of several LCM systems; for example, it could be a system that monitors these systems (it is then an instance of a MIS category). Finally, multiple LCMs may cooperate to solve a given problem. Each LCM system has its own area of expertise and cooperates with its 'colleague' systems to solve a given problem.

10.12 SUMMARY AND CONCLUSIONS

We have introduced and discussed an important class of applications that are described as lifecycle models. A lifecycle model describes what the life of an entity is from the moment of inception to when it is no longer needed in a system. Many software projects fall into this category but unfortunately are not always designed with this simple assumption in mind. This leads to large, monolithic systems that are difficult to maintain and understand. The Lifecycle category, as described in this chapter, avoids this problem by partitioning a system into simpler subsystems. Each subsystem has well-defined responsibilities (the three subsystems belong to the categories MAN, RAT and MIS). To this end, we hope that we have made a positive contribution to our field. We finish with a quote from George Polya, the famous Hungarian mathematician: when tackling a problem, try to decompose it into simpler sub-problems.

PART III

Applications (models)

11 Project resource management system: Manpower Control (MPC) system

'Trying to find the solution, we may repeatedly change our point of view, our way of looking at the problem. We have to shift our position again and again. Our conception of the problem is likely to be rather incomplete when we start the work; our outlook is different when we have made some progress; it is again different when we have almost obtained the solution.'

George Polya

11.1 INTRODUCTION AND OBJECTIVES

This chapter analyses an instance of the MIS category. We call it the Manpower Control (MPC) system and it provides planners, cost controllers and project leaders with decision-support information concerning resource usage in engineering projects. In particular, it provides them with reports in the form of charts. These charts compare the number of hours that various organizational units have spent on the project with the corresponding scheduled hours. Our aim is to show how the artefacts from Chapter 5 are instantiated. The topics in this chapter are:

- Scoping MPC by defining its context diagram
- Documenting the major use cases by the standard use case template
- Producing sequence diagrams to visualize the most difficult use cases
- Discovering and documenting UML analysis classes.

Once this high-level analysis has been completed we will be in a position to start on detailed design issues, prototypes and proof-of-concept (POC) tests. Furthermore, the initial conceptual analysis in this chapter produces a stable architecture for a fully-fledged production system that can evolve as new user requirements and features emerge. Once you understand how to analyse MPC systems you can use your knowledge to examine other MIS systems in industrial, administrative and financial application domains. Some examples are:

- Monitoring disk space usage in a large computer network
- Remote monitoring of heart patients and patients with pacemakers
- Monitoring the complexity of object-oriented software designs and code
- Monitoring the value of a financial portfolio (shares, options, bonds)
- Monitoring resources in engineering projects (this chapter).

These applications have one thing in common: they are systems that monitor what is going on in some physical or simulated world and they produce data and information that allow experts to make decisions on future action. For example, if certain financial instruments (for example IBM stock) decrease in value, a high-level report will be generated advising the owner of a portfolio to sell the shares or buy certain options to cover his or her risks.

11.2 DESCRIPTION AND SCOPE OF PROBLEM

We describe the problem to be analysed as follows. An engineering company works on projects for internal and external customers. A project represents the sequence of activities that are executed by departments and the project is deemed to be complete when each activity has been completed. A project has a start date and duration. A project can be an internal project or an external project. An employee works on several activities in a project and is allocated a certain number of hours and other resources for each activity. Each department has its own area of expertise (for example, steel design, mechanical engineering). Departments are grouped into divisions and a given division may sponsor a number of internal projects. Companies are the sponsors of external projects. The resources (in this case hours) are allocated to departments and employees on a project basis.

An employee belongs to one department. In principle, the employee's department is the cost centre for the employee's resource usage. A system needs to be built that registers, validates and monitors basis project resource usage (in this case hours) on a regular basis. In particular, the following requirements must be supported in the system:

- MPC processes transaction data once per period (e.g. per month).
- Resource utilization must be monitored.
- Status reporting capabilities must be available to stakeholders.

This is how many software systems are born, namely from an initial feature list.

11.3 CORE PROCESSING AND CONTEXT DIAGRAM

Since MPC is an instance of a MIS category the core process is concerned with the transformation of low-level transaction data into decision-support information. The transaction data in this case consists of the hours that each employee in the organization has consumed on each project for each working period. A period in this case can be a month, one-thirteenth of a year (each period lasting four weeks) or even a week. Each employee is a member of a department and a department is part of a division. Each employee is allocated a number of hours each month. For example, employee 'Jack' has worked 120 hours on project ABC in period 10 and has a schedule of 140 hours. This means that he has worked 20 hours less than what was scheduled. We now describe the kinds of reports that should be produced:

- Bar charts of used hours and scheduled hours in a given time frame
- 'S curves' of the cumulative hours (used, scheduled) up to the current period.

These reports are produced at department, division and project levels. To this end, the transaction data must be registered, validated and merged. It is then formatted and presented in Excel, for example. The activity diagram is shown in Figure 11.1. The internal objects (Validated Hours) represent the used hours and scheduled hours for each employee per period per project, while the half-products (Department Hours and other consolidated hours) represent the used and scheduled hours at

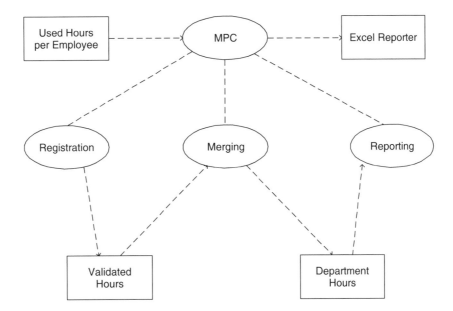

Figure 11.1   UML model activity diagram for Manpower Control.

organizational levels (such as department and division). The actions in the Registration activity are:

- Accept and process transaction data
- Validate the data (for example, check that the employee is allowed to 'book' hours on the given project)
- Notify other subsystems that the new transaction object has been created.

The actions in the Merging activity are:

- Process all the pending employee-level used hours
- Merge these objects to department and division levels
- Notify other subsystems that the new high-level objects have been created.

The merging algorithm makes use of the fact that each employee belongs to a given department and that a department belongs to a division. Finally, the actions in the Reporting activity are:

- Select the type of report or information to be displayed
- 'Format' the information to make it compatible with specific output media (for example, Excel or Oracle)
- Send and dispatch the formatted information to the specific output devices.

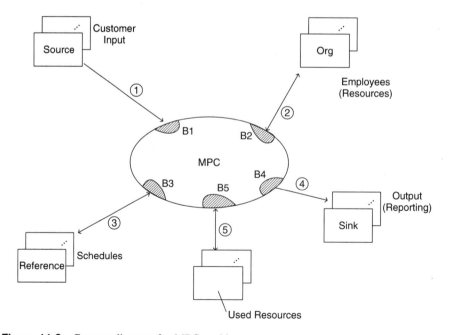

Figure 11.2   Context diagram for MPC problem.

The context diagram for MPC is shown in Figure 11.2 and is a special case of the context diagram for a MIS category. We have extended the diagram somewhat to include boundary layer objects because all communication between MPC and its actor systems takes place through them. We now discuss the roles of these systems. First, Source is the system that contains 'raw' transaction data; Org contains the information that describes the structure of the organization (for example, that an employee belongs to a department) while Reference contains project-related information including employee and department resource schedules. Thus, all basic project information is to be found in the Reference system. The Sink systems are the external hardware and software systems such as Excel and Oracle. Finally, the Used Resources system contains the store of permanent data including data at employee, department and division levels. It is similar to a data warehouse and it represents the 'long-term memory' (LTM) in MPC.

11.4 REQUIREMENTS AND USE CASE ANALYSIS

We now discuss the requirements for the MPC system. We concentrate on those requirements that realize the core process. This is not to say that the other functional and non-functional requirements are not important. However, we describe those requirements and use cases that help the reader understand MPC. The objective in this section is to demonstrate how to document use cases using the standard template mechanism and to align each use case with one system or subsystem in the MPC environment.

11.4.1 Functional requirements and use cases

The core process in MPC is to produce high-level information showing scheduled and used hours in an engineering project. The main activities are:

- A1: Process incoming transaction data
- A2: Merge and consolidate validated transaction information
- A3: Dispatch and notify clients of new consolidated information

The *strategy* to define use cases is as follows: first, the core process is realized by a use case (we call it U1) while the activities A1, A2 and A3 are realized by three 'lower-level' use cases that we call U1.1, U1.2 and U1.3.

We now document these use cases using the standard template mechanism. The descriptions tend to be minimal but accurate. Of course, use case documentation in real-life projects is (and should be) more comprehensive. The reader should keep in mind that these use cases are played out between the systems in Figure 11.2.

Use Case Name: Process Periodic Transaction Data (U1)

Actors: Source, MPC, Org, Reference, Used Resources, Sink

Preconditions: System is operational and accepting incoming transaction data.

Description of actions: The transaction data is processed, checked and validated. Then 'basic' transaction objects are created. The data must be complete and consistent with the constraints defined in the systems Org and Reference (valid employee, project and so on). The validated transaction data is then aggregated to department and division levels. Enterprise-wide business rules describe this process. Once the aggregation processes have been executed we notify interested client systems that reporting and datamining activities can begin.

We decompose U1 into three loosely coupled sub-use cases:

— Create Basic Transaction Objects (U1.1)

— Create High-level Data (U1.2)

— Notify and Dispatch to Client Systems (U1.3)

Exceptions: It is possible to give a detailed description of what can go wrong at this level but we defer these exceptions to U1.1, U1.2 and U1.3. For the moment, we note the major exceptions:

— Unable to process the transaction job (no dispatching to client systems)

— Part of the transaction job has been successful (and thus another part has been unsuccessful)

Postconditions: The transaction data has been processed. Client systems may now use the newly processed information.

We note that use case U1 brings the system from one state (as represented by the preconditions) to another state (as represented by the postconditions).

We now document the sub-use cases of U1. The reader can note that these use cases are 'played out' in one particular subsystem of MPC.

Use Case Name: Create Basic Transaction Objects (U1.1)

Actors: Source, MPC::Registration, Org, Reference, Used Resources, MPC:: Merging

Preconditions: System is operational and accepting incoming transaction data.

Description of actions: This use case is concerned with the processing of low-level external transaction data. The objective is to produce valid transaction objects at employee level. The main actions are (1) read and accept the external transaction data, (2) check and validate the data, (3) create transaction objects, and (4) notify interested systems (for example, MPC::Merging) that new objects have been created.

Exceptions:

— Source containing the transaction data is invalid (e.g. bad timestamp)

— Data is incomplete (e.g. missing field values)

— Employee is unknown (checked by Org)

— Combination Employee/Project is not correct or not allowed

The last exception has many variations; for example, the employee is not allowed to work on the project or the employee has spent more used hours (or less!) than were scheduled for the current period.

Postconditions: Basic transaction objects have been created and the merging algorithms may be executed; MPC::Merging has been notified.

Use Case Name: Create High-level Data (U1.2)
Actors: MPC::Registration, MPC::Merging, Org, Reference, Used Resources, MPC::Reporting
Preconditions: There is new transaction information waiting to be merged and it is allowed to execute merging activities at this moment in time.
Description of actions: The transaction objects from use case U1.1 contain data pertaining to individual employees and their resource profile (used and scheduled hours) for each period and project. For the purposes of high-level reporting we need to aggregate this data in different ways. We give some examples:
— Aggregate hours to department level (call it U1.1.1)
— Aggregate hours to division level (call it U1.1.2)
— Aggregate hours to project and multi-project levels (call it U1.1.3)
— Notify MPC::Reporting that it can produce reports
It is necessary to aggregate hours for each period during the life of a project and in some cases we wish to create reports based on the cumulative number of hours up to the current period.

Each of the use cases U1.1.1, U1.1.2 and U1.1.3 should be documented in general, but we concentrate on U1.1.1 for convenience only. We describe the corresponding algorithm by using a kind of mathematical shorthand. The objective is to aggregate used and scheduled hours for one department up to and including the current period. To this end, we define the following variables:
— The current period number, n
— The previous period, $n - 1$
— The current employee, e
— The current department, d
— The current project, p
We describe how to achieve the following:
— Calculate the hours for a department for the current period
— Calculate the cumulative hours for a department for the current period
The respective formulae are:
— DeptHours(n, p, d) = Sum(for all e in d) EmployeeHours(n, p, e)
— DeptCumHours(n, p, d) = DeptCumHours($n-1$, p, d) + DeptHours (n, p, d)
The notation 'Sum (all e in d)' denotes that we iterate over all employees 'e' in the given department 'd'.
Exceptions: The main exceptions are:
— A given department is not known

— A given department is not 'authorized' for a given project
— There is a discrepancy between a department's used and scheduled hours
— Unable to merge data
Postconditions: High-level data has been created and interested client systems have been notified; MPC::Reporting has been notified.

Use case U1.2 is the 'meat' in this application and it should be elaborated by using sequence diagrams in order to make clear what is taking place.

Use Case Name: Notify and Dispatch to Client Systems (U1.3)
Actors: MPC::Reporting, Used Resources, Sink, MPC::Merging
Preconditions: None. Future versions of MPC will require some form of authentication procedure. However, output data may not be accurate.
Description of actions: There are various possibilities. First, it may suffice to notify client systems that high-level information is available and where the clients can access this information. Second, MPC may send copies of the information to interested clients. The main steps in this case are:
— Determine what high-level information to send and to whom
— Format and package the information (travel request)
— Send the formatted information to the client systems
Exceptions:
— Unable to format information for dispatching
— Unable to notify interested client systems
Postconditions: Dispatching is complete and client systems have been notified of new high-level information; Sink systems have been notified.

It is a good idea to have a close look at each of these use cases as they represent our vision on how to couple use cases and structure. In particular, we can see the following emerging patterns:

• Use cases can be decomposed into smaller, loosely coupled use cases
• Use cases are closely aligned with one (sub)system (tight cohesion)
• A use case's postcondition 'dovetails' with its successor's precondition.

11.4.2 Non-functional requirements

The use cases in Section 11.4.1 are realizations of so-called functional requirements. Functional requirements are the easiest kinds of requirements to discover and document, especially when you talk to users of systems. However, non-functional requirements are just as important as functional requirements and in some cases (for example, in safety critical applications) even more important. Unfortunately, non-functional requirements tend to fall between the cracks in many projects. As far as MPC is concerned, we can use the ISO 9126 characteristics as a starting point for a discussion of *non-functional requirements* (*NFRs*). NFRs are certainly important to managers, planners and senior personnel. We have a look at some of the ISO 9126 characteristics and we give some examples.

- Reliability
  — All transaction and high-level data can be recovered (rollback)
  — Mean time between failure (MTBF) is known
- Efficiency
  — Efficient merging algorithms (in both time and resource usage)
  — Efficient throughput in system
  — System performance
- Usability
  — Users find it easy to enter and retrieve data
  — Users learn how to use the system within two weeks
  — The project manager can easily configure a new project.

Since these are NFRs it is not possible to describe them directly by use cases. However, they can be made functional by introducing new systems, objects and use cases. For example, in order to monitor system performance we create a client system that receives information from MPC on a regular basis so that it can decide whether MPC is performing well. The two systems will communicate through their boundary objects. We thus arrive at a situation whereby the two systems exchange messages and these messages are the seeds for new use cases, in particular due to the fact that two systems cooperate to solve a given problem.

11.5 VALIDATING USE CASES

Sequence diagrams are very useful for reviewing use cases and validating the class diagrams in systems. In general, we map each use case to one or more sequence diagrams. To this end, we depict the initial PAC model in MPC based on the corresponding model for the MIS category. Its context diagram is shown in Figure 11.2. Thus, we have shown what the boundary objects are and it is through these objects that information enters and leaves the system. If we examine the PAC model in Figure 11.3 we see that the Entity layers contain objects that are needed in the respective subsystems:

- Basic Objects layer: employee-based transaction objects (from U1.1)
- High-level Objects layer: department-level data (from U1.2)
- Router layer: filtered and formatted data for dispatching (from U1.3).

We restrict our attention to showing how use cases U1.1 and U1.2 are mapped to sequence diagrams. These are shown in Figures 11.4 and 11.5, respectively. We concentrate on the 'ideal' flow in the sequence diagrams; in other words, we have

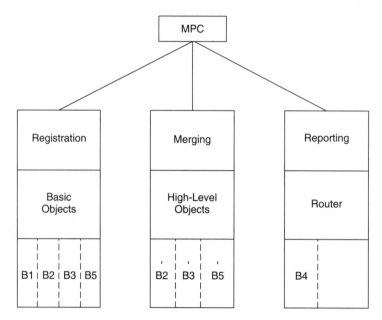

Figure 11.3   PAC model (including boundary objects) for MPC.

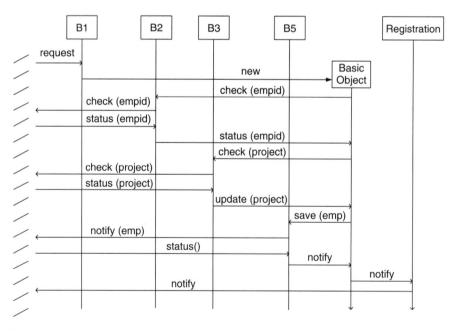

Figure 11.4   Sequence diagram for use case U1.1.

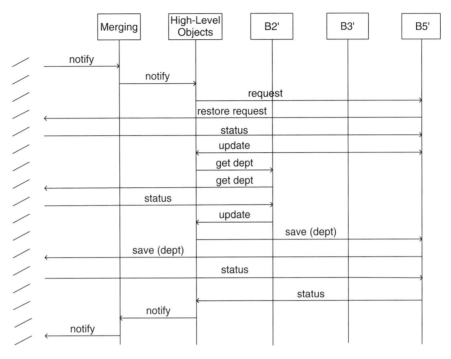

Figure 11.5 Sequence diagram for use case U1.2.

made no provisions for handling exceptions and the 'what-if' questions that arise when analysing the corresponding use cases. When extending and improving the sequence diagrams, we need to take care of the following problems:

- Timeouts and quality of service problems (for example, U1.1 fails to give a final 'notify' signal)
- Branching (if-else logic) in the case that U1.1 cannot find project or employee information
- Creation of new 'logging' systems to hold partially created transaction objects.

Attention to these and other exceptional situations will allow us to create improved and more robust sequence diagrams and hence make the transition to design more predictable and accurate.

11.6 CLASS ARCHITECTURE

We discuss and document the UML class diagrams for MPC. In particular, we look at the major actor systems in the context diagram in Figure 11.2. First, we define the responsibilities of the different systems:

- Org: contains information about the different organizational units
- Reference: project definition and project resource scheduling data
- UsedResources: information on the used hours for each organizational unit.

We discuss Reference first. This is a combination of Manufacturing (MAN) and Resource Allocation (RAT) categories because we must initialize the project and the tasks in it while we must model how project activities or tasks are allocated to resources, how tasks are related to each other and what the constraints are on individual tasks. To this end, Figure 11.6 depicts the class diagram for project-related classes such as Task, Milestone (a Task with duration zero), Task Group, Project and MultiProject (this represents a unified group of projects). Each TaskType has a Calendar that describes when hours can be used. For example, a Standard Calendar is used when we model normal working hours. Figure 11.7 depicts the classes in the

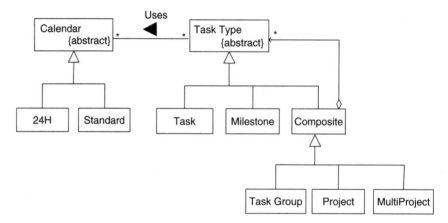

Figure 11.6   Task hierarchy.

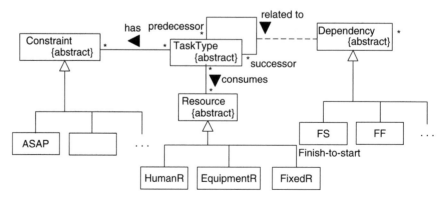

Figure 11.7   Task allocation and constraints.

RAT part of the Reference system and is concerned with allocation and scheduling activities for each TaskType. We note that Figure 11.7 is slightly more general than is needed for the current version of MPC because it has facilities for modelling various kinds of resources and not just used hours. Associated with each TaskType are zero or more constraints, for example 'ASAP' (as soon as possible) which states that the task should start as soon as is feasibly possible. Finally, we can define relationships

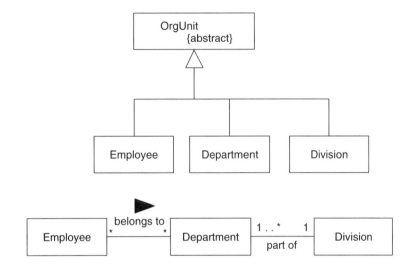

Figure 11.8   Classes in Org satellite system.

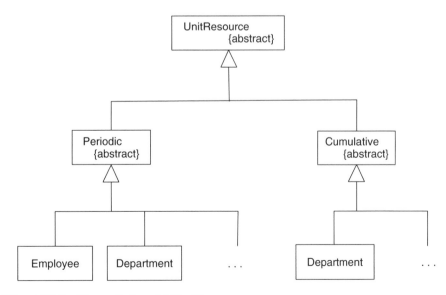

Figure 11.9   Classes that model UsedResources.

between tasks by using recursive (unary) association classes such as:

- FS (Finish to Start): task 2 should start as soon as task 1 finishes
- FF (Finish to Finish): task 2 should finish as soon as task 1 finishes, etc.

We now turn our attention to Org. This is the system that contains project-independent information about the different organizational units in the MPC environment and the corresponding structural relationships between them. This is shown in Figure 11.8. Finally, the classes in the UsedResources system are shown in Figure 11.9. We make a distinction between periodic used and scheduled hours and cumulative used and scheduled hours.

It goes without saying that the classes in Figures 11.8 and 11.9 should be populated by attributes and operations. Examining the messages and parameters in the sequence diagrams for MPC leads to these artefacts. What is important at this moment is that we have discovered the major classes and their relationships.

11.7 GENERALIZATIONS

We generalize MPC to support new resource types. This is an induction process but it should be relatively easy to do because we now have a solid basis on which to extend the class structure in MPC. Put simply, we have a basis on which to abstract. Typical examples are:

- Monitoring of cost flow in a software project
- Monitoring disk space usage in a computer network
- Monitoring the performance of a financial portfolio
- Systems for performance measuring.

11.8 SUMMARY AND CONCLUSIONS

We have carried out an analysis of a real-life application that monitors used hours in an engineering project. The used hours are compared with the scheduled hours, and reports and other presentations are created to show how well the project is doing at employee, department and division levels. It is even possible to create reports at project and multi-project levels.

Since data creation, validation and consolidation play a vital role in MPC, we have concentrated on the aspects of UML that help us understand how to realize these objectives. In particular, the use cases and the corresponding sequence diagrams are given centre stage, as are the UML class diagrams.

MPC can be generalized and 'morphed' to other systems that monitor general resources. The critical artefacts to look for when modelling a system as a MIS instance is the kind of data in the activity diagram relating to the core process, the merging algorithms and Figure 11.2.

12 Home Heating System (HHS)

'Central heating systems have three parts: the heating plant where fuel is converted into heat, a distribution system for delivering heat to where it is needed, and controls to regulate when it operates.'

Apogee Residential and Energy Systems (commercial) brochure

12.1 INTRODUCTION AND OBJECTIVES

The objective in this chapter is to analyse an instance of the PCS category using object-oriented techniques. The problem is called the Home Heating System (HHS) and it has been studied in textbooks using both structured and object paradigms (see, for example, Hatley and Pirbhai 1988, Booch 1991 and more recently Jackson 2001).

If we examine the above quotation from the Apogee organization we see that the problem domain is characterized by three major systems each of which has its own responsibilities. Each system cooperates with the other systems in order to satisfy the goals. This decomposition of the *problem* suits us fine because we immediately have decomposition in term of responsibilities and not in terms of low-level objects, for example. Furthermore, each system hides certain difficult design decisions. In keeping with the Parnas axiom:

We have tried to demonstrate by these examples that it is almost always incorrect to begin the decomposition of a system into modules on the basis of a flowchart. We propose instead that one begins with a list of difficult design decisions or design decisions which are likely to change. Each module is then designed to hide such decisions from the others.

The author started using HHS as a model problem in 1992. The approach was rather *ad hoc* and much attention was paid to finding the objects in the domain. Some time later we discovered commonality between HHS and other applications in the process control category from which we were able to generalize them and subsume them under a more general model. This is how the PCS domain architecture emerged.

The main focus is on the following issues:

- Creating a PAC model for HHS
- Discovering and documenting use cases
- Integrating use cases and the PAC model
- Creating statechart models for the objects in HHS.

Once created, the reader can decide whether the solution is understandable and extendible and what the benefits of the approach are when compared with top-down structured techniques (Hatley and Pirbhai 1988) and traditional object models (see Booch 1991).

A special feature in this chapter is that the main use cases for HHS are documented using the standard template format, and we show how to validate these use cases using a high-level statechart.

12.2 BACKGROUND AND HISTORY

The Home Heating System (HHS) has an interesting history. We describe two approaches to the problem: one uses structured analysis while the second uses traditional object-oriented technology.

12.2.1 Hatley–Pirbhai

The Hatley–Pirbhai method analyses HHS by first describing the problem in text and then moving on to a so-called Requirements Model. The Requirements Model is a list of features or high-level requirements that HHS must satisfy. Once the requirements model has been completed, Hatley and Pirbhai create Data Flow Diagrams (DFDs) and Control Flow Diagrams (CFDs) that describe the data and control in HHS, respectively (for an overview of this method, see Appendix 3). Finally, we create a state machine that describes the lifetime of the HHS when viewed as an entity.

The author has been influenced by this method because his customers were using the method in the 1990s to analyse real-time and process-control systems. The Hatley–Pirbhai method is not object-oriented and the author attempted to extend the method to align with object-oriented models. Some shortcomings of the Hatley–Pirbhai method are:

- The informal requirements and features in the Requirements Model can be interpreted in different ways. It was not structured and the mixing of optative and indicative moods (as described in Jackson 2001, page 295) makes the text difficult to understand. We resolve this problem by structuring the requirements model according to the guidelines in this book. In particular, partitioning the problem into well-defined use cases adds to understandability.

- Data flow and control flow are described in separate diagrams. This makes integration of these two models difficult to realize in practice. Furthermore, it is not clear when to stop with process decomposition. We resolve these problems by combining data and control flows in a single sequence diagram.
- The Hatley–Pirbhai method does not support an Information Model; this makes it difficult to align with the object-oriented way of thinking.
- The mapping to architecture and design is weak. In fact, the Architectural Interconnect Diagram (AID) as shown in Figure 12.1 is in essence the same model as the PAC model for the HHS except that the AID describes the hardware and software interfacing between the subsystems. The AID can be described as a diagram that describes the physical partitioning of the system into its component parts, the information flow between these components and how this information flows from one component to another component.

Notwithstanding the above problems, the author used this method as a basis for new improved models. We have used HHS since 1992 as a typical example of a process control system in courses and development work. Initial production prototypes using C++, design pattern and traditional object-oriented technology were developed in 1995. At the time of writing we now model HHS and other similar applications as instances of a Process Control System (PCS).

We shall see that analysing and designing an instance of PCS is reduced to 'filling in the blanks', as it were. This means that structural, functional and behavioural templates are in place and it is more or less a question of instantiating their contents by the classes and use cases for the current problem (SUD).

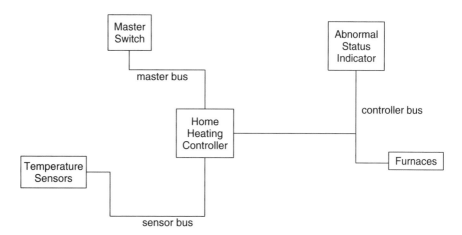

Figure 12.1 Architectural Interconnect Diagram (AID) for Home Heating System.

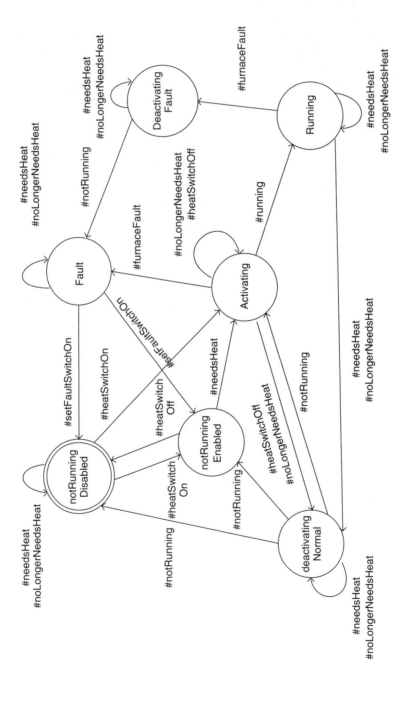

Figure 12.2 Heat flow Regulator State Transition Diagram.

12.2.2 The Booch approach

Grady Booch (1991) describes HHS in some detail. He takes an object-oriented approach by first looking for the tangible entities in the given domain. He then constructs an object model. The dynamics in the systems are modelled by the external events to which HHS must respond. These events help us define the boundaries of the system. Traditional 'flat' state machines (STDs) are used to model object state. Some of the problems in this approach are:

- The approach is bottom-up in the sense that Booch discovers the main objects in the problem domain and then determines what the behaviour of these objects should be. This approach was quite common in the early days of the object-oriented paradigm when people thought that it was enough to find the objects and then everything else would follow ('objects for the picking').
- Traditional state machines (State Transition Diagrams, STDs) are used to model object state. The essence of the corresponding STD in Booch (1991) is given in Figure 12.2 for the Regulator object. Each state can have a name as well as a number.

Finally, an account of the HHS is given in Jackson (2001) where attention is given to its context diagram. This defines the boundaries between the system and the external stakeholder systems. The approach in the Jackson method is very close in spirit to that taken in this chapter, especially at the context level.

12.3 DESCRIPTION OF PROBLEM

In general, a heating system converts fuel or other energy form into heat. The conversion takes place in one or more locations and the heat is then distributed throughout the living space.

Gas-fired heating systems generate heat in either a furnace or a boiler. A furnace heats air that is blown through air ducts and delivered to rooms through registers or grills. A boiler heats water to steam that then circulates through pipes to radiators.

The block diagram for HHS (taken from Booch 1991) is given in Figure 12.3. We can use this diagram as a basis for initial discussions with the sponsor of the project in order to discover requirements and use cases.

12.4 GOALS, PROCESSES AND CONTEXT

Since HHS is an instance of PCS, the basic goal or objective is to maintain a particular relationship or function over time between the input to the system and the output from the system in the face of disturbances in the process. In this particular

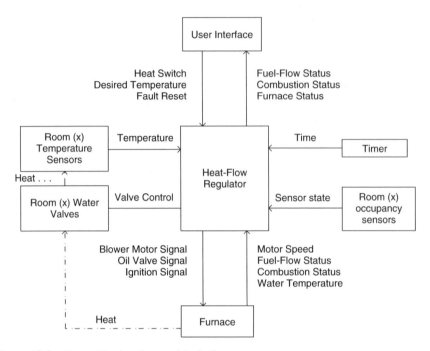

Figure 12.3 Home Heating System block diagram.

case we qualify this statement by saying that the goal is to ensure that the (current) temperature in the rooms remains between predefined levels. How do we achieve this goal? The answer is by burning enough fuel! This physical process corresponds to the core process in HHS and this core process has three activities:

- A1: Burn oil to produce warm water (the Delivery activity)
- A2: Distribute warm water to the rooms that need it (the Regulator activity)
- A3: Inform the operator of the status of the warming process (the Control activity).

A simple example of a home heating system is shown in Figure 12.4. The boiler (or furnace) contains warm water that is circulated to terminal units (or radiators). These radiators are situated in the rooms. Each terminal unit has a modulating valve; the valve opens when the room needs heat and closes when heat is not needed. In general, warm water is distributed to the room and circulates back to the boiler to be reheated. Based on this discussion and Figure 12.3, we depict the context diagram for HHS in Figure 12.5. This contains the following external stakeholder systems:

- *Physical Actuators*: the systems representing boilers, furnaces and their components.
- *Physical Sensors* (*synonym Environment*): the systems containing sensors (they measure the current temperature in the rooms).

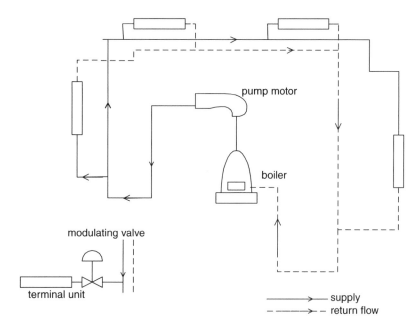

Figure 12.4   Two-pipe reverse–return circuit.

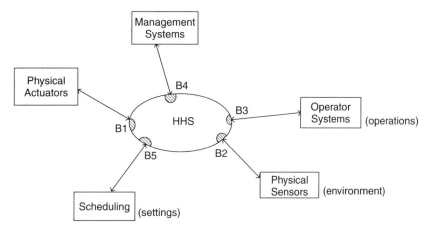

Figure 12.5   Context diagram for HHS.

- *Scheduling*: the systems that define the set point and other attribute values of the entities in HHS (for example, the reference temperature in the Room class). This is a RAT system.
- *Operator Systems* (*synonym Operations*): the systems that allow the owner to start and stop the system as well as receiving status readings.

- *Management Systems*: usually instances of MIS (or to a lesser extent, PCS); for example, we could define a system that models trending and historical behaviour in the rooms.

We have shown the Boundary objects that communicate with the external stakeholder systems in Figure 12.5. These will be needed when we construct the PAC model for HHS.

12.5 SYSTEM DECOMPOSITION AND PAC MODEL

Since HHS is an instance of the PCS category it is relatively easy to produce a PAC model for it based on the context diagram in Figure 6.8 (in Chapter 6). The current diagram is shown in Figure 12.6. We have documented the Boundary objects by name and by number. Notice that the responsibilities of each agent (such as Delivery, Regulator and Control) determine where the Boundary objects should be placed. In other words, each Boundary object plays its part in helping to realize the responsibilities of its corresponding agent. Similar remarks hold for the Entity and Control objects, of course. In general, the responsibilities of the agents are:

- Delivery: provide heating services
- Regulator: distribution of heat to living areas (for example, a Room)
- Control: strategic input and output operations.

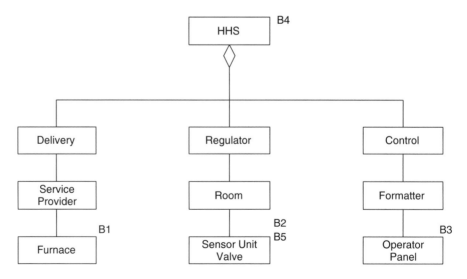

Figure 12.6 PAC for Home Heating System, version 1.

In general, Boundary objects are service providers to Entity objects while these latter objects communicate with the Control objects. The Boundary objects are:

- Furnace: provides heat (in the form of warm water) (boundary object B1)
- SensorUnit: tells us what the state of the environment is (B2)
- OperatorPanel: Input/output devices that control the system (B3)
- Management systems (B4)
- Scheduling systems (B5).

The Entity objects represent the abstractions of interest in this problem. First, ServiceProvider is a virtual machine that informs clients how much heat is available and what the current service levels are. The Room class models everything that we need to know about a room, such as:

- The name of the room (for example, 'living room')
- The setpoint values (reference temperature) and occupancy pattern
- The sensors in the room (the association between Room and SensorUnit).

Finally, the Control objects are the virtual machines to the other agents. These objects' interfaces should be so generic that other agents cannot peek into each other's internal structures. For example, clients can communicate with Regulator but they have no knowledge of what is going on behind the walls of this black box. All access is by means of standardized interfaces.

12.6 VIEWPOINTS AND REQUIREMENTS ANALYSIS

The main viewpoints in this case are Reliability and Functionality. Some requirements are:

- R1: The ability to control the operational life of the HHS system (Functionality)
- R2: Alarm and escalation management (Reliability).

We now discuss the requirements for each of the stakeholder systems in Figure 12.5. We look first at Management Systems. There are two specific systems in this group called 'Management System'. First, the data is aggregated to produce trending information and historical records. The main viewpoints are Functionality, Reliability and Efficiency. The major requirements are:

- R3: Save critical data to persistent storage
- R4: Compute trends
- R5: Monitor resource utilization.

Second, personal settings and preferences are defined in Pattern and are down-loadable to HHS. The main viewpoints are Efficiency and Functionality and the requirements are:

- R6: Must be possible to customize HHS
- R7: Calibrate HHS to take account of owner's living pattern.

HHS is the source system that sends low-level transaction data to Management System.

Physical Actuators are the systems that actually transform resources into energy. For example, a furnace burns kerosene and uses the generated energy to produce warm water that is distributed to the rooms in the home. The main viewpoints are Reliability and Efficiency. The resulting requirements are:

- R10: Heating units must be reliable
- R11: Efficient use of energy.

Lastly, Physical Sensors (synonym Environment) are the systems (usually sensors) that monitor the environment in which HHS operates. The main viewpoint is Reliability. The main requirement is:

- R12: Reliable sensor information.

12.7 USE CASES

We now realize the requirements from Section 12.6 by use cases. By definition, requirements are general and are always true while use cases represent specific interaction sessions in the system.

In this chapter we discover the use cases based on the events in the system. In this sense our approach is similar to the approach taken in Booch (1991) and the so-called event–response list as discussed in Umphress and March (1991). This technique is useful for small and medium-sized systems (HHS is a medium-sized system). Each event–response pair serves as a functional description of how one or more objects behave. For example, the use cases to be described shortly are discovered using events and responses. To take an example, if we press the start button (an event) the response will be a use case to turn heat on (in this case UC2).

We review the main use cases and we shall then document them using the standard template format.

We have discovered the following use cases by examining the different events in the system in chronological order. Other strategies are of course possible but they are not discussed here.

We summarize the main use cases in HHS for convenience:

- UC1: Bring HHS to Standby Mode
- UC2: Turn Heat On
- UC3: Turn Heat Off
- UC4: General Change in Environment (during normal operational mode)
  — UC4.1: Change in Reference Temperature
  — UC4.2: Change in Actual Temperature
  — UC4.3: Download Owner Preferences
  — UC4.4: Owner enters Room (leaves Room)
- UC5: Fuel Flow Abnormality occurs
- UC6: Hardware Abnormality occurs
- UC7: Reset System
- UC8: Upload Data to Management System
- UC9: Shutdown System
- UC10: System reaches Equilibrium
- UC11: Activation of Heating Units
- UC12: Deactivation of Heating Units.

All of the above use cases (with the exception of UC11 and UC12 which are played out in the Delivery agent) are termed system-level use cases because they affect all entities in HHS. Also, use case UC4 is a generalization of use cases UC4.1 to UC4.4.

Use Case Name and ID: Bring HHS to Standby Mode ('Power up') UC1.
Precondition: System is Off.
Short Description: The system is 'cold-booted'. This means that the system's hardware and peripheral systems are activated.
Detailed Description: The master switch is pressed. The system investigates what its peripheral hardware is, what resources it needs and what is available. The system is ready for service provision when all resources and hardware have been enabled.
Exceptions: Hardware and resource availability problems. We enumerate specific exceptions (based on the actors in the context diagram), for example:
— Not enough oil supply
— Actuator system not functioning properly (boiler/furnace system)
— Sensors defective
— System unable to arrive in Idle mode (timeout problems).
Postconditions: System in Idle mode and ready for startup or shutdown command.

Use Case Name and ID: Turn Heat On (Start HHS) UC2.
Precondition: System is Idle.
Short Description: The command is given to start heating the home.

Detailed Description: The start/stop button in the operator's panel is toggled. It is activated if the system is not in the cool-off period. The system checks the rooms in the home to determine whether they need heat. The heating units are activated if any room in the home needs heat.

Exceptions:
— Defect hardware due to previous malfunction
— System malfunction during startup process
— Oil supply depletion when starting.

Postconditions: System is Enabled and is ready for 'steady-state' commands.

Remarks: This use case represents the only service that is offered by HHS.

Use Case Name and ID: Turn Heat Off (Stop HHS) UC3.

Precondition: System is Enabled.

Short Description: The command is given to stop heating the home.

Detailed Description: The start/stop button in the operator's panel is toggled. All hardware systems and resources are notified. This use case corresponds to a 'graceful' shutdown.

Exceptions:
— System unable to shut down (e.g. timeout problems)
— Hardware problems during shutdown.

Postcondition: System is Idle.

Remarks: This use cases implies that it is possible to stop the system at any time.

Use cases UC4.1, UC4.2, UC4.3 and UC4.4 are concerned with changes in the environment and document what should be done when such changes occur. We document UC4.1 but not UC4.2, UC4.3 and UC4.4 because they are similar. We leave them as an exercise for the reader. Each of the above use cases refers to a single room.

Use Case Name and ID: Change the Reference Temperature UC4.1.

Precondition: System is Enabled.

Short Description: This use case describes what should happen when a room's reference temperature changes.

Detailed Description:
— Value changed in thermostat
— Check in room if action is needed
— Room requests heat services.

Exceptions: No action needed if the reference and actual values do not drift too far apart; this is the so-called *delta value*.

Postconditions: System is (still) Enabled and waiting to reach equilibrium state.

Remarks: This use case represents a disturbance to the system.

We have examined use cases UC4.1 to UC4.4 and see that there is much commonality between them. In general, a disturbance occurs in the environment and this is made known to a Room that then calculates what should be done next. We embody this common behaviour in the following more general use case.

Use Case Name and ID: General Change in the Environment UC4.
Precondition: System is Enabled.
Short Description: This use case describes what should happen when a room is affected by some change in the external environment.
Detailed Description:
— Value changed in the Environment (physical sensor unit)
— Check in room if action is needed
— Request heat services.
Exceptions: No action needed (not really an exception as such).
Postconditions: System is Enabled and waiting to reach equilibrium state.

Use Case Name and ID: Fuel Flow Abnormality occurs UC5.
Preconditions: System is Enabled and no hardware errors.
Short Description: This use case describes what happens when the oil supply in HHS becomes depleted.
Detailed Description:
— Value changed in fuel flow indicator
— Heating units informed of change
— Operations notified of fault.
Exceptions: Not applicable.
Postconditions: System is in abort mode (soft failure) and waiting on repair (reset) actions.
Remarks: Once the oil supply has been replenished it is possible to start heating again (use case UC2).

Use Case Name and ID: Hardware Abnormality occurs UC6.
Preconditions: System is Enabled and no hardware errors.
Short Description: This use case describes what happens when the combustion sensor in HHS is not functioning or the motor is defective.
Detailed Description:
— Hardware problem discovered
— Inform Operations.
Exceptions: None at this moment in time.
Postconditions: System is in abort mode and waiting on repair (reset) actions.
Remarks: It should be possible to amalgamate UC6 and UC5 into a single, more general use case.

Use Case Name and ID: Reset System UC7.
Precondition: System is in abort mode.

Short Description: This use case describes the actions to be taken in order to start up HHS after a hardware fault has been repaired or fuel has been replenished.
Detailed Description:
— Reset button pressed
— Determine what parts of system need to be repaired
— Configure new hardware and settings.
Exceptions:
— Unable to repair
— Timeout problems
— Attempting to reset in the cool-down period.
Postcondition: System is brought to Idle mode.

Use Case Name and ID: Upload Data to Management System UC8.
Precondition: System is Enabled.
Short Description: This use case describes the periodic uploading of transaction data from HHS to the Reporting system. Attention points are the frequency of uploading, what to upload and how uploading is triggered. In general, it is possible to upload operating data such as the temperature in the rooms and energy usage.
Detailed Description:
— New transaction data arrives/is produced in HHS
— Dispatch data to Management Systems.
Exceptions: Data is not being produced or data is incorrect.
Postcondition: System is Enabled.
Remarks: A detailed analysis and design of the data interfacing and interoperability between it and HHS needs to be carried out. Another use case will be needed to configure HHS so that it delivers the necessary data to Reporting. Data is reinitialized after uploading.

Use Case Name and ID: Major Shutdown of System UC9.
Precondition: System is Enabled.
Short Description: This use case describes the actions when the HHS is to be taken out of service.
Detailed Description:
— Press master ON/OFF switch
— Wait for pending requests to complete
— Notify external systems of request (all units must be shut down).
Exceptions: Unable to shut down (for example, HHS is in the cool-down period).
Postcondition: System is Off.
Remarks: UC9 is the shutdown equivalent of UC1.

Use Case Name and ID: System reaches Equilibrium UC10.
Precondition: System is Enabled.

Short Description: This use case describes the actions to be taken after the rooms in the home have reached their desired temperatures.

Detailed Description:

— Desired temperature is reached
— Stop physical actuator
— Inform Operations of new status
— Shut down physical actuator.

Exceptions:

— System does not reach equilibrium before the deadline (timeout)
— Defective hardware.

Postconditions: System is Enabled and Idle.

Remarks: UC10 resolves the disturbances induced by use case UC4 and its special cases.

Use Case Name and ID: Deactivation of Heating Units UC12.

Precondition: Heating Unit is active.

Short Description: This use case describes the actions that are taken when the heating unit is deactivated. It involves deactivation of various hardware components in the unit.

Detailed Description: The main actions are:

— Close oil valve
— Wait for valve to close
— Stop the motor control
— Wait for ACK from motor control
— Deactivate igniter
— Wait for ACK from igniter
— Inform clients that heating unit has been deactivated.

Exceptions:

— Motor control acknowledges with a hardware error
— Timeout while waiting on motor control
— No ACK from igniter.

Postcondition: Heating unit is deactivated.

Remarks: The time needed to stop the motor in the motor control is 5 minutes while the time to close a valve is 5 seconds. A motor cannot be started again while it is in this 'cool-off' mode.

Use case UC11, Activation of Heating Units, is the converse of UC12.

12.8 VALIDATION EFFORTS

The use cases must be aligned with the PAC model in Figure 12.6. The objective is to discover and document object interfaces. In this section we concentrate on Room

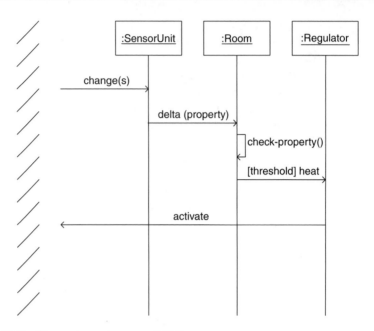

Figure 12.7   Change in environment (UC4).

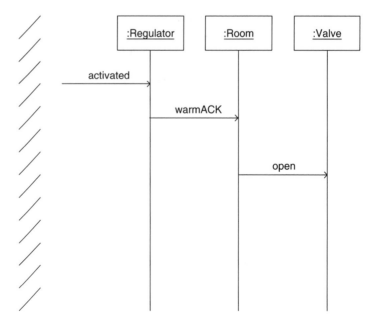

Figure 12.8   Room is informed of availability of warm water.

as an example. We focus on UC4 and the role that Room plays in relation to it. In general, the Room requests heat (Figure 12.7) if the delta value is beyond a certain threshold and an acknowledgement is given at some later stage (Figure 12.8). This leads to the initial list of input and output methods:

- delta (property): something has changed in the environment
- warmACK: Room is informed of warm water

- heat: Room requests heat
- open: Room opens its valve

'Mirror images' of Figures 12.7 and 12.8 can be created for the cases in which Room requests that no more heat be delivered and its corresponding acknowledgement (we call these 'noheat' and nowarmACK, respectively).

Having found Room's input and output functions we group these into interfaces. An example is

```
interface IRequest
{
        // input methods
        delta(Property)

        // output methods
        heat
        noheat
}


interface IResponse
{
        // input methods
        warmACK
        nowarmACK

        // output methods (commands to Room's valve)
        open
        close
}
```

It is possible to create a sequence diagram for UC4.4 that describes the owner's coming and going. The reader may like to try this as an exercise.

12.9 CREATING STATECHARTS

Having created the interfaces for Room (this is the syntax part) we now embark on the job of defining the corresponding semantics. To this end, we create several

statecharts that model the dynamic behaviour of Room. In keeping with experience in this specific area (see Selic *et al* 1994, Chapter 13) we model Room as
an entity object that is separated from its hardware interfaces. Furthermore, we
model it by two orthogonal states called OccupyState and WarmingState as shown
in Figure 12.9. Notice the presence of stub states (vertical bars) which when zoomed
into lead to the states in Figures 12.10 and 12.11.

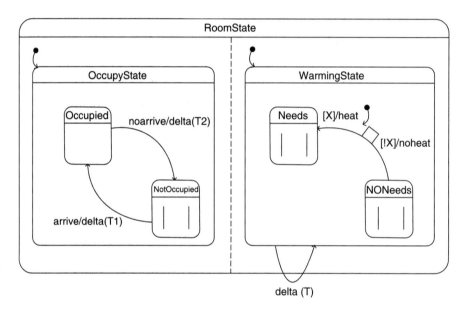

Figure 12.9   Room top-level state.

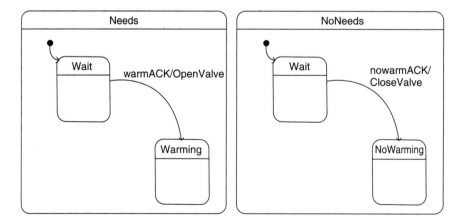

Figure 12.10   Substates of Warming state.

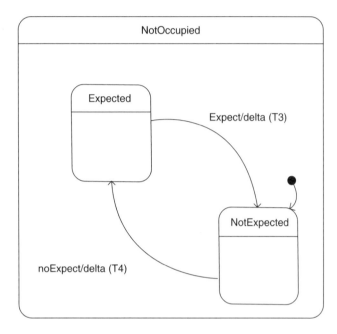

Figure 12.11 Details of NotOccupied state.

The reader might like to compare the present results with the traditional STDs for the Room class in Booch (1991). In the latter case Booch identifies six top-level states:

- NeedsHeat and Occupied
- NeedsHeat and Not Expected
- NeedsHeat and Expected

- NoNeedsHeat and Occupied
- NoNeedsHeat and Not Expected
- NoNeedsHeat and Expected

There are in total 15 transitions between these states. The McCabe complexity metric in this case gives us a value of 10; the state machine is difficult to maintain.

How do we design objects and their corresponding statecharts? The design patterns literature has a lot to say about this problem. First, a Room (when viewed as a component) realizes a number of interfaces (such as IRequest, for example). This is the syntax part only. The semantics of the interface is realized by a statechart. Now, Gamma (in GOF 1995) describes how to design a statechart using the State pattern and the problem of implementing interfaces is easily done in languages such as C# and Java. The design is documented in UML as in Figure 12.12.

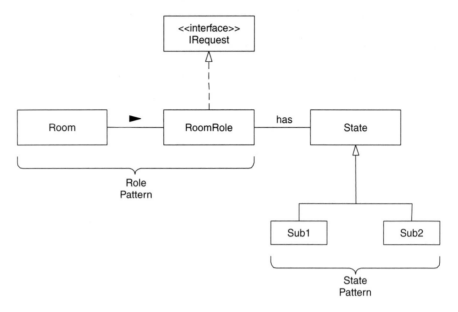

Figure 12.12 High-level design of Room class.

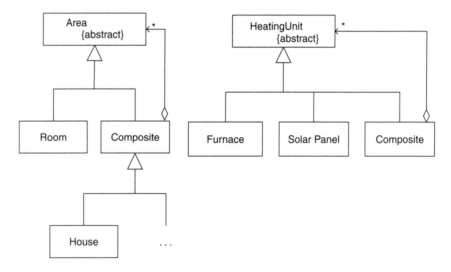

Figure 12.13 Generalizing Entity and Boundary classes.

12.10 GENERALIZATION EFFORTS

We discuss in short some of the new requirements that may arise in future versions of HHS. We cannot describe all possibilities but we mention a few:

- HHS for Rooms, Homes and Streets
- Different kinds of heating units (for example, solar panels).

Not only do we have to create new classes and class hierarchies but also new use cases will need to be discovered and documented. In the first case we envisage the class diagrams as in Figure 12.13. Of course, the PAC model in Figure 12.6 must be changed to reflect the fact that we are no longer working with hard-coded Room and Furnace classes.

12.11 SUMMARY AND CONCLUSIONS

We have analysed a soft real-time problem using UML. This is the Home Heating System problem that is well known in the literature and has been discussed using both structured analysis (Hatley–Pirbhai) and traditional object-oriented technology (Booch).

We have modelled HHS as an instance of a PCS category, thus effectively giving us its PAC model for free. Furthermore, we modelled the dynamics in the problem by use cases that are then validated by sequence diagrams. Finally, we have shown by means of an example (the Room class) how to create and design statecharts based on the output from the corresponding sequence diagrams.

HHS can be used as a model problem for other applications in the same category. It is our experience that a proof-of-concept (POC) model will be up and running in a matter of weeks if you can discover the analogies between HHS and your current problem.

13 Elevator Control System (ELS)

'Everything is possible if you wish hard enough.'

Peter Pan

13.1 INTRODUCTION AND OBJECTIVES

This chapter analyses the well-known Elevator Control System (ELS) as described in Yourdon and Argila (1996). We adopt a top-down approach, moving from goals to core processes and eventually to requirements and use cases. There is a strong emphasis on requirements analysis in this chapter. Furthermore, we decompose ELS (as a system) into its subsystems.

We have found it necessary to do justice to the problem of documenting ELS in terms of stakeholders, viewpoints, requirements and use cases on the one hand and processes, systems and the PAC model on the other hand. Furthermore, we show that the approach taken in this chapter is more robust and less fragile than other object-oriented approaches.

This chapter is structured as follows: in Section 13.2 we introduce ELS as an instance of the RAT category by defining its context diagram. Section 13.3 describes the hardware objects in ELS based on the text in Yourdon and Argila (1996). Section 13.4 describes the goals and core processes in ELS while Section 13.5 documents the major stakeholders. In Section 13.6 we document several requirements. Having described high-level functionality in the system we then direct our attention to decomposing ELS into subsystems and PAC models in Sections 13.7 and 13.8. Finally, Section 13.9 discusses a number of important use cases in ELS, including the documentation of exceptional use cases.

The added value of this chapter in our opinion is that we analyse a well-known application by first examining the problem, its core processes and major requirements and then mapping these to the objects and classes. In this way we produce artefacts that are more adaptable and maintainable than an arbitrary set of classes that we hope will somehow satisfy the requirements. We have in a sense eliminated some of the risk inherent in traditional object-oriented applications.

13.2 DOMAIN CATEGORIES AND ELS

ELS is an instance of a Resource Allocation and Tracking (RAT) category. ELS processes customer requests, allocates resources to realize those requests and monitors the status of requests at all times. In this sense it is in the same category as some other systems such as:

- Helpdesk System in a computer department (customer problem tracking)
- Order Processing System in the manufacturing industry and business domains (order tracking)
- Customer Request System (customer course request tracking).

Using these systems as guidelines we can construct the basic context diagram for ELS as shown in Figure 13.1. The main external systems are:

- *ELS*: the system under discussion (SUD).
- *Source*: mainly customer groups (passengers and would-be passengers) who wish to travel between floors in a building.
- *Sink*: This system contains functionality that displays the status of a customer request.
- *Knowledge Base (KB)*: the management system that determines which floors are accessible to customers and what services are on offer.

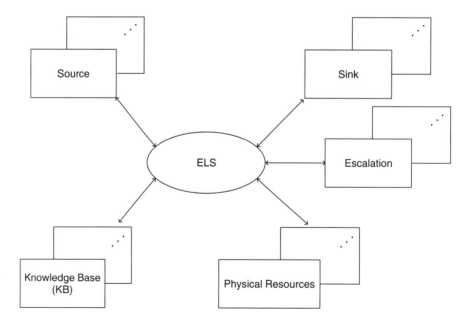

Figure 13.1   Context diagram for ELS environment.

- *Physical Resources*: This system contains all the hardware pertaining to the physical units in the system. For example, this system contains the UP, DOWN and STOP motors as described in Yourdon and Argila (1996). This is a separate system that is to be analysed and designed.
- *Escalation (ESC)*: This is the system that is responsible for ensuring safety in the ELS system. It is also responsible for service level agreements (SLAs).

We concentrate on the ELS system in this document and not its satellite systems. However, in real-life situations it may also be necessary to analyse the other systems that interface with ELS. Each of these is an instance of some domain category. In this particular case, we have an idea about each of the 'satellite' systems of ELS (again, see Figure 13.1):

- *Source* can be an Access Control System (ACS); in this case access to the system is via humans. Furthermore, all customer requests need to be validated and checked.
- *Sink* could be a Manufacturing (MAN) or Management Information System (MIS) because internal commands and information are converted to some other format.
- *Knowledge Base* is an instance of a Management Information System (MIS) because this is where all configuration data and historical information are stored.
- *Physical Resources* is a RAT system because this is where the customer request is assigned to a physical elevator (this is a common pattern where one RAT system cooperates with another RAT system). This system is responsible for the allocation of physical resources that satisfy the needs of the 'higher-level' logical requests from the ELS system.
- *Escalation* is primarily an instance of a Process Control System (PCS). It monitors exceptional and abnormal situations in the system.

Knowing the reasons why ELS is an instance of a RAT category gives us insights into its functional and non-functional requirements. Furthermore, we are able to reason about its structure because the decomposition of any instance of a RAT category is well known at this stage.

13.3 A TRADITIONAL OBJECT-ORIENTED REQUIREMENT SPECIFICATION

We develop ELS as a system to schedule and control a number of elevators in a building. The elevators transport people from one floor to another. Sketches of the exterior and the interior of the elevator are shown in Figures 13.2 and 13.3, respectively (taken from Yourdon and Argila 1996).

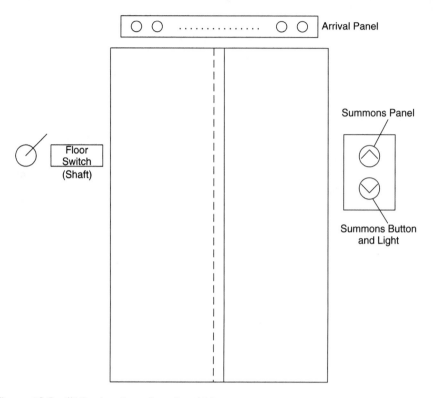

Figure 13.2   ELS: view from floor (outside).

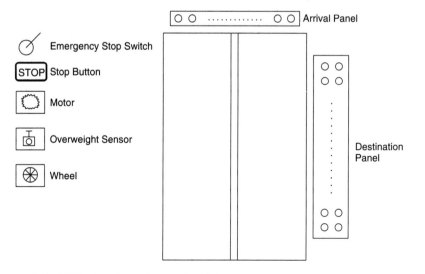

Figure 13.3   ELS: view from elevator (inside).

Major goals in ELS are efficiency and customer safety. Elevators do not change direction of travel until the passengers travelling in them have reached their destination. The system has no knowledge of passenger boarding and exits. An elevator that is filled to capacity should not respond to a new summons request (there is an 'overweight' sensor for each elevator).

We now describe the major hardware entities in ELS (many of them will later be modelled as boundary objects in UML and/or external actor systems). It is useful to refer to Figures 13.2 and 13.3 when reading the text below.

1. Summons buttons

Each floor has a panel containing two summons buttons. One button is for the 'up' direction while the other button is for the 'down' direction. The ground floor has no 'down' button while the top floor has no 'up' button. Would-be passengers press these buttons in order to summon an elevator. It is the responsibility of the scheduler to summon a particular elevator. The summons buttons can be illuminated.

2. Summons button lights

The illumination of a button tells the passenger(s) that the system has taken note of the request. Further interrupts caused by additional pressing of the button are ignored. The light in the button is turned off as soon as an elevator arrives at the floor.

3. Arrival lights

The interior of each elevator is furnished with a panel consisting of illuminable indicators. Each indicator corresponds to a floor. The panel tells the passengers which elevators will be visited. The indicator is illuminated when the elevator arrives at the floor and the indicator is extinguished when it leaves the floor. There are also arrival lamps on each floor.

4. Floor sensors

Each floor has a floor sensor switch for each elevator shaft. When an elevator is within eight inches of a floor a wheel on the elevator closes the switch for that floor. The system knows what the floor number is corresponding to the generated interrupt.

5. Destination button

The interior of each elevator is furnished with a panel consisting of an array of buttons, one button for each destination floor. These buttons may be illuminated.

6. Destination button lights

When a passenger presses a button the panel sends an interrupt to the computer. The illumination of the button notifies the passenger that the system has taken note of the request and prevents further interrupts caused by additional pressing of the button. The button panel is turned off when the elevator stops at a floor.

7. Elevator motor controls

There are three motors (UP, DOWN, STOP). The elevator mechanism does not obey any unsafe or inappropriate commands. The computer issues a stop command when the elevator is within eight inches of a floor (in which case the floor switch is closed). The elevator is 'levelled', opens its door and then closes it. Open and close commands are ignored until the conditions for movement are met. Each elevator's panel contains a stop button. Its purpose is to hold the elevator at a floor with its door open when the elevator is currently stopped at a floor. An emergency stop switch stops and holds the elevator at the next floor that it reaches irrespective of the scheduling. The red switch may optionally turn on an audible alarm.

13.4 RE-ENGINEERING ELS: GOALS AND PROCESSES

Traditional object-oriented approaches to ELS tend to search for objects and classes and from these they create class diagrams and use cases. This approach leads to brittle systems. This chapter takes a completely different approach, namely by starting with goals and core processes.

There are two main goals or business concerns. The first goal is efficient transport of passengers from one floor to another in a building and the second goal is safety. There may be some other (hidden) goals but we conclude that Efficiency and Safety are the two most important ones at this moment. We now describe these goals in detail using the standard template structure.

Goal name and ID: Efficiency (ID is G1)

Short description: This goal is concerned with the efficient transportation of people in a building. Delay times should be reduced to a minimum.

Detailed description: One of the main reasons for the installation of ELS is to transport people between the different floors in a building. This saves people having to use stairs and it allows less mobile people to get to their destination in the building. The energy that is needed to power the elevator system should be used in an optimal way. To this end, elevators should be on 'standby' during non-peak hours.

Value to the organization if goal is achieved: In a building with many floors and different companies, personnel are transported as quickly as possible to their destination. In what sense is the goal strategic? The realization of this goal ensures the proper functioning of a modern building. In particular, it is important that customers are given the level of service that they require.

Possible sub-goals: Transport efficiency, waiting time efficiency, energy usage efficiency.
Related system: ELS (this goal applies to the current system).

Goal name and ID: Safety (ID is G2)

Short description: Passenger safety should be guaranteed at all times.
Detailed description: The safety of passengers and would-be passengers is important. Loss of life must be avoided at all costs and ELS should be designed in such a way that it does not endanger the well-being of passengers. Furthermore, ELS should conform to the standards and procedures as laid out by the appropriate regulatory authorities.
Value to the organization if goal is achieved: Realization ensures that the system functions according to the regulations. Non-conformance entails disciplinary action from regulators. Lawsuits will follow if passengers are injured. In what sense is the goal strategic? It concerns passenger safety. It is in every stakeholder's interest that no accidents occur.
Possible sub-goals: Safety of those already in a building.
Related system: ELS (this goal applies to the current system).

The main core processes have to do with the actual transportation of people from one floor to another and with ensuring their safety at all times. These processes realize the goals in ELS:

- P1: Elevator Reservation (passengers embark and disembark)
- P2: Elevator Utilization (transport passengers to their destination)
- P3: Elevator Safety (safety of passengers)
- P4: Elevator Efficiency.

We see these as core processes because they are visible to customers and other important stakeholders. We now document each process using the standard template structure.

Process name and ID: Elevator Reservation (ID is P1)

Process category: Core.
Short description: Would-be passengers make it known that they want to use the services of an elevator. It is not possible to reserve a specific elevator. Instead, a would-be passenger indicates whether she or he wishes to travel 'up' or 'down' from a given floor. In this case an elevator will be scheduled to travel to the floor where the summons request originated.
Detailed description: A would-be passenger wishes to use the services of an elevator. The passenger must identify himself or herself in some way. Validation checks are carried out to determine whether the request can be fulfilled. Once the request

has been accepted an elevator will be scheduled. The would-be passenger is kept informed of the whereabouts of the elevator, for example by deploying arrival panels above the elevator door. The elevator arrives and the door opens.

Major input and output: Input is a request, output is the status of a request.

Related goals: G1 (Efficiency) and G2 (Safety).

Possible core processes that process depends on: There is a relationship with core process P2 because would-be passengers may interact with disembarking passengers.

Process name and ID: Elevator Utilization (ID is P2)

Process category: Core.

Short description: An occupant of an elevator makes known his or her wish to travel to a certain floor.

Detailed description: An occupant (passenger) wishes to use the services of an elevator. The passenger makes known which floor she or he wishes to travel to. Validation checks are carried out to determine whether the request can be fulfilled. The passenger is kept informed of the whereabouts of the elevator. The elevator arrives, the door opens and the passenger may disembark.

Major input and output: Input is the elevator sensing that a passenger has embarked. Output is the current position of the elevator and in particular the intervening floors that are visited.

Related goals: G1 (Efficiency) and G2 (Safety).

Possible core processes that process depends on: Process P1.

Process name and ID: Elevator Safety (ID is P3)

Process category: Core.

Short description: All disturbances and changes to the system must be monitored. Preventive and corrective action is needed to ensure safety of passengers at all times.

Detailed description: The ELS system must ensure the safety of passengers at all times. No loss to life or limb may occur. All changes to the system must be registered and monitored for possible breaches of safety. Possible breaches can occur when passengers are embarking or disembarking or while they are in the elevator.

Major input and output: Input is represented by change in the system state. Output can be a return to a normal state, a warning message or an alert message. In other words, input is a change request and output is some kind of status message.

Related goal: G2 (Safety).

Possible core processes that process depends on: Closely related to processes P1 and P2. If P1 and P2 are not present then there is no need to implement P3.

Process name and ID: Elevator Efficiency (ID is P4)

Process category: Core. This process is realized by the Physical Resources system that interfaces with the system ELS (see context diagram, Figure 13.1)

Short description: This process is responsible for handling all requests from would-be passengers and passengers. The output is some kind of status.

Detailed description: Process P4 is responsible for elevator scheduling and dispatching. The current kinds of requests are:

— Summons request (reserve some elevator)
— Destination request (travel to a given floor).

Summons requests contain information concerning the source of the request (on which floor the summons button was pressed) and the desired direction of travel (up, down). Process P4 attempts to satisfy this request by scheduling an elevator. Once an elevator has arrived at a floor it is then possible to select a destination floor, assuming that the floor is in the elevator's 'trajectory' path. To give a specific example, if an elevator is travelling in the 'up' direction and the elevator is currently at the sixth floor then requests from the seventh floor and higher will be honoured while requests to travel from floors one to five will be ignored. The customer is mainly interested in queue time (how long he or she must wait for an elevator) and transport time (the time between embarking and disembarking, for example).

Major input and output: Input is some kind of request (originating from process P1 or P2). Output is the current status of a request.

Related goal: G1 (Efficiency).

Possible core processes that process depends on: Processes P1 and P2.

13.5 STAKEHOLDERS AND THEIR REQUIREMENTS

We introduce the most important groups of people and systems that benefit directly or indirectly from ELS. We do not discuss viewpoints in this chapter due to space considerations. Instead, we introduce the most important stakeholders and their specific requirements.

Stakeholder name and ID: Customers (would-be passengers and passengers) (ID is ST1)

Stakeholder type: Interactor (because they interact directly with ELS).

Short description: The persons who wish to avail of the services that ELS offers.

Detailed description: ELS is a system that transports persons from one floor to another in a building. Each customer group has its own ways of interacting with the system, for example:

— Reserving an elevator
— Receiving feedback on request status
— The ability to send alarms and help messages to the external world
— Efficient transportation to a given destination.

Typical activities and jobs: Typically, customers interact directly with the system and receive status messages on elevator scheduling and dispatching progress.

Possible sub-categories: It is possible to create specializations based on how customers interact with the system. Furthermore, we can group passengers based on the type of access to a floor or an elevator that they use. We note that the group of would-be passengers is not necessarily the same as the set of passengers. In some situations it is possible for an elevator to visit a floor at regular intervals, in which case no summons buttons are needed.

Relationships with other stakeholder groups: Not applicable in this version.

Stakeholder name and ID: Elevator Mechanism (ID is ST2)

Stakeholder type: Interactor (this is the system that represents the allocated physical resources in the system).

Short description: This is the stakeholder that actually realizes the customer requests. It is the physical motor system in this version of ELS. This stakeholder is synonymous with the Physical Resources actor in the context diagram in Figure 13.1. This is a RAT instance in its own right.

Detailed description: This stakeholder is responsible for scheduling all customer requests (would-be passengers and passengers). For example, it is possible to send an elevator to a given floor and it is able to place a destination request in the 'attention list' of a reserved elevator. We speak of two related issues here:
— Elevator scheduling
— Elevator dispatching.

We define scheduling as reserving an elevator and sending it to a given floor to pick up a would-be passenger, while dispatching is defined as transporting a passenger to a given floor.

Typical activities and jobs: The responsibilities of this stakeholder are to provide would-be passengers and passengers with a service (in this case by transporting them as efficiently and safely as possible to their destinations).

Possible sub-categories: Not applicable in this version.

Relationships with other stakeholder groups: Customers.

Stakeholder name and ID: Notification Mechanism (ID is ST3)

Stakeholder type: Stakeholder.

Short description: This is the system that informs would-be passengers and passengers of the initial status of a given request. This stakeholder is synonymous with the Knowledge Base (KB) actor in the context diagram in Figure 13.1.

Detailed description: It must be possible to determine the status of a request at all times. Typical examples are:
— Is it allowed to travel from a floor?
— Can I travel to a given destination?

Typical activities and jobs: The main responsibility of this stakeholder lies in configuring ELS to define what the 'access paths' are in the building. For example, we define which floors are accessible from other floors, which floors are 'off-limits' and so on.

Possible sub-categories: Notification mechanism outside elevator; notification mechanism inside elevator.

Relationships with other stakeholder groups: There is a relationship between the Customer groups (passengers and would-be passengers) and this group because customers are informed about the status of a request via this mechanism.

Stakeholder name and ID: Safety and Service Level Management (ID is ST5)

Stakeholder type: Domain. This is a domain stakeholder group because ELS is an application where human safety is all-important. Hence ELS must comply with all rules and regulations concerning safety.

Short description: ELS must comply with all safety rules and regulations.

Detailed description: The owners must abide by the rules as laid out by agencies and governments concerning passenger safety. Safety is defined as freedom from accidents or losses.

Typical activities and jobs: Service Level Management (SLM) is responsible for the safety of would-be passengers and passengers. For example, an overweight sensor is situated in each elevator and this sets a limit on the maximum number of passengers that may be in the elevator at any given time. Furthermore, the interior of each elevator contains a stop button and an emergency stop button. Finally, it should be possible to 'audit' the elevators on a regular basis, for example a REM (Remote Elevator Monitoring) system.

Possible sub-categories: This group can be subdivided into the group that is concerned with customer safety and the group that is responsible for customer service (quality of service issues).

Relationships with other stakeholder groups: Customers.

13.6 REQUIREMENTS

The most important requirements have to do with the Customers and Service Level Management stakeholder groups:

- R1: Efficient Embarkation and Disembarkation
- R2: Safe Embarkation
- R3: Efficient Arrival at Destination
- R4: Safe Arrival at Destination
- R5: Efficient Scheduling and Dispatching of an Elevator.

We document R1, R2 and R3 in this section. Not all fields in a requirements description have been filled in this version of ELS. In these cases we have used the term 'Not applicable'. Furthermore, we consider each requirement to have a high risk factor because this is a new domain for the IT team charged with developing the system.

Requirement name and ID: Efficient Embarkation (ID is R1)

Short description: Since there are many would-be passengers and passengers using the elevators, it is important to schedule the elevators in such a way that as many passengers as possible can embark and disembark as efficiently as possible. For example, each floor could be provided with two doors, one for embarking passengers and the other for disembarking passengers.

Detailed description: It must be possible for would-be passengers to summon an elevator and be assured that an elevator will arrive. For example, it should be possible to determine whether a request can be honoured. Furthermore, it should be possible to determine the status of an elevator request. Finally, once an elevator arrives at a floor it should be possible to embark as quickly as possible.

Rationale: The ELS system will be installed in buildings with many floors. Passengers wish to get to their destination as efficiently and as safely as possible.

Source: Service Level Management (SLM) and Customers.

Customer importance (priority): Medium.

Risk factor: High.

Quantitative description of requirement: The most important system attribute is Performance with metrics 'number of passengers transported per hour' and 'response time for user input'. Values can be assigned to these metrics.

Possible sub-requirements: Not applicable in this version.

Requirement name and ID: Safe Embarkation (ID is R2)

Short description: The safety of would-be passengers and passengers is of paramount importance at all times. ELS should be designed in such a way that nothing can happen to injure passengers. If something does go wrong passengers should be able to alert the central security service (for example, by the use of an emergency button). In general it should be difficult to get into a hazardous state and it should be easy to return to a safe state (Leveson 1995).

Detailed description: ELS should be designed in such a way that the safety of would-be passengers is assured at all times. Each elevator should be configured and designed in such a way that the safety of would-be passengers is not compromised. For example, a limit to the maximum number of passengers could be defined for each elevator (by using overweight sensors). Furthermore, an elevator should be inactive until all doors have been closed. This is to ensure that a would-be passenger does not get stuck in a door. Providing separate doors for embarkation and disembarkation can enhance safety.

Rationale: Safety is all-important.

Source: Service Level Management (SLM) and Customers.
Customer importance (priority): High.
Risk factor: High.
Quantitative description of requirement: The most important system attribute is Reliability with metrics 'mean time to failure' and 'rate of occurrence of failure'. Values should be assigned to these metrics.
Possible sub-requirements: Not applicable in this version.

Requirement name and ID: Efficient Arrival at Destination (ID is R3)

Short description: It is important to schedule the elevators in such a way that as many passengers as possible are transported to their destination as quickly and efficiently as possible.
Detailed description: If an elevator has no passengers or would-be passengers then it parks on the last floor that it visited. An elevator should not reverse its direction of travel until all its passengers who want to travel in the 'current direction' have reached their destination.
Rationale: Customers become annoyed and frustrated when it takes too long to get to their destination.
Source: Service Level Management (SLM) and Customers.
Customer importance (priority): High.
Risk factor: High.
Quantitative description of requirement: The most important system attribute corresponding to this requirement is performance of the elevator. This attribute has corresponding metrics 'number of transported passengers per hour' and 'response time to passenger input' (how long it takes to get to destination).
Possible sub-requirements: Not applicable in this version.

As an exercise, the reader might like to document requirements R4 and R5 using the above structure.

13.7 SYSTEM DECOMPOSITION OF ELS

ELS can be modelled as one or more instances of a Resource Allocation and Tracking (RAT) system. We now address the problem of decomposing it into subsystems. There are a number of possibilities, two of which are:

- Option 1: Treat ELS as a basic RAT category
- Option 2: Decompose ELS into two loosely coupled RAT systems.

Option 1 demands that we decompose ELS into three subsystems that we call Registration, Assignment and Presentation. All requests (whether they be elevator

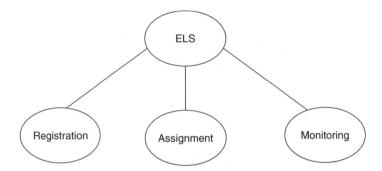

Figure 13.4   System decomposition of ELS (option 1).

summons requests or destination requests) enter the system via Registration (see Figure 13.4), the requests are assigned to physical resources in Assignment and the status of all requests is shown in Presentation. Option 2 is based on a *separation of concerns* strategy, the assumption that ELS is really a combination of two simpler and more or less independent systems belonging to the RAT category. One system is responsible for elevator summons requests while the other is responsible for floor destination requests. System RES (Request Elevator System) registers and resolves requests for would-be passengers, while RDS (Request Destination System) registers and resolves requests for passengers who are already in an elevator. The structural decomposition of ELS in terms of RES, RDS and their respective subsystems is shown in Figure 13.5. Notice the similarities between RES and RDS; each is an instance of a RAT category.

We now summarize what we think are the advantages and disadvantages of the two options. We benchmark each option against *two* ISO 9126 quality characteristics,

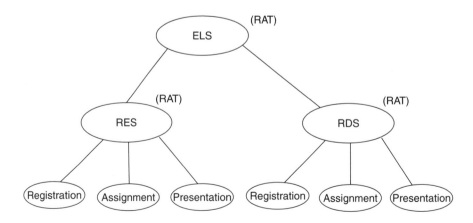

Figure 13.5   System decomposition of ELS (option 2).

namely Maintainability and Functionality. The first characteristic is concerned with the stability of the system when modifications take place and how easy it is to effect these changes, while Functionality refers to how a system supports stated and implied needs. The latter characteristic also has to do with how easy it is to 'extend' and 'contract' functionality.

Option 1 clusters the functionality for both elevator summoning and passenger transportation into one system. No distinction is made between a request for an elevator and a transportation request to travel to a given floor. This has the advantage that functionality is grouped around three logical subsystems (instead of six as with option 2) and to this end we say that option 1 results in a tightly coupled system. The main disadvantage is understandability, especially when different teams work on the system. For example, confusion may arise when we start to discuss the concept of a request: one group may be thinking about elevator summons requests while the other group consider a request as being a request to transport a passenger to a given floor (floor destination request).

The main advantage of option 2 is that concerns are separated: subsystem RES is responsible for dispatching an elevator to a given floor while RDS is responsible for transporting a passenger to a given floor. Each subsystem can be independently planned, analysed and designed. Furthermore, changes and extensions to one subsystem have little or no impact on the other subsystem. The main disadvantage is that the two subsystems must be integrated at some stage and it is then that performance, interfacing and reliability problems may arise.

We choose between options 1 and 2 by how they address each ISO 9126 viewpoint. We give a plus or minus to each option. Of course, there is a certain amount of subjectivity involved, but we have created the matrix based on the judgements of several independent experts. The matrix is shown in Figure 13.6. Based on these results, we choose option 2 as the preferred architecture for this problem. This is the option that will be discussed in more detail in the next two subsections.

	Option 1	Option 2
Functionality	–	+
Reliability	+	+
Usability	–	–
Efficiency	++	+–
Maintainability	–	–
Portability	–	++

Figure 13.6 Making high-level design decisions in ELS.

13.8 PAC DECOMPOSITION OF ELS

Since the subsystems RES (Request Elevator System) and RDS (Request Destination System) are both of RAT category, it is possible to create an initial PAC model for them. In keeping with the RAT philosophy we know that the control objects are called Registration, Assignment and Presentation in both cases.

For the subsystem RES the responsibilities of these control objects are (see Figures 13.7 and 13.8):

- Registration: accept and register a validated elevator summons request
- Assignment: allocate an elevator for the current request
- Presentation: notify interested parties of request status.

For RDS the control objects are:

- Registration: accept and register a validated floor destination request
- Assignment: allocate a plan for the current request
- Presentation: notify interested parties of request status.

We now deal with the boundary objects in RES and RDS. For RES the boundary objects and their responsibilities are:

- Summons panel (floor object): allows would-be passengers to select an elevator
- Elevator requestor: interfaces with external Physical Resources system
- Door actuator and alarm bell.

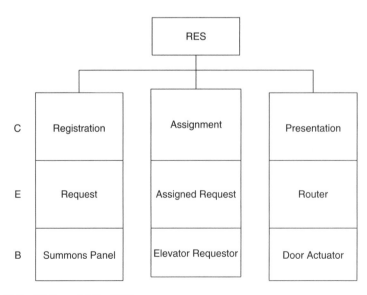

Figure 13.7 PAC model for RES.

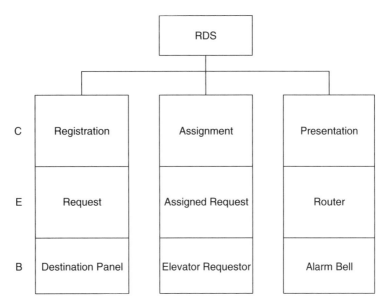

Figure 13.8 PAC model for RDS.

For RDS the boundary objects and their responsibilities are:

- Destination panel: allows a passenger to select one or more destinations
- Elevator requestor: interfaces with Physical Resources system
- Door actuator and alarm bell.

It now remains to discuss the Entity objects in each subsystem. This is not always easy to do at this stage of the analysis because it is easier to discover them, their attributes and methods during OOA. However, we give some idea here of their names and responsibilities. The Entity objects for RES are:

- (Summons) Request: contains information on source and direction of request
- Assigned request: request receives the attention of some elevator
- Router: translates internal commands to external commands (and vice versa).

The Entity objects for RDS are:

- (Destination) Request: contains information on destination floor
- Assigned request: request commits an elevator to a floor
- Router: translates internal commands to external commands (and vice versa).

One of the activities during object-oriented analysis is to add more detail to these Entity objects.

The PAC models for RES and RDS are shown in Figures 13.7 and 13.8 respectively.

13.9 MAJOR USE CASES

We describe several use cases in order to gain insight into the generic requirements from Section 13.6. For completeness we document both normal and exceptional cases according to the UML standard.

13.9.1 Normal use cases

The normal use cases are:

- U1: Customer requests an elevator
- U2: Customer wishes to travel to some floor
- U3: Schedule an elevator
- U4: Dispatch an elevator.

We now describe use cases U1 and U3. The reader might like to document U2 and U4 along similar lines.

Use case name and ID: Customer requests an elevator (ID is U1)

Associated requirement: R1 (Efficient Embarkation) and R2 (Safe Embarkation); R5 (Efficient Scheduling).
Actors in use case: Would-be passengers and passengers in the elevator.
Preconditions: ELS system is operational.
Short description: The would-be passenger summons an elevator (up or down) from the current floor. The elevator arrives and the floor door opens.
Detailed description: An elevator is summoned by pressing one of the buttons in the summons panel. This request is validated to determine whether it is allowed to use the elevator from the current floor. The summons button light becomes illuminated if the request is satisfied. We note that the 'up' button does not function at the top floor while the 'down' button does not function at the 'ground' floor (in fact, they may even be absent). It is not possible to summon a particular elevator; the scheduler (Physical Resources actor) selects the most suitable elevator that satisfies the customer request. This is determined by the scheduling algorithms in the system. The would-be passenger can see which elevator will arrive and where it is at any given moment by examining the arrival panel that is situated above each door. When the elevator arrives the door opens for a number of seconds and customers can embark and disembark. Some floors have one door while others have two doors. Some floors have no elevator doors.

Exceptions:
— Not possible to use elevator from this floor
— Summons button does not respond to request
— Door fails to open
— Summons panel has already been pressed: this new request is ignored because a similar request is already pending.

Other concurrent activities: Other passengers are issuing destination requests while yet others may have pressed stop buttons or emergency stop buttons. Other would-be passengers may be trying to access the same elevator.

Postconditions: Door has been opened and waiting for embarkation.

Use case name and ID: Schedule an elevator (ID is U3)

Associated requirement: R5 (Efficient Scheduling).
Actors in use case: Physical Resources.
Preconditions: Current floor not in attention list of any elevator.
Short description: A request originates from a floor. A would-be passenger hails an elevator.
Detailed description: A request originates from a given floor. This is realized by pressing the summons button (up or down direction). The request is modelled as the source of the request (that is, from which floor the request came) and the desired direction of travel. This information is sent to the Physical Resources actor that then attempts to place the request in its 'attention list'. Once this has been realized the summons button light will be illuminated.
Exceptions:
— Unable to schedule an elevator
— Elevator already scheduled.

Other concurrent activities: Other would-be passengers are summoning the same elevator; passengers are travelling to their destinations.

Postconditions: Current floor in attention list of some elevator.

13.9.2 Exceptional use cases

We now document several abnormal or exceptional use cases. They represent situations that should not occur but seeing that safety is a major goal of ELS we document them using the standard template mechanism.

Use case name and ID: Elevator becomes dangerous (because of overweight)
(ID is U5)

Associated requirement: R2 (Safe Embarkation).
Actors in use case: Would-be passengers, passengers.
Preconditions: Elevator door has been opened.

Short description: The elevator becomes dangerous if too many people are in an elevator. Each elevator has a maximum number of passengers that it is allowed to carry.

Detailed description: For safety reasons, each elevator is provided with an over-weight sensor that measures the weight of the total number of passengers in it at any moment in time. As soon as a would-be passenger embarks and just before the elevator door closes, the total weight in the elevator is measured. If this value is above a certain threshold the elevator door will not close, the elevator will not move and a continuous alarm will be sounded indefinitely until one or more passengers disembark. A message should be sent to the Service Level Management group if the overweight situation persists for too long.

Exceptions:

— Overweight situation takes too long to rectify.

Other concurrent activities: Would-be passengers are requesting the elevator.

Postconditions: Door remains open and elevator is temporarily disabled.

Use case name and ID: Passenger registers alarm situation (ID is U6)

Associated requirement: R2 (Safe Embarkation), R4 (Safe Arrival at Destination).

Actors in use case: Passengers, Service Level Management.

Preconditions: None.

Short description: A passenger presses the emergency stop button. This is a signal that something is wrong and help should be sent to the elevator as soon as possible.

Detailed description: Each elevator is provided with an emergency stop button. If a passenger presses the emergency stop button the elevator stops at the next floor in its trajectory. When the elevator arrives the door is opened automatically and all further requests are ignored. An alert message is sent to the Service Level Management group who should send someone to investigate the problem. The door remains open until reset.

Exceptions: Not applicable.

Other concurrent activities: Would-be passengers are requesting the services of the current elevator.

Postconditions: Passenger alert message has been registered with Service Level Management.

Use case name and ID: Elevator malfunctions in some way (ID is U7)

Associated requirement: R2 (Safe Embarkation), R4 (Safe Arrival at Destination).

Actors in use case: Hardware in system (actors in context diagram).

Preconditions: None.

Short description: A piece of hardware ceases to function properly. The Service Level Management group should be notified.

Detailed description: It is important that the hardware in the ELS system functions according to the specifications. In particular, all vital physical units should function properly. The most important hardware consists of the following:
— The physical units in the elevator (motor, vital sensors)
— Summons and destination panels
— Arrival panels (interior and exterior).
One way to realize this use case is to deploy a Watchdog system (see Douglass 1998). Such a system receives messages from ELS on a periodic or sequence-key basis. If messages arrive too late or out or sequence the Watchdog takes some corrective action. This action might be a reset, a system shutdown, an alarm message or even some more elaborate recovery procedure.
Exceptions: Not applicable.
Other concurrent activities: Customers have requested or are requesting services of the elevator. Other passengers may be pressing stop buttons, emergency stop buttons or the red button.
Postconditions: ELS enters degraded or in failure mode.

In general, as discussed in Leveson (1995), the feasibility of building effective fail-safe protection systems depends on the existence of a safe state to which the system can be brought and the availability of early warning. A general design rule is that hazardous states should be difficult to get into while the procedures for switching to safe states should be simple.

13.10 SUMMARY AND CONCLUSIONS

We have carried out an analysis of a well-known problem in the literature: the Elevator Control System (ELS). Several authors have examined this problem from various perspectives. We distance ourselves from traditional object-oriented approaches because we think that they are inappropriate in this context. The main problem is that describing a problem domain such as ELS in terms of hardware and data objects in the initial stages of analysis will lead to brittle systems, that is systems with low Usability, Functionality, Maintainability and Portability levels.

APPENDIX 13.1: DEFINITIONS

We define the most important concepts and terms in ELS. The emphasis is on the nouns in the documentation. It is important that all stakeholders are clear on what these concepts really mean, hence the reason for definitions.

Accessible floor: A floor that may be travelled to by a passenger. It may also refer to the floor from which a would-be passenger may travel.

Customer: Those people and groups of people who use the services of the ELS. Customers include would-be passengers and passengers.

Delay time: The time it takes for an elevator to arrive at a given floor after a summons button has been pressed. There are various kinds of delay in ELS, for example the times would-be passengers must wait on an elevator and the time it takes to close an elevator door.

Destination request: Request to travel to a given floor (called the destination).

Efficiency: A general term referring to how well ELS is functioning in terms of energy usage, delay times and transportation times.

Elevator: The machinery that transports passengers from one floor to another floor. An elevator has attributes such as serial number, date of installation, maximum number of passengers allowed in it and so on.

Elevator direction: The direction in which an elevator is currently travelling. Possibilities are up, down and 'none' (elevator is stationary).

Elevator dispatching: Sending an elevator to a given floor after the elevator has been summoned.

Floor: That part of a building where customers embark and disembark. Elevators stop at floors. A floor is furnished with summons panels and a number of doors.

Passenger: Those people and groups of people who wish to travel to a given floor or destination.

Request: A general term to describe how customers interact with ELS and what kinds of service they expect from it.

Request scheduling: The action that involves reserving an elevator in order to satisfy a summons request from a person.

Request time: The time needed to satisfy a given request. This is a generic term. For example, it could refer to the time it takes to hail an elevator after the summons button has been pressed. Request time is similar to delay time.

Scheduler: A general name to denote algorithms in the Physical Resources system. These algorithms ensure that elevators are reserved and that passengers are transported to their destinations.

Would-be passenger: A person or group of persons who summons an elevator.

14 Order Processing Systems (OPS)

> 'In many companies, cross-functional situations are perceived as conflicts and are addressed from the standpoint of conflict resolution rather than problem solving. The lack of predetermined criteria for solving cross-functional problems and the jealously guarded "turf" make the job all the more difficult.'
> Masaki Imai, *Kaizen, The Key to Japan's Competitive Success*

14.1 INTRODUCTION AND OBJECTIVES

This chapter analyses an order-tracking system. Before we go into details, let us describe the organization in which this system will operate. The organization is the sum total of all processes and activities that take place at Datasim Education, a company that develops software products (including training courses, customized software toolkits using object-oriented, component and agent technologies). The Datasim organization has three core processes:

- Order Processing System (OPS)
- Product Profile System (PPS)
- Customer Profile System (CPS).

Each of these systems is an instance of a Lifecycle Model (LCM, see Chapter 10). The organization interfaces with three major actor systems:

- *Customers*: Organizations that avail themselves of the products and services that Datasim provides. Typical examples are IT system houses, software development companies and companies that design and manufacture products.
- *Suppliers*: Organizations that deliver products and services to Datasim. Typical examples are catering and cleaning services, computer and software manufacturers, accountants, and companies offering facilities (for example, office space).

- *Environment*: This is a kind of 'catch all' group and includes systems such as the tax office, competitors, market forces and the law. It could also include cultural norms and values and process documentation. This is the group of indirect stakeholders.

We focus on the system OPS in order to reduce the scope. This lifecycle model is responsible for everything that happens to a customer request from the moment it enters the supply chain to the time that it is no longer used. OPS is a composite of three domain architecture types:

- Order Creation System (OCS) (Manufacturing)
- Order Realization System (ORS) (Resource Allocation and Tracking)
- Order Management System (OMS) (Management Information System).

We reduce the scope even further in this chapter by examining ORS in detail. We shall describe OCS and OMS by their context diagrams and main requirements. The high-priority and high-risk system for us is ORS. Reducing the scope even further, we concentrate on a number of important issues:

- A Customer Requirements Specification (CRS)
- Inventory of the major stakeholders and requirements in ORS
- The use cases that implement the core process
- The major class diagrams
- Hints and tips for the designers of ORS.

Once we have discussed these topics we can justifiably say that we understand the problem at a high level, that many risks have been identified and mitigated and that we, as requirements analysts, UML analysts and architects, are in position to hand over the artefacts to the designers and developers.

The OPS system is a good prototype example of a *data-intensive application*; data is created, stored and accessed by different stakeholders and much of the functionality in such applications is geared to producing suitable user interfaces to business data and business logic. Thus, OPS can be used as a baseline example for similar applications. In fact, order processing is fundamental to many organizations and tends to be the first object-oriented test case that these organizations undertake.

In Section 14.2 we list the main features that OPS should provide. In Section 14.3 we describe the lifecycle model for OPS by describing its context diagram and interfaces to its external systems. Section 14.4 introduces the behavioural elements in OPS by introducing stakeholders and their corresponding requirements. The class architecture is discussed in Section 14.5 and to this end we describe it as a set of PAC models. Having produced analysis artefacts we have thought it appropriate to pay some attention to the design of OPS, in particular to how we model the lifecycle of data in the system. This is discussed in Sections 14.6 to 14.8.

14.2 CUSTOMER REQUIREMENTS SPECIFICATION (CRS): THE PRODUCT MANAGEMENT VISION OF OPS

This section describes the Customer Requirements Specification (CRS) for the OPS system. Datasim is a company that provides software services and to this end the product management group has come up with a number of features that the new order processing system should support. In particular, they have seen how the current system works and they have come up with the following list of features that the new system should have:

1. Efficient flow of information, materials and funds from initial customer request through to request closure and archiving.
2. Higher usability levels, in particular user-friendly input screens and report-generating facilities. The Front Office works with Commercial Off-The-Shelf (COTS) software such as Word and Excel and there should be some provision for automatic coupling between OPS and these software packages.
3. OPS should be an 'open' system in the sense that it interoperates with other systems in the Datasim organization.
4. Provision for escalation policies and procedures. This is needed by the service level management group who need to know where things are going wrong before they actually get out of hand.
5. Senior management has placed restrictions on the budget: the first production system must be ready in a year's time and a team of three staff must implement the system. These personnel have other duties and not all personnel will be involved full-time on the project.
6. An up-to-date and accurate customer database including product-buying history, customer request and statistical information concerning critical attributes.
7. Interdepartmental communication improvement. In particular, once a request has been registered it should be accessible to all relevant departments. By 'relevant' we mean those stakeholders in the Datasim organization who schedule the request, allocate resources and have contact with customers and suppliers. In general, traceability is important.
8. The new OPS system should benchmark similar allocation and tracking systems in other disciplines, for example Federal Express, DHL or similar organizations (Bogan and English 1994). We should learn from the best in class and not reinvent the wheel.

14.2.1 Business concerns and stakeholders' viewpoints

Senior management has a number of goals and objectives for OPS. There is a wish to improve efficiency, shorten cycle times and have accurate information concerning orders, products, customers and suppliers. To this end, the requirements analyst has discovered three major business concerns:

- Accuracy
- Responsiveness to customer wishes
- Usability.

Accuracy has to do with the quality of the information in the OPS system. In this case it refers to the usefulness of the data in the system. For example, a customer database in which 95% of the information is accurate and up-to-date will be more useful and less wasteful of resources than a database in which only 60% of the information is accurate. Responsiveness relates to the speed with which customer requests are processed. Usability refers to how long it takes for Front Office personnel to learn how to use the system. These are the most important concerns because their realization will lead to improved performance and higher customer satisfaction levels.

The sub-concerns for each of these concerns can be discovered by using the Inquiry Cycle model (see Potts *et al* 1994 and Appendix 1 of this book). In this case we can pose the question 'what-kinds of':

- *What kinds of accuracy?*
    — C1: Accurate and up-to-date customer profile information
    — C2: Accurate and up-to-date product profile information
    — C3: Accurate stock control
    — C4: Accurate information concerning customer orders
- *What kinds of responsiveness?*
    — C5: Performance measures of customer request resolution
    — C6: Efficient escalation procedures
- *What kinds of usability?*
    — C7: Audit trail of customer requests
    — C8: Logical build-up of user input screens.

Each of these sub-concerns can be decomposed into viewpoints and we eventually arrive at the level of requirements. These issues are of fundamental importance and the requirements analyst should ensure that these requirements are realized.

14.3 OPS AS A LIFECYCLE MODEL

The OPS system is an instance of a Lifecycle Model (LCM) because we are interested in tracking a customer request from the moment the request enters the system to when the corresponding order is closed. The scope is well defined. We already know from Chapter 10 that there are three major systems in Lifecycle Models, namely a Manufacturing (MAN) system that creates the basic objects to be processed, a Resource and Tracking (RAT) system that allocates resources for these objects, and a Management Information System (MIS) that monitors the status of the objects and clusters of objects. We have already seen that the OPS system has subsystems Order Creation System (OCS), Order Realization System (ORS) and Order Management System (OMS). OCS creates basic order entities, ORS assigns resources to fulfil the order, while OMS allows high-level management reports to be created and dispatched to interested parties. Thus, OPS is responsible for everything that happens to an order. Of course, orders have to do with customers, products and other environmental factors and to this end we must construct a suitable context diagram if we are to make clear what OPS expects as a client, what it delivers as a server and how it collaborates with other systems. The context is shown in Figure 14.1 where we have explicitly shown the three systems of OPS, the external stakeholder systems and some (though not all) of the boundary objects that give an

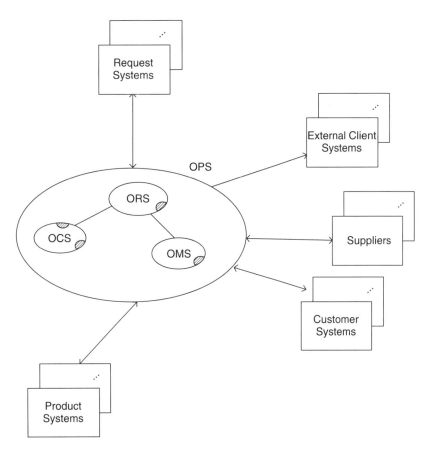

Figure 14.1   Context diagram for OPS.

indication of how OCS, ORS and OMS communicate with the outside world. The major external systems in this version of OPS are:

- *Request Systems*: systems that send basic request data to OPS
- *Product Systems*: systems that are responsible for product lifecycles
- *Customer Systems*: systems that contain information about customers
- *External Client Systems*: other systems that benefit from OPS in some way
- *Supplier Systems*: systems that consume resources, and produce products and services.

Examples of client systems that benefit from OPS are invoicing, archiving and decision-support systems that need multi-dimensional information pertaining to orders.

We need to consider how data enters the OPS systems, how it is processed and how it is transferred to other systems.

We have drawn connecting lines between OCS, ORS and OMS in Figure 14.1. The lines mean that one system is related to another one in some way. Their precise meaning will become clearer as we progress in this chapter. Having understood the high-level environment of OPS, we now zoom into each of its subsystems in the next three subsections.

14.3.1 Order Creation System (OCS)

OCS is an instance of a MAN category and its main responsibility is to create basic request entities. These are not fully-fledged orders because we do not yet know if the request can be satisfied (this is ORS's job). The extended context diagram is shown in Figure 14.2. We call it an extended diagram because we show the boundary objects that communicate with OCS's external systems.

We motivate the roles of OCS and its external systems by noting the activities that realize the core process 'Create Request Entity':

- Accept request data (via B1)
- Check and validate request data (via B2); is it a valid request?
- Notify MIS of new request data (via B3)
- Allocate resources for request (via B4)
- Notify and dispatch (via B5), for example to ORS.

These are the main activities that realize the core process. We shall see how to find the subsystems and UML analysis objects in OCS in Section 14.5.

The reader might like to compare Figure 14.2 with the context diagram for the MAN (Figure 8.11) category to persuade herself or himself that OCS is indeed an instance of MAN. See Chapter 8 for more details.

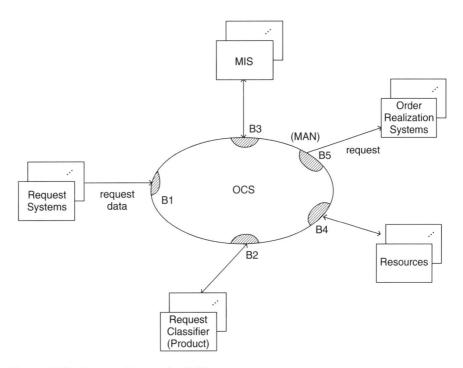

Figure 14.2   Context diagram for OCS.

14.3.2 Order Realization System (ORS)

This is an instance of a RAT category and its main responsibility is to create orders and allocate resources in order to realize them. In particular, it checks the requests from OCS by first identifying the sender of the request, in this case a customer who wishes to request services or purchase products, and second by checking whether Datasim can actually execute or realize the order. Examples of constraints could be price, time to deliver, customer credit rating, quality and other non-functional requirements. The context diagram is shown in Figure 14.3.

We motivate the roles of ORS and its external systems by noting the activities that realize the core process 'Create Order Entity':

- Accept order data (via B1)
- Check and validate order data (via B2); it is a valid customer?
- Notify MIS (possibly) of new order (via B3)
- Allocate resources for order (via B4)
- Notify and dispatch (via B5), for example to OMS.

ORS schedules each order and it will be the responsibility of OMS to determine whether the order planning and scheduling has been realized.

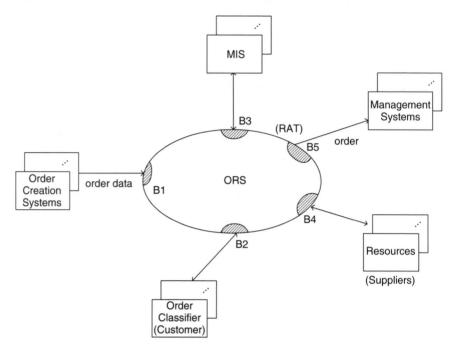

Figure 14.3   Context diagram for ORS.

The reader might like to compare Figure 14.3 with the context diagram for the RAT (Figure 7.4) category to persuade herself or himself that ORS is indeed an instance of RAT. See Chapter 7 for more details.

14.3.3 Order Management System (OMS)

This is a Management Information System (MIS) and is concerned with order fulfilment after orders have been scheduled. In particular, we are interested in consolidating orders in different ways, for example:

- All orders for a given customer/region/city
- All orders that were created in a given month
- Outstanding and unfulfilled orders.

In fact, OMS is similar to the Manpower Control (MPC) system and it is a good idea to use MPC as a baseline architecture for OMS. We can compare the two systems based on functionality, structure and behaviour. Figure 14.4 shows the context diagram for OMS.

We motivate the roles of OMS and its external systems by noting the activities that realize the core process 'Create Decision Support Information':

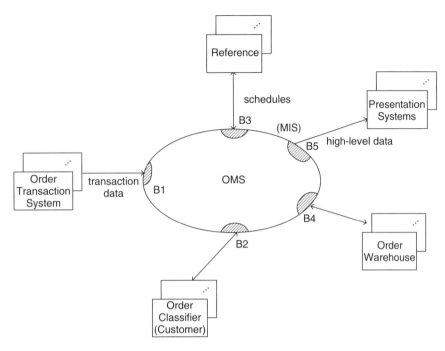

Figure 14.4 Context diagram for OMS.

- Accept transaction data (via B1)
- Classify transaction data (via B2); in which group does it belong?
- Notify Reference of new transactions (via B3)
- Consolidate transaction data and store in a data warehouse (via B4)
- Notify and dispatch (via B5) to external client systems.

The reader might like to compare Figure 14.4 with the context diagram for the MIS (Figure 5.5) category to persuade herself or himself that OCS is indeed an instance of MIS. See Chapter 5 for more details.

14.4 BEHAVIOURAL ASPECTS

We now discuss the stakeholders, viewpoints and requirements for OPS. We classify stakeholders by using a three-level scheme:

- Internal stakeholder groups
- External stakeholder groups
- Domain stakeholders.

The first group represents all those personnel within the Datasim organization that are involved in processing customer requests. We further subdivide the internal group into three categories:

- The Front Office
- The Middle Office
- The Back Office.

We now discuss these three internal groups in more detail.

14.4.1 Front Office

The Front Office is concerned with those activities that have to do with initial contact with the customer. The Back Office is involved in ensuring that customer requests are realized. The Middle Office is the bridge between the two other groups and is concerned with those issues that have a direct bearing on the products and the quality of products and services that the customer requires.

The stakeholders in the Front Office group are those in daily contact with customers. Their main duties are as follows.

- *Operational level*
  - Registering customer requests
  - Forwarding requests to appropriate support personnel
  - Keeping the customer database up-to-date
- *Tactical level*
  - Providing feedback to customers on request performance
  - Creating an infrastructure for effective communication
  - Market research on new prospects, leads and customers
- *Strategic level*
  - Defining policies and procedures
  - Customer satisfaction levels and service level management (SLM)
  - Defining new customer groups, services and products.

The Front Office is dependent on the Middle Office and Back Office and when something goes wrong it is the Front Office that is responsible for escalation policies and procedures.

14.4.2 Back Office

The Back Office is responsible for functions such as human resource management and procurement of goods. The main roles of each sub-group are:

- *Operational level*
  - Ensuring availability of resources and supplies

— Feedback to the Middle Office
— Distribution of resources that are related to a customer request
- *Tactical level*
  — Contact with suppliers and quality of service issues
  — Resource planning and scheduling
  — Line management functions
- *Strategic level*
  — Category management (new products and raw materials)
  — Organizational cost control management
  — Financial planning.

The Operational group is responsible for the smooth running of the organization while the Tactical group is responsible for ensuring that all resources are ordered, delivered and consumed. Finally, the Strategic group is responsible for the overall financial health of the organization in the medium and long terms.

14.4.3 Middle Office

The Middle Office is populated by the stakeholders that have intimate knowledge about the products and services that the organization offers. These are key stakeholders because without them there is no product to sell.

- *Operational level*
  — Training and pre-sales activities
  — Product deployment
  — Provide feedback on product acceptance
- *Tactical level*
  — Product development
  — Benchmarking competitors' products
  — Skills improvement
- *Strategic level*
  — New business opportunities and new products
  — Benchmarking competitors' products
  — Provide feedback to upper management.

14.4.4 External groups

The external groups represent those persons and organizations that interact directly and indirectly with Datasim:

- *Customers*: those organizations that receive services or products from Datasim.
- *Suppliers*: those organizations that provide services, products and raw materials to Datasim.

- *Regulators*: those organizations that audit the services, products and processes in the Datasim organization.

In general, each group can be further classified according to how they relate to customers. In particular, we define three sub-categories based on the type of information that the group wishes to see:

- Operational (daily duties, ensuring that customer requests are satisfied)
- Tactical (short-term duties, ability to adapt to new events)
- Strategic (long-term planning and goals of the organization).

We give a summary of the main information flows:

- *From OPS to customer*
  — Response to a request
  — Direct mailing
  — Special actions
- *From customer to OPS*
  — Information request
  — Product request
  — Other feedback
- *From OPS to supplier*
  — Order resources (resource request)
  — Define new policies
- *From supplier to OPS*
  — Request status
  — New resources announced
- *From OPS to regulators and other external client systems*
  — Status of product/customer delivery
  — Quality assurance
  — Financial and accounting information
- *From regulators to OPS*
  — Audits
  — Information requests.

14.5 COLLECTING REQUIREMENTS FROM MULTIPLE STAKEHOLDER VIEWPOINTS

We concentrate on ORS in this subsection. Once the different stakeholder groups have been found, the next step is to determine the requirements of each group. In other words, we elicit the requirements by examining the ORS system from the perspective of each of these groups. This approach has the advantage that we can focus on one group at a time without being distracted by the requirements from other groups. In general, the requirements from the internal and external groups can be found by interviewing the key stakeholders, while a large number of requirements in ORS can be found due to the fact that ORS is a RAT instance (see Chapter 7). In this chapter we concentrate on a subset of stakeholder requirements. We discuss the following stakeholder groups:

- S1: The Front Office Operational Group
- S2: The RAT Group in the Domain group
- S3: The Back Office Operations Group.

These groups have been chosen (for the purpose of this chapter only) because they have the highest priority and are closely aligned to the critical business processes that ORS must support.

After interviewing the stakeholders in each of the groups S1, S2 and S3 we managed to arrive at a preliminary list of requirements for each group. We stress that the list is not complete and there may be conflicts, overlaps and other problems associated with the resulting requirements. These activities are part of the requirement analyst's duties and are outside the scope of this book (for more on these topics, see Sommerville and Sawyer 1997). We settle for the following requirements:

- *The Front Office Operational Group*
  — R1: User-friendly registration of a customer order
  — R2: Accessing customer and customer category information
  — R3: Automatic generation of customer reports and letters
  — R4: Accessing order data
- *The RAT Group in the Domain group*
  — R1: Scheduling a customer request
  — R2: Knowing the status of a request at all times
  — R3: Escalation procedures and rerouting policies
  — R4: Efficient throughput in system
- *The Back Office Operations Group*
  — R1: Stock Control status
  — R2: Capacity planning (what to order, when to order and from whom).

14.5.1 Critical use cases

In order to reduce the scope even more, we concentrate on the most important use cases. In particular, we adopt the strategy of first searching for those use cases that are closely related to the core and supporting processes. The main core processes will suggest *architecturally important use cases*:

- OCS: Create basic request entities (use case U1)
- ORS: Create order planning and scheduling (use case U2)
- OMS: Create high-level decision-support information on orders (use case U3).

Note that each use case is tightly coupled to a subsystem and loosely coupled to other use cases. In fact, the postcondition of one use case in many applications is the precondition of another use case! This avoids overlap and promotes understandability. We decompose U1, U2 and U3 into lower-level use cases and we assign each new use case to a subsystem of OCS, ORS or OMS. This assignment may not always be possible. These sub-use cases are realizations of the activities in each core process:

- U1.1: Create embryonic request entity (in OCS::Preprocessing)
- U1.2: Create internal request entity (in OCS::Conversion)
- U1.3: Dispatch and format internal request entity (in OCS::Postprocessing)

- U2.1: Create basic order entity (in ORS::Registration)
- U2.2: Schedule order and assign resources (in ORS::Assignment)
- U2.3: Dispatch and display order status information (in ORS::Presentation)

- U3.1: Create basic transaction object (in OMS::Registration)
- U3.2: Consolidate transaction objects (in OMS::Merging)
- U3.3: Dispatch and display decision support information (in OMS::Reporting).

It is possible to document each of these use cases using the standard UML template structure. We give one worked example in Appendix 14.1 of this chapter, namely U2 as well as its sub-use cases U2.1, U2.2 and U2.3.

14.6 CLASS ARCHITECTURE

We now 'zoom' into the internal structure of the OCS, ORS and OMS systems, as it were. We create PAC models for each one. This is a relatively straightforward process at this stage because the models have been thoroughly explained in Chapters 8 (for MAN), 7 (for RAT) and 5 (for MIS).

14.6.1 Class models and diagrams

Figure 14.5 shows the PAC model for OCS. The boundary objects and systems have already been found from the corresponding context diagram in Figure 14.2. The names in the control layers are standard and have been reused from the resulting

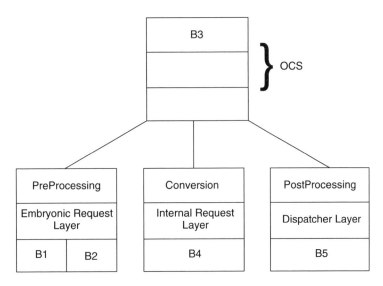

Figure 14.5 PAC model for OCS.

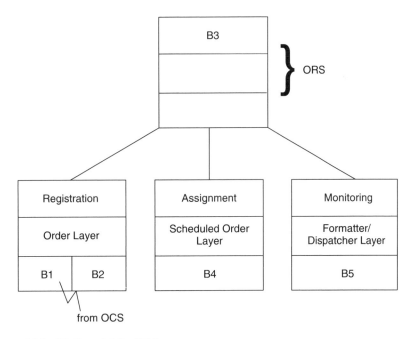

Figure 14.6 PAC model for ORS.

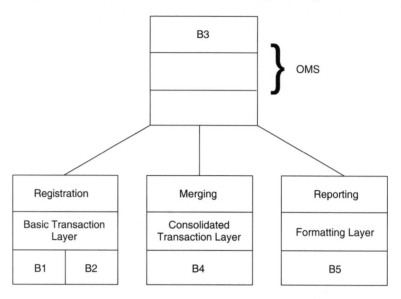

Figure 14.7   PAC model for OMS.

domain category. The entity layers deserve attention and must support the following classes and corresponding class associations:

- A request has a sender
- A request has attributes
- A request belongs to a certain category
- A request can be part of another request.

We can document these as UML class diagrams.

Figure 14.6 shows the PAC model for ORS. The boundary objects and systems have already been found from the corresponding context diagram in Figure 14.3. The names in the control layers are standard and have been reused from the RAT domain category. The class diagrams will be similar to those in OCS. Appendix 14.2 gives a simplified class diagram example for the ORS system.

Figure 14.7 shows the PAC model for OMS. The boundary objects and systems have already been found from the corresponding context diagram in Figure 14.4. The names in the control layers are standard and have been reused from the RAT category. The PAC model is shown in Figure 14.7.

14.7 DESIGN GUIDELINES FOR OPS

It is intuitively obvious that data and data management will be the life-blood in OPS. The data in the system must be accurate, up-to-date and secure. In particular, we must understand detailed design issues and propose a strategy for their implementation using standard design patterns, for example. The following discussion pertains to all kinds of UML analysis objects in principle, but the most important category is the set of Entity objects because they are the objects that contain the persistent data in the system. The main use cases for these objects are suggested by applying the Lifecycle Model to Entity objects:

- Creating Entity objects from different data sources
- Structuring Entity objects so that they become part of a class model
- Saving Entity objects to data stores.

There is a myriad of questions that we can ask concerning these three major action points. For example, we can apply the Inquiry Cycle model (see Appendix 1) to gain insights into the design problems that arise. Some questions are:

- What is a data store?
- What kinds of data stores are there?
- What is the relationship between Entity objects and data stores?
- What is the relationship between Boundary objects and data stores?
- What is the relationship between the Boundary and Entity objects?
- How are Entity objects created, structured and made persistent?

To this end, the rule is that we must add new external actor systems that will contain the data in the systems. Here we think specifically of real-world relational database systems (such as Oracle and SQL/Server), object-oriented databases, disk files, flash memory and other proprietary formats. Each new external data store will have its own specific service interfaces whereby it can (and must!) be accessed from our PAC model. In particular, we design new Boundary objects (one for each specific physical data store). A generic example is shown in Figure 14.8 where each PAC agent communicates with its own specific data store. This gives us the freedom to work in a heterogeneous database environment, but this level of flexibility comes at a price and may be overkill in many real-life situations. An alternative is shown in Figure 14.9 where we now have only two external physical data stores.

A good introduction to the design of data-intensive applications by using reusable design patterns is given in Fowler *et al* 2003.

14.7.1 Data patterns

We now define what we mean by the data and Entity object lifecycle in relation to design. First of all, the data that resides in the Entity layer is stored in external databases and is brought into the system by special Boundary objects as already seen from Figures 14.8 and 14.9. These objects can have various synonyms depending

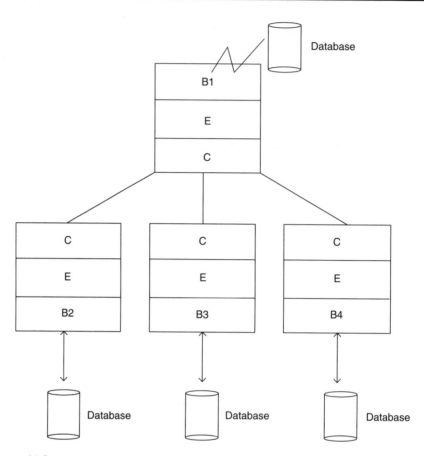

Figure 14.8 Introducing physical database: option 1.

on which particular database technology you are using. For example, Microsoft uses the term 'data objects' for those Boundary objects that save data to, and restore data from, commercial database systems such as Oracle, SQL Server and Access.

Incidentally, the Client/Server model can be viewed as a special case of the software architecture that is described in this section. In other words, our model subsumes C/S and other models. For example, the PAC model can be viewed as a more flexible and understandable alternative to the somewhat outdated Model-View-Controller (MVC) pattern (see POSA 1996).

Once we have determined how external data enters and leaves the system we must now determine where this data is to reside. This is usually in the Entity layer and objects will need to be created and the relationships with other objects will be defined. For example, the Entity layer consists of a graph of object associations, aggregations and other UML-based relationships. Finally, once the structure of the Entity layer (and, of course, other layers in general) is determined we must decide

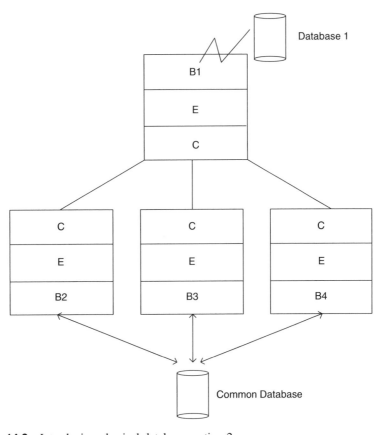

Figure 14.9 Introducing physical database: option 2.

how the different objects and layers communicate with each other. In other words, we must decide how to design and implement the messages in the sequence diagrams. Even more crucial to the discussion is how a receiver object acquires data from a sender object (the data is to be found as the parameter fields in the message). The options are:

- The sender sends the data to the receiver (push model)
- The receiver actively pools the sender object (pull model).

Which option to use in a particular situation depends on the application's functional and non-functional requirements. These requirements are to be found in the Software Requirements Specification (SRS) in general.

Summarizing this section, we see that there are three main issues involved with data management during design, namely:

- Creational patterns

- Structural patterns
- Behavioural patterns.

The specific requirements in an SRS will determine which specific design patterns (e.g. from GOF 1995 or POSA 1996) to use.

Examining Figures 14.8 and 14.9 again we must now decide how the different agents in OPS communicate with each other. We sketch a number of alternatives. This so-called design dimension is concerned with whether communication between objects occurs using shared state (in this the external data stores), events or both. The options (see Shaw and Garlan 1996 for a more extensive treatment of design dimensions for interactive applications) are:

1. *Events*: No shared data (all communication relies on events).
2. *Pure state*: Shared data (objects must repeatedly inspect state variables to detect change).
3. *State with hints*: Shared state but the receiver is informed of changes. Hints correspond to signals from a sender object to a receiver object.
4. *State plus events*: Both shared data and events are used (events deliver information not available from state monitoring).

The current application is best modelled as a repository system so the first option is not useful (this is more applicable to process control and event-driven systems). We use option 2 or 3 when creating an initial prototype.

We qualify the remark on option 3 by stating that we separate control flows and data flow; control flow is via the top-level mediator ORS while data flow occurs via the boundary layers to external database systems. These two flows should not be mixed, otherwise we shall inherit a system that is difficult to maintain and to understand.

14.8 FUNCTIONAL AND NON-FUNCTIONAL REQUIREMENTS AND THEIR REALIZATION

We have already introduced the ISO 9126 characteristics in some detail in this book. We now use the six characteristics as baseline software requirements. Experience has shown that the characteristics subsume many of the software design decisions that confront IT development teams. Having determined which characteristics to investigate we show how to realize them using the famous Design Patterns (see GOF 1995).

14.8.1 ISO 9126 revisited

We now discuss the ISO 9126 characteristics and their applicability to the PAC models in OPS. The question is: is a given ISO 9126 characteristic an issue in the current design and if so where does it affect the structure of the PAC model?

1. *Functionality*: Security and Interoperability are important. In the first case we must define groups of users and how these users access the data in the system, what data they are allowed to read, write and modify. In fact, we must define access control policies and the security viewpoint would suggest a front-end Access Control System (ACS) to OPS. For Interoperability we must define universal message names and data formats between the Boundary objects in OPS and the outside world, for example using XML (Extensible Markup Language). The data in the systems should always be up to date and hence Accuracy will play a role. We see opportunities for application of XML as a standard for data interoperability.

2. *Reliability*: It is doubtful whether fault tolerance is absolutely necessary but recoverability in the form of database restore and transaction rollback are important.

3. *Efficiency*: This is a relevant characteristic, particularly in the context of a hybrid object/relational database world. For example, instead of converting table records into objects, we might consider working directly with record sets and cursors without going through the process of mapping them to a list or array of objects in the Entity layer. In some cases you may decide to keep the Entity layer empty and do all data processing via the boundary layer to the external database system. This improves performance, especially when working with composite objects.

4. *Portability*: This has mainly to do with the Boundary layer. This layer is populated by user interfaces 'screens', data objects (that communicate with the physical data stores), and other hardware interface entities (for example, hardware drivers). Portable database systems are in abundance, for example ODBC (Object Database Connectivity) and JDBC (the Java equivalent of ODBC), and in the last resort you can always make your own portable drivers using the Bridge design pattern (see GOF 1995).

5. *Usability*: In the case of user interfaces, we imagine that OPS should function with several variants (see Shaw and Garlan 1996):
   (a) Command language (artificial, symbolic language)
   (b) Natural language (based on a subset of English)
   (c) Menu selection (select from a group of alternative menu items)

(d) Form filling (entry of values from a given set of variables)

(e) Direct manipulation (direct graphical representation).

For example, the Front Office stakeholders could be provided with options (c) and (d) while planners and more advanced users (for example, those in the Middle and Back Offices) could use options (a) and (b) for advanced searching and query manipulation. Finally, senior management and other novice computer users could be provided with eye-catching options for direct manipulation via icons. The above five options promote Understandability, Learnability and Operability (the three sub-characteristics of Usability).

6. *Maintainability*: We get this one almost for free, especially since we have decomposed the systems into loosely coupled subsystems. An extra condition is that the system interfaces are generic and 'pluggable'. To this end, we advise using component technology to implement these interfaces.

14.9 DATABASE REPOSITORY: AN ARCHITECTURAL STYLE FOR DATA-DRIVEN SYSTEMS

We design and implement the databases in OPS by using the so-called 'Database Repository' architectural style as advocated in Shaw and Garlan 1996. In the current situation we design OPS as a set of agents or systems that access a global repository as shown in Figure 14.10. It has been shown that this style is useful for a broad class of problems. Each external system should be able to access the data in the database. In particular, we wish to know which systems are the 'owners' of the data

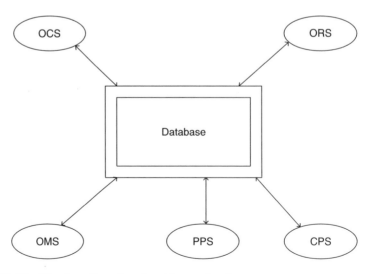

Figure 14.10   'Database Repository' architectural style.

in the repository, which systems are able to read data and which systems have no access to the data. Examples are:

- PPS is the owner of the product database
- CPS is the owner of the customer database
- OPS is the owner of the order database (in particular, OCS, ORS and OMS).

An owner system is responsible for the complete lifecycle of its data.

The access control policies must be defined at stakeholder level. In particular, different users may be assigned different access rights to the data. This is an analysis project in its own right and it could be modelled as several Access Control Systems (ACS). For example, the Front Office and Back Office groups have read access but no write access to the product database.

14.10 SUMMARY AND CONCLUSIONS

We have analysed and designed an order processing system. We have modeled it as a lifecycle model and have concentrated on the tracking part of the system. In particular, we have identified the major stakeholder groups, their requirements and the corresponding use cases. Furthermore, we have paid special attention to the class architecture in the system and we have given guidelines on how to design and implement the architecture as a database repository system.

The OPS system can be used as a reference model for other applications in the same domain architecture. Typical examples are call handling systems, helpdesk systems, material, products and entity registration, resource allocation and monitoring.

APPENDIX 14.1: DOCUMENTING USE CASES

We now document use case U2.

Name and Identifier: Process a new Customer Request from beginning to end, U2.
Preconditions: Order is new (i.e. it has not already been registered).
Description: This use case affects all departments in the organization. The Front Office registers the customer request. When the information has been validated it is dispatched for scheduling to the Middle and Back Offices. These are responsible for checking whether the order is feasible. In particular, the stakeholders in these groups assign and reserve resources. Once these have been taken care of, the Front Office will be in a position to inform the customer about the status of the order. From this description we can decompose use case U2 into three lower-level use cases:
— U2.1: Register the customer order
— U2.2: Schedule the customer order
— U2.3: Inform customer of order status.

Exceptions:
— Unable to dispatch order
— Timeout problems (service level agreements).
The first exception refers to the fact that it was not possible to satisfy the customer order, for example not enough resources are available or customer input is incomplete. The second exception refers to the fact that no response concerning the order has been given within some given period of time. For example, service level management policies demand that all customer orders should be addressed within three days of their entry into the OPS system.
Other concurrent activities: Other orders for the current customer are being entered. New orders are contending for the same resources.
Postconditions: The customer order has been dispatched to the customer. The system is waiting on possible feedback from the customer.

We now document use cases U2.1, U2.2 and U2.3.

Name and Identifier: Register a customer order, U2.1.
Preconditions: This is a new order.
Description: The input data from the customer is entered into the system. Customer profile information is checked to determine whether the customer exists and whether there are any special considerations to be taken into account. The order is checked against the product and service offerings to determine whether there are any restrictions.
Exceptions:
— Register an existing order
— Customer input is incomplete
— Customer does not exist
— Timeout problems (takes too long to process registration order)
— Unable to dispatch order for scheduling.
Other concurrent activities: Other related orders are being processed. It is possible that the customer order belongs to a group of logically related orders.
Postconditions: The customer order has been registered and can now be scheduled.

Name and Identifier: Schedule a customer order, U2.2.
Preconditions: Customer order information has been registered.
Description: This is the phase in which an attempt is made to satisfy the customer order by checking whether the product is available. If the product is available we must determine what resources need to be allocated in order to distribute the product to the customer. Some of the activities in this use case are:
— U2.2.1: Register the product
— U2.2.2: Store the order
— U2.2.3: Check whether the current order can be merged with other orders from the same customers.

This is one of the most important use cases because it is here that many of the business processes and business rules are defined.

Exceptions:
— Timeout problems (takes too long to schedule order)
— Unable to dispatch order for scheduling
— Customer order information has arrived after expiry date.

The last exception is concerned with the problem of attempting to schedule a customer order that has arrived too late. We shall either reject the order or execute some emergency procedures to ensure that the order can be scheduled.

Other concurrent activities: Other related orders are being scheduled. Other orders from the same customers are being registered and other orders are being dispatched and transported to the customer.

Postconditions: The customer order has been scheduled.

Name and Identifier: Inform customer of order status, U2.3.

Preconditions: The product and its related resources are in stock and ready for distribution.

Description: The status information (including distribution and transportation information) is edited and formatted. Different stakeholders will be notified of the order status. Some possible examples are:
— 'Snail mail' and e-mail confirmation
— Write status information to historical database (for data warehousing)
— Coupling with financial and accounting systems.

Exceptions:
— Incomplete dispatching details (e.g. unknown contact person)
— Timeout problems (takes too long to dispatch order status).

Other concurrent activities: Other related orders are being scheduled. Other related orders are in the dispatching phase.

Postconditions: The customer order has been dispatched to the customer. The system is waiting on possible feedback from the customer.

APPENDIX 14.2: SOME UML CLASS DIAGRAMS

We give one example of how to document the Entity objects in the ORS system using UML. The classes are placeholders for attributes. The classes will be 'glued together' by the associations that are found from the actions in the use cases. The classes and their associations can be discovered from each subsystem in ORS:

- Subsystem Registration
  — A company is the sender of an order
  — An order concerns a product

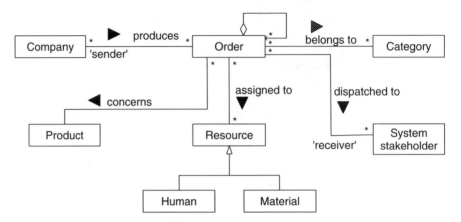

Figure 14.11 Class model in ORS.

- — An order may consist of order items
- Subsystem Assignment
  - — An order uses resources
  - — An order belongs to some category
- Subsystem Monitoring
  - — An order is dispatched to an external system.

The UML class diagram is shown in Figure 14.11. In real life this diagram would be much more comprehensive but the underlying issues will be the same as in the present example. However, this is the level where CRC cards can be used to discover classes and document the relationships between them.

15 Drink Vending Machine (DVM)

'The specification by itself, whether verbal or written, whether a page of text or a thousand pages, can never express all that is required.'

Dr W. Edwards Deming

15.1 INTRODUCTION AND OBJECTIVES

In this chapter we create a stable and extendible PAC model for an interactive system that dispenses products (for example, cans of soft drink) to customers. It is a medium-sized system and we focus on class-level structures and architectures that are flexible enough to support future and *unpredictable* requirements. The system is called Drink Vending Machine (DVM) and is modelled as an instance of an ACS category. In general, real-life systems are a combination of MAN, RAT, MIS and ACS instances and we shall discuss this in Section 15.7. For the moment, however, we reduce the scope in order to concentrate on the man–machine and user-interface aspects in the system. Thus, our wish is to construct a UML model that can be modified to support new hardware, software and customer environments. The ISO 9126 characteristics of interest in this application are Functionality, Usability and Maintainability. The main stakeholders are Customer and Vendor.

There are relatively few use cases in this problem because we focus on the customer. This has advantages because it reduces the scope of the problem since we are interested in documenting the classes and their relationships in UML using the following modelling techniques:

- Aggregation
- Composite aggregations and nested objects
- Associations
- Generalization of Boundary, Entity and Control classes.

Once this has been done and when each class's attributes and operations have been discovered, we can commence with the design of DVM.

Some readers may think that DVM is a toy problem but it can be used as a baseline application for other Access Control Systems such as:

- Coffee machines
- The well-known ATM problem
- Petrol pump system (Coleman *et al* 1994)
- Interactive database systems
- All sorts of gambling machines.

Furthermore, it is instructive to analyse DVM in some detail because it serves as an excellent model to help novice analysts learn how to document a problem using the visual techniques that UML offers.

15.2 DESCRIPTION OF PROBLEM

The Drink Vending Machine (DVM) is a well-known problem (see Hatley and Pirbhai 1988) in the literature and has been used in both object-oriented and non-object-oriented literature as a test case. The problem is understandable to most readers and at the same time challenging enough to analyse. Furthermore, we can generalize DVM to other applications and domains. In fact, we know that it is an instance system of the ACS domain architecture type (see Chapter 9). Those readers who develop interactive applications will hopefully find the solution of DVM to be useful because there are many similarities between the features of DVM and those of other interactive applications.

We came across the DVM problem in Hatley and Pirbhai (1988) where it was analysed and designed using structured analysis techniques. We include the original list of *ad hoc* features from that book:

- F1: Accept objects (candidate coins) from the customer in payment for purchase.
- F2: Check for slugs (not real coins), for example by validating size, weight, thickness and serrated edges.
- F3: Accept euros only.
- F4: The system cannot be tricked by conniving people.
- F5: The customer should be able to select a product.
- F6: Check product availability: if not available, return coins to customer.
- F7: Products may change from time to time.
- F8: Return the customer's payment on request if she or he decides not to go through with the transaction.
- F9: Dispense product if it is available and enough coins have been inserted.
- F10: Return the correct change if the amount deposited is greater than the product price.

- F11: Disable the product selection after the product has been dispensed and until the next validated coin is received.
- F12: Make deposited coins available for change.

The danger of using features to drive the software process is that they sidestep a decent requirements analysis. Use of features leads to brittle and inflexible systems in general.

15.2.1 Scope and span of problem

In order to model the DVM as a system we must define what we are modelling in order to avoid 'creeping featuritis'. To this end, we try to identify all the variable factors or dimensions in this problem. For example, the dimension that represents the selection type that is used to choose a specific product has the following options:

- Touchscreen
- Buttons
- Command line
- Batch input
- Remote input (for example, Web services).

Each source of volatility represents an opportunity for development work and is at the same time a source of risk. For these reasons we must keep our eye on the ball. We examine the context diagram in Figure 15.1 to determine the sources of volatility:

- Selection systems (for example, different kinds of input devices)
- Enabling systems (coin units, pin units and other hardware)
- Product supply systems (cans of beer, coffee, hot meals, etc.)
- MIS systems (all kinds of clients of DVM).

Furthermore, another dimension is represented by how the customers interact with the system. We must take the following issues into consideration:

- Which products a given customer is allowed to purchase
- How the customer selects products
- How products are dispensed
- How a transaction is committed.

The reader might like to compare Figure 15.1 with the context diagram for the ACS category in order to determine whether the fit is good.

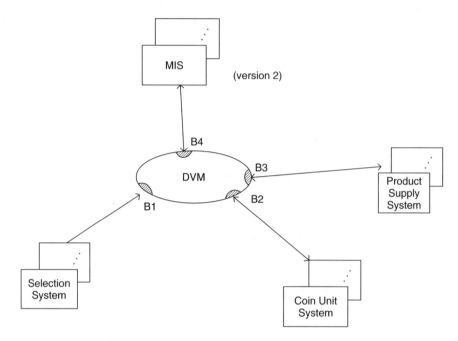

Figure 15.1 DVM (initial) context diagram.

15.3 GOALS, PROCESSES AND CONTEXT

The main goal is to allow authorized customers to use the services of a drink vending machine. There are a number of secondary goals but they do not concern us in this chapter. The most important viewpoints for the customer are Usability and Accuracy, while the drink vendor is usually interested in Efficiency (sell as much as possible), Reliability (in particular, fault tolerance) and Security (remember feature F4 concerning conniving people).

The context diagram for DVM in Figure 15.1 is deduced from the corresponding context for the ACS domain category. Here we see that DVM (when viewed as a black-box system) has a number of satellite systems that cooperate with it to satisfy its core, supporting and management processes:

- *Selection Systems*: These systems allow active subjects (in this case customers) to select drinks. These systems are strategic and have input and output functionality.
- *Product Supply Systems*: These systems contain the passive objects (in this case cans of drink). In general, these systems are instances of the MAN category because they need to be created and/or replenished at regular intervals. Product Supply dispenses drink to customers. We may wish to provide services in the form of coffee and hot meals in the future.

- *Coin Unit Systems*: Specializations of authentication systems; if the customers insert a sufficient number of valid coins they may be served by the drink machine. Otherwise, the DVM will remain disabled and/or refuse to dispense drink.
- *MIS*: These systems are client systems of DVM. They monitor DVM or are interested in receiving transaction information from DVM, for example at what times of day drink is sold, which drinks are selling well and so on. In general, these client systems are instances of the PCS and MIS categories.

The core process is described as an activity diagram involving the different stakeholders in Figure 15.2. We also describe the activities in textual form:

1. Selection system requests a drink; check the choice.
2. DVM checks product status.
3. DVM checks amount of inserted coins.
4. Determine whether transaction can be committed.
5. Eject change in Coin Unit.
6. Dispense drink in Product Supply.

The activity diagram contains two examples of forking and merging. First, to check the customer request we ensure that the customer has inserted enough valid coins and that the desired product is in stock. Second, during the commitment phase the product is dispensed and the change is ejected. Finally, once the transaction has been committed an acknowledgement is sent to the Selection System.

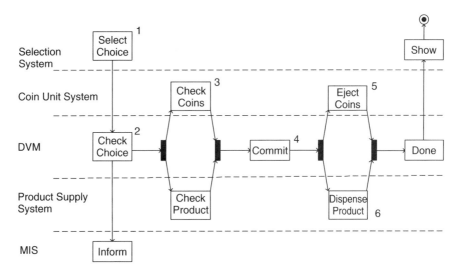

Figure 15.2 Activity diagram for core process in DVM.

15.4 USE CASES

We model two high-priority use cases in some detail in this section. These are use cases that directly affect the customer of the system and are in fact realizations of the activities in the core process. The use cases are called:

- U1: Authenticate the customer (by inserting coins)
- U2: Select a drink (by means of a selection panel).

Use case U1 is concerned with the enabling of the machine before a drink is selected while use case U2 describes how the customer selects a drink.

Use case name and ID: Customer Authentication, U1.
Actors in use case: DVM, Coin Unit system, Selection system.
Preconditions: System is in Disabled mode; the peripheral actors systems are operational and the system is waiting for authentication.
Short description: Valid coins are inserted into the Coin Unit. The first valid coin enables the system (including the Selection system).
Detailed description: It is possible to authenticate the customer by inserting one or more coins. The first valid coin enables the system and from this moment it is possible (in principle) to select a drink. The customer may insert more coins if he or she wishes.
Exceptions:
— Invalid coin inserted
— Hardware breakdown during coin insertion
— Customer cancels authentication process.
Other concurrent activities: Not applicable in this version since this is a single-user system. In future versions multiple users may wish to simultaneously access products. Furthermore, a maintenance engineer may need to inspect the machine on a regular basis. This will lead to new satellite systems in the future and (unfortunately) more opportunities for use case conflicts.
Postconditions: System is now in Enabled mode; this means that it is now possible to select a drink.

Use case name and ID: Select Product, U2.
Actors in use case: DVM, Selection system, Coin Unit System, Product Supply system.
Preconditions: System is in Enabled mode.
Short description: The customer selects the drink. The system checks to determine whether the transaction can be committed. The change (if any) is ejected and the drink is dispensed.

Detailed description: We give a detailed description of the actions that are executed in order to dispense a drink. The description is suitable as input for sequence diagrams and helps in the discovery of exceptions.

1. Selection system requests a drink.
2. DVM checks product status.
3. DVM checks amount of inserted coins.
4. Determine whether transaction can be committed (enough inserted coins).
5. Eject change in Coin Unit.
6. Dispense drink in Product Supply.
7. Return to disabled mode.

Exceptions: We examine what can go wrong at each stage (action) in the use case:

- Problems with Product Supply
  — Product Supply malfunctioning
  — Desired product not available in Product Supply (low capacity)
- Problems with Coin Unit
  — Coin Unit malfunctioning
  — Low capacity in Coin Unit (not enough change)
  — Overcapacity in Coin Unit
- Problems with carrying out Transaction
  — Not able to carry out Transaction (insufficient funds entered)
  — Transaction fails to commit (some kind of timeout)
- Problems with completing Transaction
  — Problems with Coin Supply
    - Coin Unit malfunctioning
    - Unable to return change
  — Problems with Product Supply
    - Product Supply malfunctioning
    - Unable to dispense product.

Other concurrent activities: Not applicable in this version of the software. See remarks in the corresponding field in use case U1.

Postconditions: Drink and change (funds) have been dispensed; system reverts to Disabled mode.

15.5 CREATING AN INITIAL PAC MODEL

The initial PAC model for this problem is shown in Figure 15.3. Each layer is a composite black box and that is the reason why the multiplicities of associations between the components in each agent are 1:1. Furthermore, we model the top-level *mediator* object DVM as a single entity. In other words, DVM contains boundary, entity and control functionality. Thus, we analyse and design the mediator as a single monolithic class in this version of DVM.

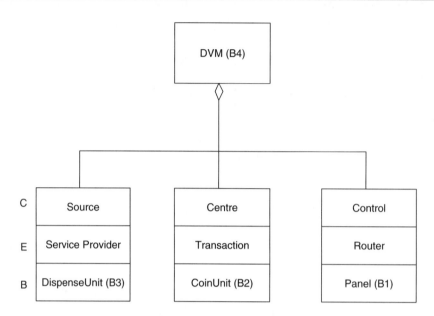

Figure 15.3 PAC model for DVM problem.

We model the relationship between the top-level DVM object and its agents as an assembly parts relationship (see POSA 1996). The multiplicity is 1:1. Strictly speaking, this is a composition because the lifetimes of DVM and its agents are coincident.

We couple the context diagram and the PAC model for this problem by aligning the Boundary objects from Figure 15.1 with Figure 15.3. Furthermore, we rename the generic names B1, B2 and B3 so that developers can understand them. We note that each Boundary object adds value to the agent of which it is a part. For example, CoinUnit (B2) helps us to enable the transactions in the (transaction) Centre agent. In general, deciding where to place Boundary objects is an iterative process: do not be surprised if you do not get it right on the first or second attempt!

15.6 CLASS STRUCTURE

We describe some of the classes in Figure 15.3 as UML diagrams. Other classes, notably the Entity and Control layers, will be modelled as black boxes. We describe the following Boundary classes:

- DispenseUnit
- CoinUnit
- Panel.

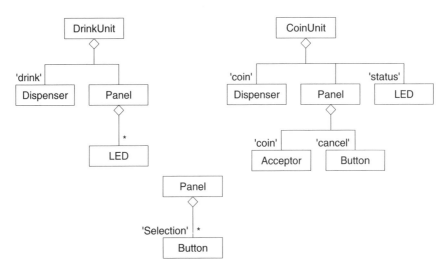

Figure 15.4 Structure of Boundary objects in DVM.

These objects communicate with the external stakeholder systems. The structure of the three Boundary classes is shown in Figure 15.4. Notice that DrinkUnit and Coin-Unit are multi-levelled aggregate objects. This approach promotes maintainability and information hiding.

15.7 INTERACTION DIAGRAMS AND INTERFACE DISCOVERY

UML supports visual techniques that display how objects interact. They are called *interaction diagrams* and the specific variants are called sequence diagrams and collaboration diagrams. We shall show how these two techniques complement each other to help the analyst understand the event flow between the different objects in DVM. The main attention points in this section are:

- Mapping use cases to sequence diagrams
- Prioritizing sequence diagrams (external and internal, variants and exceptions)
- Taking maintainability issues into consideration
- Creating collaboration diagrams (see Rumbaugh 1999)
- Optimization (discovering object interfaces).

15.7.1 Sequence diagrams

We first concentrate on use case U1 (Authentication) and we create the corresponding sequence diagrams based on the initial external events that enter the system.

The main sub-use cases and the corresponding sequence diagrams are:

- U1.1: Insert coin into CoinUnit (Figure 15.5)
- U1.2: Enable transactions to be carried out (Figure 15.6)
- U1.3: Notify appropriate clients that system is ready (Figure 15.7).

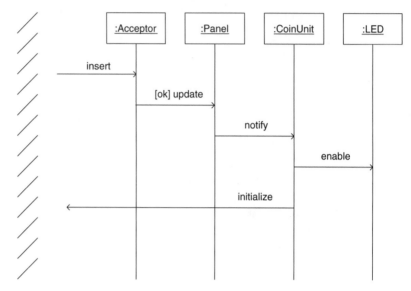

Figure 15.5 Enable transaction by inserting coin.

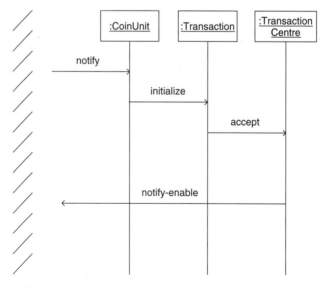

Figure 15.6 Inform Transaction Centre of Enable.

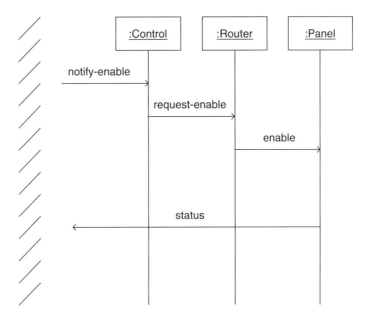

Figure 15.7 Notify Control System of Enable.

Our assumption is that all external events enter via a Whole's part, for example in Figure 15.5 where the first external message 'insert' is sensed by Acceptor. In this figure we see the sequence of messages in the CoinUnit. A similar relationship exists between the Acceptor (fingers) and the CoinUnit (brain).

Once U1 has completed we will be in a position to select a product. However, we may insert more coins (and more may be needed). In this case we show the sequence diagram in Figure 15.8. Notice that no messages percolate to the Entity layer in this case (why?).

Another variant is the cancel option. It is possible to cancel the transaction in which case the customer will receive his or her money back (see feature F8 in Section 15.2). The customer can press the cancel button in CoinUnit as shown in Figure 15.9. Notice that the coins are ejected (via the message 'button-pressed' to the Panel) and the transaction is aborted.

We now discuss use case U2 (Select Product). The sub-use cases are:

- U2.1: Choose product
- U2.2: Commit transaction.

The sequence diagrams corresponding to U2.1 are shown in Figures 15.10 and 15.11 and are played out in the Control agent. The sequence diagrams for U2.2 are to be seen in Figures 15.12 to 15.15.

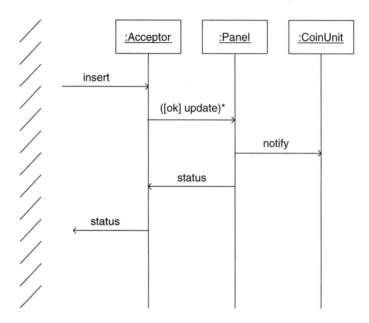

Figure 15.8 Insert more coins.

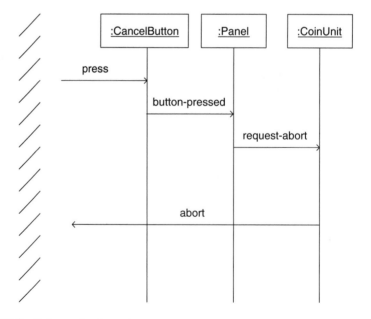

Figure 15.9 Return coins to customer.

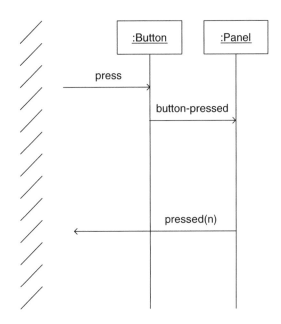

Figure 15.10 Choose a particular drink.

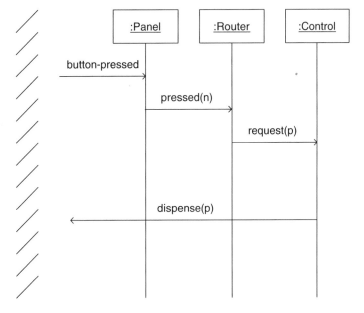

Figure 15.11 Request to dispense a product.

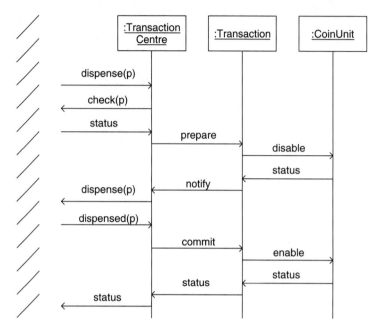

Figure 15.12   Commit transaction.

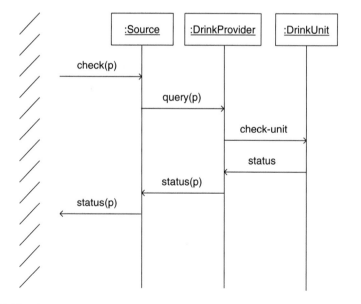

Figure 15.13   Check availability of Source system.

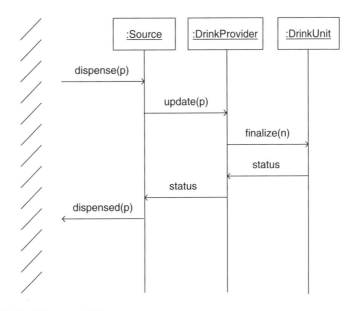

Figure 15.14   Dispense drink.

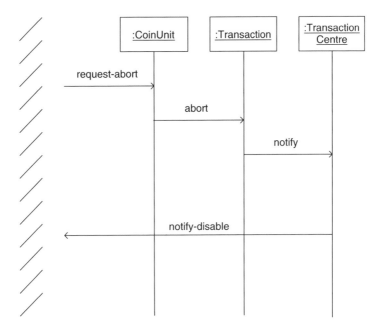

Figure 15.15   End transaction.

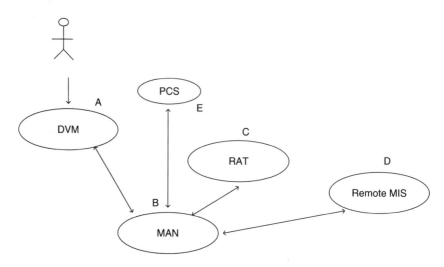

Figure 15.16   Extended Drink Vending Machine.

15.8 SUMMARY AND CONCLUSIONS

We have analysed a model problem that can be used and adapted to many different applications. We have shown how to analyse this problem using UML class diagrams, sequence diagrams and collaboration diagrams. We have created an understandable, portable and maintainable product. The approach represents an improvement on *ad hoc* strategies.

In general, product vending machines are complex things and a simple ACS instance is not enough. In fact, it is a composite system consisting of the following instance systems as shown in the sketch in Figure 15.16:

- System B (MAN): produces the products
- System C (RAT): tracks the manufacturing process
- System A (ACS): user interface system to the product
- System D (MIS): monitoring and management system
- System E (PCS): monitors and controls threshold and exceptional values in the manufacturing system B.

This context diagram can be used as input to a requirements engineering study.

APPENDIX 15.1: COLLABORATION DIAGRAMS IN A NUTSHELL

A collaboration diagram (CD) is similar to a UML class diagram but instead of defining structural relationships between the classes we display inter-object interaction by the use of sequence numbers. Thus, each message is assigned a number that tells what its order is in the list of messages in the use case.

The main components in a CD are:

• Named objects
• The relationships between objects (message-passing)
• Messages.

Each message can have the following attributes:

• Its sequence number (its number in the pecking order)
• Its identifier (usually its name)
• The message direction (from sender to receiver)
• Preconditions (must be true if the message is to be executed)
• Role names
• Message qualifiers (for example, message parameters)
• Guard conditions.

Some examples of messages are:

```
 2: send(p, r): retValue
23: query(A) [isOK()]
```

The first message has sequence number 2, is called send(), has two parameters and the return value is placed behind the colon. The second message has a guard condition in the form of the Boolean function isOK(). If this function evaluates to true then the body of the function query() will execute.

In considering whether we should use sequence diagrams (SDs) or collaboration diagrams (CDs), both are concerned with the same basic information, namely creating a visual representation of a use case. In this book, we can use SDs and CDs to depict object interactions at four different levels, namely:

• When it is not clear how a use case is documented
• When we are not sure whether the use case is accurate or complete
• When we wish to validate the structural integrity of class diagrams and PAC models
• When we wish to discover object interfaces.

A sequence diagram is a two-dimensional graph where the horizontal axis represents the objects that participate in the corresponding use case while the vertical axis represents time. A SD focuses on the sequence of messages that are discovered from the corresponding activities in the use case, while a CD focuses on the static structure of collaborating objects in the use case. In other words, when you view

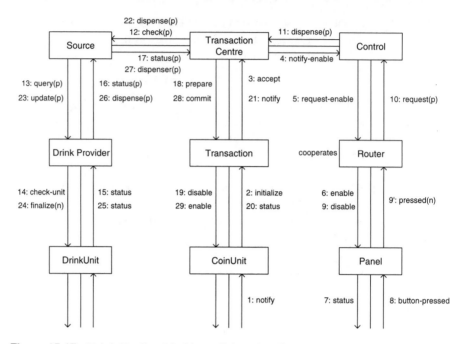

Figure 15.17   Drink Vending Machine collaboration diagram.

a CD you can see the structure of, and the relationships between, the participating objects as well as the sequence of messages between those objects. SDs, on the other hand, display the messages between objects but do not display the structural relationships between them. It is in theory possible to break the Information Hiding principle in an SD by sending a message between objects whose classes have no structural relationship. Some common errors in sequence diagrams are:

- Entity objects that communicate with external stakeholder systems
- Boundary objects that communicate with Control objects
- Control objects that communicate with external stakeholder systems
- Some people tend to create complex sequence diagrams.

We have brought the sequence diagrams together to produce the collaboration diagram in Figure 15.17 for the DVM problem. We have left out the details of how we arrived at this diagram; it was an iterative process.

16 Multi-tasking lifecycle applications

> *'We may consider ourselves lucky when, trying to solve a problem, we succeed in discovering a simpler analogous problem.'*
>
> George Polya

16.1 INTRODUCTION AND OBJECTIVES

This chapter discusses an instance of a Lifecycle Model (LCM, see Chapter 10). The application is quite technical but what it produces is well known: plastic. We describe how raw materials (in the form of coloured plastic pellets) are melted to produce a liquid that is then inserted into a bubbling chamber. The bubbling chamber produces half-products in the form of film. This film is trimmed and then transported to a winder.

There are many analogies to be found between the current problem and lifecycle models for other kinds of entities. Thus, the reader can use this as a 'baseline' system for other systems.

The emphasis in this chapter is on showing how a large and somewhat intractable problem can be decomposed into simpler sub-problems. As is always the case in this book, we motivate our choice of decomposition by looking at the workflow in the system. In other words, we describe the production process in the language of the customer. The specific system in this chapter (we call it the Plastics Extrusion System, PES) is concerned with the realization of customer batch jobs. For example, a customer may have a request to produce a number of metres of film of a certain width, thickness, colour and quality. PES processes this request by producing an amount of processed film that the customer wants. We attempt to provide some insights into how this is achieved. To this end, we include a number of sections that describe the application lifecycle, starting with a high-level description of the problem and finally describing which architectural and design patterns satisfy the software requirements for PES. Section 16.2 is an introduction to plastics manufacturing. In Section 16.3 we review some of the features that the system should support and we also introduce the main system stakeholders as they will be the sources of all major requirements in the system. Section 16.4 deals with the problem of finding the context diagram for PES. We also motivate why PES is an instance of a Lifecycle Model. In particular, we define the scope and span of each of its subsystems in the system:

- Blending (MAN instance): produces 'physical' products from batch jobs
- Extrusion (RAT instance): produces the 'finished' product from physical products
- Reporting (MIS instance): produces reports and presentation information at various levels of detail.

These systems will be examined in some detail and in order to reduce the scope we pay particular attention to the Extrusion subsystem as an example of how UML and software patterns can be effectively used to produce design blueprints. Sections 16.5 to 16.7 introduce the problem of designing PES and how to apply software patterns from the handbooks by Schmidt *et al* (2000), Buschmann *et al* (POSA 1996) and Gamma *et al* (GOF 1995) to produce a flexible and maintainable software system.

We have included an appendix that introduces the topics of multi-tasking applications and generic models for such applications. This appendix may be skipped without loss of continuity.

16.2 THE PROBLEM DOMAIN

The problem in this chapter is an instance of a Lifecycle Model (LCM) that describes how to produce plastic film.

16.2.1 General description of problem

We summarize the essence of PES as follows: plastic pellets of different colours and qualities are fed into a blending machine that then mixes the pellets using the force of gravity. The pellets are fed into an extruder where they are melted. Once the plastic pellets have been melted the molten plastic is injected into a bubbling chamber. The bubbling chamber produces raw plastic. The plastic is then trimmed, rolled up and finally transported to a nearby warehouse for storage. The product is now ready for distribution. The manufacturing process must be carefully monitored and controlled to ensure that the final product satisfies customer and regulatory standards (for example, the US Food and Drug Administration). It should also be possible to produce management reports using Excel and other software tools.

A rough sketch (artist's impression) of the physical PES environment is shown in Figure 16.1. It consists of a number of key components. First, blenders mix plastic

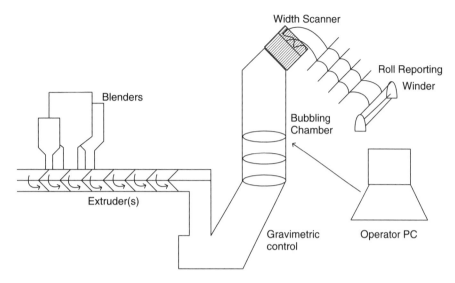

Figure 16.1 Physical layout of extruder system (simplified).

pellets of differing quality using the power of gravity. The pellet mix is then fed into several extruders where it is warmed to form molten plastic. The molten plastic is injected into a so-called bubbling chamber where a chemical process takes place and where 'half-products' (unfinished plastic film) are produced. Special sensors measure the width of the plastic that is then trimmed. Finally, a winder system rolls the finished product that is then removed from the system. Management reporting is also possible.

We model PES as a Lifecycle Model because we see clear elements of manufacturing, tracking and management functionality. To this end, Figure 16.2 shows the high-level activity diagram for this problem. The primary output consists of high-level reports on what the PES has produced; in particular, this output contains historical, real-time and exceptional reporting information. The primary input is a batch request order from a customer (usually a company). The format of this input should be well documented and contains information pertaining to how much plastic the customer wants and what its quality should be.

Looking at Figure 16.1 helps us to identify three major processes in PES:

- Blending: mix and blend 'raw' plastic pellets
- Extrusion: produce molten plastic
- Reporting: report on the status of current production job.

The objects in the activity diagram in Figure 16.2 should be mentioned. Physical Products describes the pellet mix while Usage Information is another name for the amount of molten plastic that has been produced by the Extrusion process.

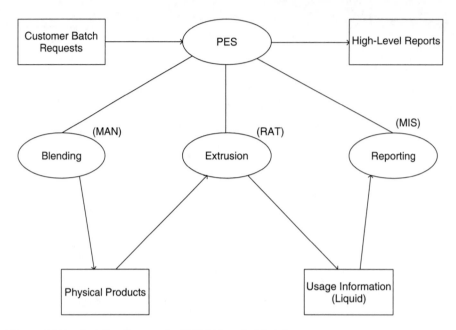

Figure 16.2   Activity diagram for PES Lifecycle Model.

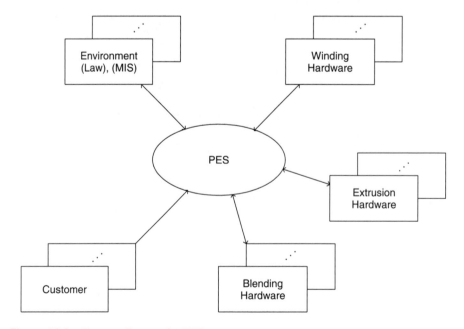

Figure 16.3   Context diagram for PES.

16.2.2 System stakeholders

The context diagram for PES is shown in Figure 16.3. It shows PES as a 'black box' that is surrounded by its satellite systems. The main systems are those that are hardware-related, for example Blending, Extrusion and Winding. Of course, there are other less obvious stakeholders such as the Customer (where the batch request originates) and the Environment (this is needed because we must keep a record of all production jobs). Finally, we will need to take into account the fact that the PES will be controlled and monitored by operators and to this end we must develop interactive user interfaces to the system. These are usually ACS instances. We will also need one or more instances of the PCS category to monitor and control the real-time production process.

16.3 SYSTEM FEATURES

Strictly speaking, a full requirements analysis should be carried out for PES but in practice the development team has to be content with a list of product 'features' that customers (and managers) wish to see. This is a far from ideal situation and many projects have failed because this approach leads to highly fragile systems. On the other hand, we must accept this fact and we try to localize each feature in one subsystem of PES. We must live with these risks and try to mitigate them.

The product manager and salesperson have interviewed the customer and have arrived at a list of major features that the system should offer. The most important features are:

- F1: Gravimetric control of the blending process
- F2: Gravimetric blending
- F3: Width control (width of plastic)
- F4: Thickness control and profiling (of plastic)
- F6: Temperature control of molten plastic in extruder barrel
- F10: Power monitoring in the extruder
- F16: Long-term storage of production variables and data
- F18: Waste reporting.

Notice that some features have been left out in order to keep the problem manageable for the sake of this chapter. The relationships are shown in Figure 16.4. For example, feature F6 is concerned with the monitoring and control of the molten plastic in the Extrusion subsystem.

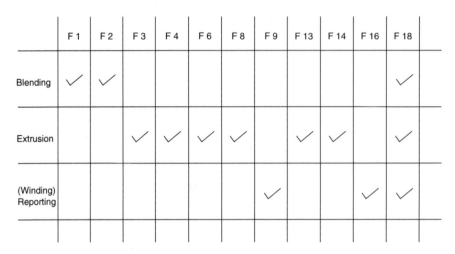

	F 1	F 2	F 3	F 4	F 6	F 8	F 9	F 13	F 14	F 16	F 18
Blending	✓	✓									✓
Extrusion			✓	✓	✓	✓		✓	✓		✓
(Winding) Reporting							✓			✓	✓

Figure 16.4 Requirements and subsystems for PES.

16.4 SYSTEM ARCHITECTURE

Since PES is an instance of a Lifecycle Model we document it in UML as an aggregation as shown in Figure 16.5. We thus have a centralized control model. Furthermore, we model each component as a 'black box'. To this end, we model each component 'from the outside to the inside' by defining its context diagram. These diagrams are shown in Figures 16.6, 16.7 and 16.8 for the three major subsystems. Note that the Boundary objects have been explicitly modelled because they are the interfaces to and from the other external systems and they can be designed and implemented using the concurrent and network patterns due to Dr Douglas Schmidt (see Schmidt *et al* 2000). In particular, we show how to extend the PAC model to accommodate multi-threading producer–consumer applications.

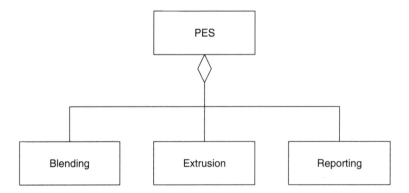

Figure 16.5 UML class model.

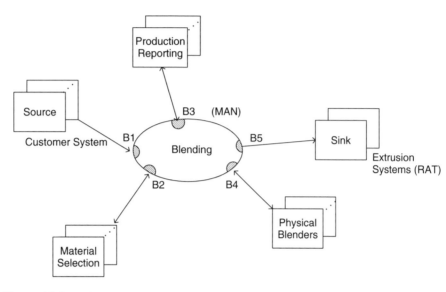

Figure 16.6 'Blending' context diagram (MAN).

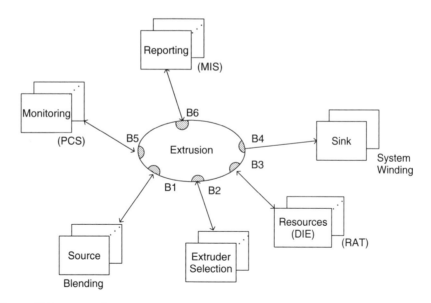

Figure 16.7 'Extrusion' context diagram (RAT).

We do not explain the responsibilities of the different satellite systems in Figures 16.6, 16.7 and 16.8. The names should indicate what each satellite system does and the reader should consult the context diagrams in Chapters 8 (MAN), 7 (RAT) and 5 (MIS) and compare them with these specific instances in PES.

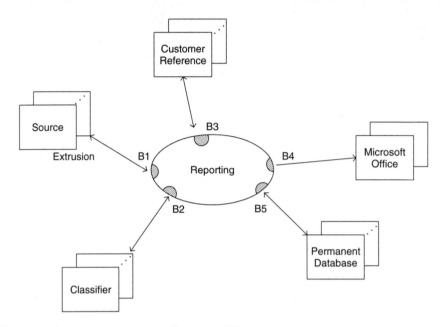

Figure 16.8   'Reporting' context diagram (MIS).

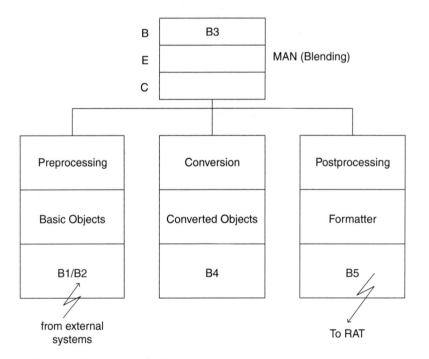

Figure 16.9   PAC model for Blending.

16.4.1 The PAC models

The PAC models for the subsystems in PES are shown in Figures 16.9, 16.10 and 16.11. The reader can note how the boundary objects that we have depicted in the context diagrams have been incorporated into the Boundary layers in each subsystem. The reader should also verify that the 'correct' boundary objects have been placed in the appropriate agent. In order to reduce the scope, we now deal with the Extrusion subsystem as shown in Figure 16.10 in more detail. We defend its system decomposition by appealing to activity diagrams. The internal objects correspond to some kind of request object while the half-products correspond to molten plastic that has been 'assigned' to one or more extruders.

It is possible to create UML diagrams for all classes that appear in the layers in Figure 16.10. To this end, we discuss the structure of the Boundary layer in the Extrusion subsystem. This is in fact the layer that contains the extruders (logical boundary objects!). The UML class structure is shown in Figure 16.12. Here we see that each extruder is decomposed into a number of zones. A zone consists of several temperature controllers. This is needed because we wish to satisfy feature F6.

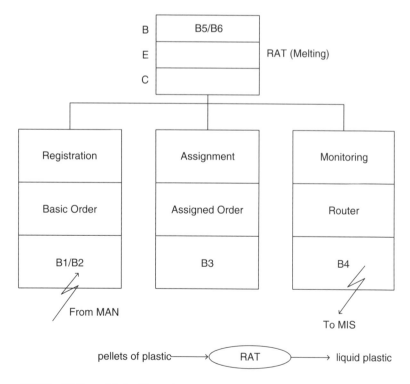

Figure 16.10 PAC model for Extrusion.

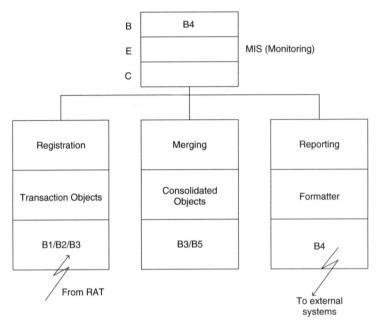

Figure 16.11 PAC model for Reporting.

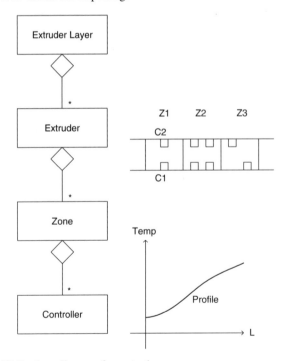

Figure 16.12 UML class diagram for extruder.

16.5 DESIGN ISSUES: OVERVIEW

Most of the discussion in this chapter has been devoted to conceptual analysis and high-level architectural issues in PES. Not all details have been filled in. We feel that the time has come to devote some attention to design issues. We know that the mapping of a PAC model to the design pattern of GOF (1995) is feasible and it is quite easy to realize once you know the rules. Our concern in this chapter, however, is to describe the design of multi-threaded and multi-tasking applications. To this end, we give an introduction to threading and we introduce several common threading models in the appendix to this chapter. Continuing, we apply Dr Schmidt's patterns to synchronizing communication between systems. Particular attention will be paid to showing how these patterns are integrated with the PAC model.

16.6 THE PROOF OF THE PUDDING: ENTER THE ACE LIBRARY

The Adaptive Communication Environment (ACE) is the brainchild of Dr Douglas Schmidt and is a library of C++ classes that allow developers to create portable, efficient and usable distributed and networked-based software applications. The library is based on network and communication patterns (see Schmidt *et al* 2000, Schmidt and Huston 2002). The library consists of a number of frameworks:

- Event multiplexing and dispatching framework
- Connection establishment/service initialization framework
- Concurrency framework
- Service configuration framework
- Streams framework.

A complete discussion of these frameworks is beyond the scope of this book. The main relevance of the ACE library to this chapter is that the library supports active objects that communicate over a computer network. This is needed when two instances of a domain architecture communicate with each other via the active objects in their respective Boundary layers.

Objects in the object-oriented paradigm are passive by default. When an object's method is called it is run in some other thread, but an active object has several threads and these threads are used to execute the active object's methods. To this end, ACE defines the class `ACE_Task` and your own active classes should be derived from it. ACE defines communication mechanisms between tasks. The model is based on Hewitt's Actors model (see Agha 1986). A task (in ACE) has one or more threads and an underlying message queue through which tasks communicate. Messages are 'enqueued' and 'dequeued' as shown in Figure 16.13. Thus, we see

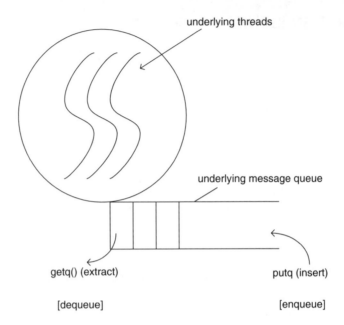

Figure 16.13 Tasks in ACE.

that clients of the task class do not need to know about the underlying thread structure.

Our interest is in defining a communication channel between a client and a server, for example between instances of domain architectures as shown in Figure 16.14. This involves the creation of new active objects in the Boundary layers of the respective systems. To this end, we must introduce some new concepts and patterns (see Schmidt *et al* 2000):

- The Reactor pattern
- The Acceptor and Connector pattern
- The steps in creating and using a task.

The intent of the Reactor pattern is to demultiplex and dispatch service requests to an application from one or more distributed clients. The advantage of the pattern is that it can handle different types of events in one API (Application Programming Interface). The Acceptor and Connector pattern deals with the problem of communication between a client and a server. Its main use is to decouple connection establishment from the services that are performed after the connection has been established. In ACE, the connection establishment is achieved using sockets or some other InterProcess Communication (IPC) mechanism. The Acceptor component in this pattern is situated in the server and is used for passive connection

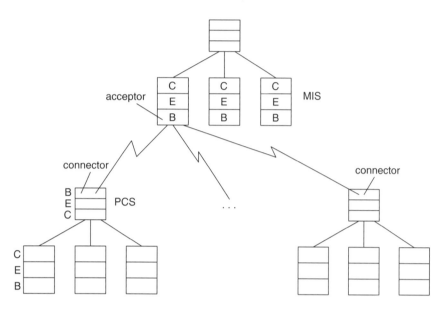

Figure 16.14   Using ACE with domain categories.

establishment and handling of connections after establishment from the Connector (that is situated on the client). The Connector component is responsible for active connection establishment and also for connection handling after establishment.

Having given a bird's-eye view of some ACE patterns, we must deal with them in more detail as preparation to their application to the plastics extrusion problem. The Acceptor component encapsulates the BSD `accept()` function in the base class `ACE_Acceptor`. This is a factory class and your specific acceptor class should be derived from it. Instances of this class listen for clients that wish to establish a connection. You must create your own service handler by deriving from the class `ACE_Svc_Handler`. The Connector component encapsulates a BSD `connect()` function call and you should create your own connection class by deriving it from `ACE_Connector`.

16.7 THE CHALLENGE: APPLYING THE ACE LIBRARY IN THE EXTRUSION APPLICATION

We have created a prototype, proof-of-concept (POC) solution to test the following assumptions:

- Is it possible to use ACE libraries in a distributed application?
- Is it possible to integrate ACE and domain architectures?

The answer to both questions is yes. We have found that the ACE library is easy to use once you have understood the API function details. To answer the second question, it is just a matter of defining `ACE_Task` instances in the respective Boundary layers.

The test case in this section can be used in many situations. The basic problem is to send data from several instances of a domain architecture (for example, PCS or RAT systems) to a central system (typically, an instance of a MIS system).

The following discussion is rather complex and may be skipped without loss of continuity.

The UML class diagram for the component that sends readings (in this case the Boiler object) is shown in Figure 16.15. Here we see our own implementations of the classes `ACE_Task` (active object) and `ACE_Method_Object` (this class encapsulates methods or commands in objects). This is achieved by subclassing. `StatusLogger` is the most important class in this diagram and it is responsible for the entire logging process.

We deploy a Visitor pattern to send parameters to the logger class. The structure is extensible and it is possible to extend the Visitor hierarchy to handle spreadsheet output, for example. The Active Object pattern is implemented by placing command objects in a queue. These commands are then retrieved and executed by another thread, the `svc()` method.

The central management component environment is depicted in Figure 16.16. We identify two main tasks. First, the `UDPListener` object runs in its own threads and listens for UDP broadcasts from (Boiler) clients using an `ACE_SOCK_Dgram` object. Once it receives some data it replies using another `ACE_SOCK_Dgram` object. This enables the client to determine the IP address of the central management component and further communication will be based on that address. The second task is called `DataProducer` and this also runs in a separate thread. This class, in conjunction with its 'helper' classes, is responsible for receiving data from clients. The incoming data will then be sent to a dialog box called `CCentralObserverDlg`. A visual example of such a dialog box is shown in Figure 16.17. This has been created using Microsoft Foundation Class (MFC) technology. It contains a list view that displays the temperature-related parameters for each connected client.

Going back to Figure 16.16, we use the Acceptor–Connector pattern to receive data from clients. The `ClientAcceptor` task listens for clients that wish to establish a connection. Once the connection has been established a `ConnectionHandler` object is created that has the responsibility for handling the connection. An instance of `ConnectionHandler` is created for each connected client. All connections are processing using multiplexing.

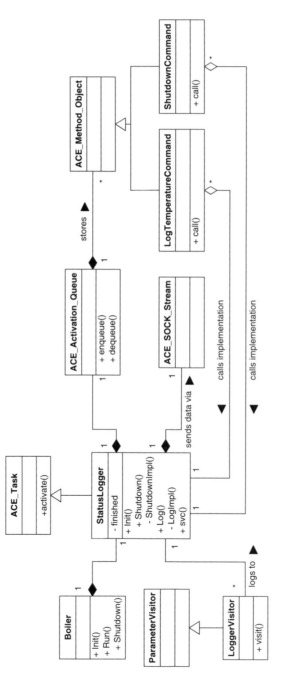

Figure 16.15 Logging class diagram.

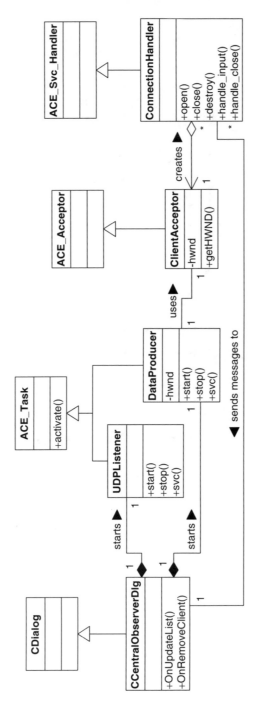

Figure 16.16   Central Observer class diagram.

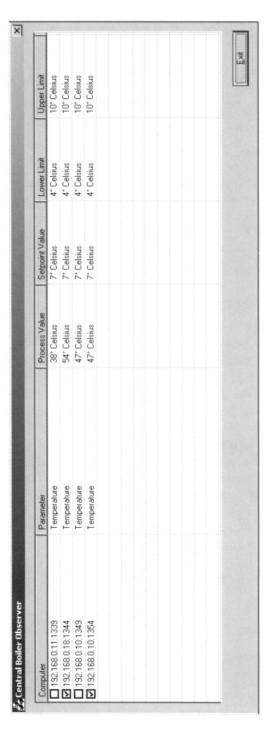

Figure 16.17 Central Observer dialog box.

16.8 SUMMARY AND CONCLUSIONS

We have given an introduction to the problem of analysing and designing a large, distributed, real-time application. We have included it because it shows how to decompose a system into loosely coupled subsystems where each subsystem is responsible for one specific and well-defined task. The system is an instance of a Lifecycle Model (LCM) and we scope the system and its subsystems by defining context diagrams and corresponding Boundary objects. Having analysed the problem domain we must devise a strategy for designing the solution to the problem. To this end, we introduced the concepts of multi-threading, multi-tasking and the ACE library. Finally, we gave an example of how the ACE library and domain architectures can be integrated. This is an area of future research and holds great promise, in the author's opinion: mapping reusable architectures in the problem domain to patterns in the solution domain.

APPENDIX 16.1: AN INTRODUCTION TO MULTI-THREADING

This book is concerned with the discovery and documentation of high-level architectures that can be seamlessly integrated with the UML artefacts. In general, we are not concerned with design issues because we are more interested in the problem. The design topic is outside the scope of this book. We make an exception in this chapter because here we are interested in *how* objects and systems communicate with each other. In particular, we model objects and systems as active entities. To this end, we need to introduce the topics of multi-threading and multi-tasking.

A thread is a unit of execution in a (software) process and represents a sequence of CPU instructions. It has a specific structure consisting of registers, stacks and private storage areas. In general, a software process will have one or more threads. Each thread is assigned a time slice (or quantum) in which it may use a portion of CPU time. When the time slice expires the thread goes back to sleep. In fact, a thread may find itself in different mutually exclusive states:

- *Ready*: The thread is able to run and is waiting for the processor to give it a time slice.
- *Running*: The thread is currently running and executing its tasks.
- *Blocked*: The thread is not running (because it is waiting on a resource to be freed).
- *Terminated*: The thread has served its function and is no longer available.

We describe a thread by a Lifecycle Model. One possibility is to document it by means of a Harel statechart (Harel and Politi 2000) as in Figure 16.18. As soon as

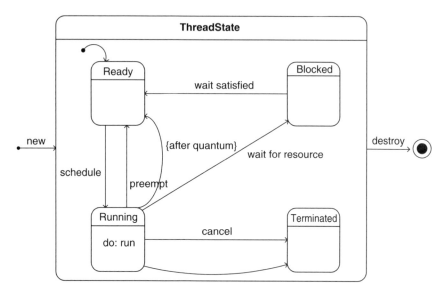

Figure 16.18   The life of a thread.

a thread is created it goes into Ready mode and it remains in that state until the processor makes it active, after which time it is in the Running state.

There is only one running thread on a uniprocessor machine while true multi-threading is achieved on multi-processor machines: each processor has a thread assigned to it. The latter case allows us to achieve true parallelism. In other words, each processor executes independently of the other processors. Concurrency, on the other hand, is the illusion of parallelism because it does not imply that operations execute simultaneously. For example, it is possible to define a concurrent solution on a uniprocessor machine while parallel applications are only possible on multi-processor machines. A complication with threaded applications is that multiple threads may compete for resources and unexpected things may occur unless we take precautions. The main concern is thread safety and we must ensure that multiple threads do not simultaneously compete for the same resources. In particular, we must ensure that code operates safely in multiple threads and we say that existing code must be made *thread-safe*. Two major problems are called deadlock and race condition. A *deadlock* occurs when two threads are waiting on each other to free resources. Both threads are in their respective Blocked states and a program will 'hang' if such a situation occurs. Another problem is the infamous *race condition* problem. This situation occurs when two or more threads share data. Race conditions occur when two use cases are attempting to access the shared data concurrently. The main problem is one of synchronization: the value of the data depends on unpredictable timing factors. Let us give an example in a standard ATM application and let us suppose that two customers wish to simultaneously withdraw

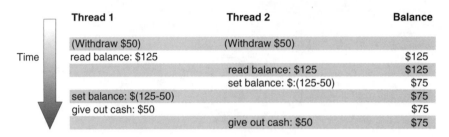

Time	Thread 1	Thread 2	Balance
	(Withdraw $50)	(Withdraw $50)	
	read balance: $125		$125
		read balance: $125	$125
		set balance: $:(125-50)	$75
	set balance: $(125-50)		$75
	give out cash: $50		$75
		give out cash: $50	$75

Figure 16.19 Race condition: what happens when two customers simultaneously withdrawn $50 from the same account?

$50 from a single account that initially has a balance of $125. The operations that each customer carries out (see Figure 16.19) are:

- Operation 1: Read balance ($125)
- Operation 2: Set new balance ($75 = $125 − $50)
- Operation 3: Dispense cash.

As can be seen in Figure 16.19 the operations are 'interleaved' between the two customers, thus leading to unpredictable results.

In order to resolve deadlocks and race conditions we must define some synchronization mechanisms. The main objective is to eliminate all race conditions and avoid deadlock while at the same time ensuring that there is no performance degradation caused by the introduction of these mechanisms. The main mechanisms are as follows.

- *Mutex*: a synchronization mechanism that controls access to data. Use of a mutex ensures integrity of a shared resource because only one thread can access the mutex at any given time.
- *Critical section*: a mechanism that provides exclusive access to a code path. The code in the path modifies data in general and we thus see that use of a critical section is an indirect way of protecting shared data. Only one process can execute a critical section at any one time.
- *Condition variable*: a mechanism that allows a thread to wait until it is safe to proceed. Its main use is in the synchronization of threads.
- *Semaphore*: a special kind of mutex which can be seen as a synchronization primitive in concurrent environments.

Novice developers sometimes think that a multi-threaded application is more efficient than a single-threaded equivalent. This is not necessarily so. In fact, on single-processor machines a multi-threaded application may perform less well than a single-threaded one because of context switching.

We are unable to give a detailed account here of synchronization mechanisms. For an account, see Nichols *et al* (1996) or any good book on operating systems theory.

We now give an introduction to threading models. In particular, we discuss how these techniques are used to define a number of generic models for multi-threaded applications. Our wish is to integrate them with domain architectures and with the Schmidt patterns. Before we can do this we need to address a number of important issues:

- How an application delegates work to its threads
- How threads communicate
- How to integrate threads and object technology.

In short, we wish to structure and document a threaded solution to a problem. The major models (see Nichols *et al* 1996) are:

- The Boss/Worker model
- The Peer model
- The Pipeline model.

In the Boss/Worker model (also known as Master–Slave, see POSA 1996) one boss thread accepts input for the program and then passes specific tasks to one or more worker threads. The boss is responsible for each worker's lifecycle. In general, its responsibilities are:

- Creation/destruction of worker threads (either dynamically or from a pool of threads)
- Assigning tasks to workers
- Optionally, waiting for tasks in the slaves to finish
- The boss loops/listens if there are no input requests.

An example of this model is shown in Figure 16.20 while a possible application to the PAC model is given in Figure 16.21. In this latter case we see that all the Control components are multi-threaded while the top-level component plays the role of boss and the other control components play the role of workers.

A variant of the Boss/Worker model is called the Peer model. In this case the boss places tasks in a queue. Workers periodically check the queue and take tasks from it. The situation is similar to a manager/secretary relationship in a business environment. The peers work independently as shown in Figure 16.22. An application to the PAC model is shown in Figure 16.23 in which we display three active objects in a Boundary layer; each object is responsible for getting input from the external stakeholder systems in its own way and then sending it on to the 'data objects' in the entity layer. We must be careful with possible race conditions because this is

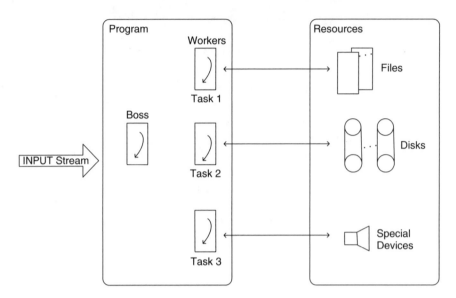

Figure 16.20   The Boss/Worker model.

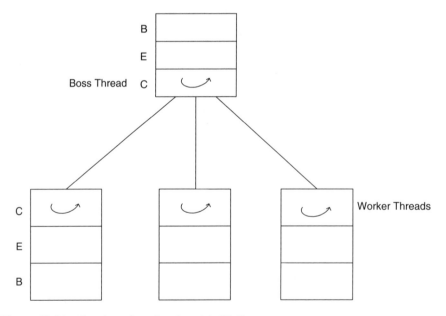

Figure 16.21   Creation of worker thread in PAC.

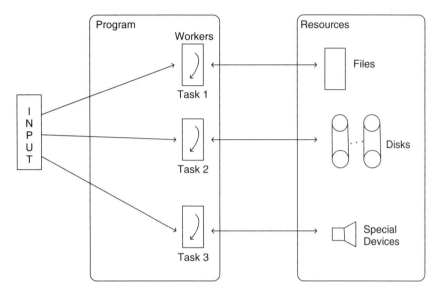

Figure 16.22 The Peer (Work Crew) model.

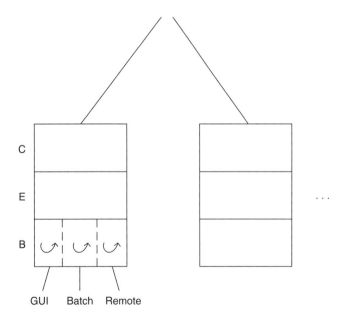

Figure 16.23 The Peer model in PAC.

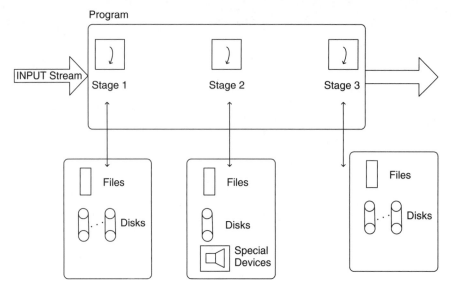

Figure 16.24   The Pipeline model.

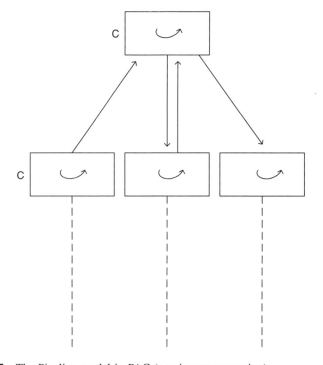

Figure 16.25   The Pipeline model in PAC (e.g. image processing).

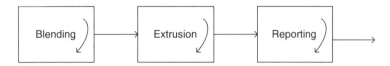

Figure 16.26   The Pipeline model for the PES application.

where problems occur when Entity objects are simultaneously updated by different Boundary and Control objects.

The last model that we discuss in this section is called the Pipeline model. In this case we divide a tasks into steps. The tasks are then performed in sequence. The work in each step is based on the input from the 'previous' step and the steps are designed to work in parallel. A good example of where this model can be applied is in an image scanning application (this is an instance of a MAN application). We have three subsystems, each of which is implemented by a thread (we call them A, B and C). The major/primary input is an image array and the major output is a report displaying decision-support information. The threads carry out the following duties:

- Thread A: process the image array and produce a processed image
- Thread B: search the processed image for patterns
- Thread C: collect and aggregate patterns in order to produce decision-support information.

We give an example of the pipeline model in Figure 16.24 while a possible application to PAC is given in Figure 16.25. In this case each agent is modelled as a thread in the pipeline. Finally, Figure 16.26 gives an example of the model for the plastics extrusion application. Notice the absence of the top-level mediator stage in this case.

PART IV

Domain architecture summary and 'how to use' documentation

17 Summary of domain architectures

'All models are wrong, some are useful.'

Dr W. Edwards Deming

17.1 INTRODUCTION AND OBJECTIVES

We have written two short chapters in Part IV to help readers find their way in this book. The chapters are appropriately devoid of detailed analyses and you can read them without getting bogged down in architectural details. Instead, they provide guidelines and pointers on using the book. Furthermore, they bring a number of results and conclusions together in one place.

This chapter summarizes the essential features of the different domain architectures (see also Figure 1.2). We gather all relevant information in order to help the reader get a correct and high-level impression of what each domain architecture is and what its applications to software development are. Chapter 18 is a practical guide to using domain architectures because it deals with issues that software developers are confronted with in their working lives, which is how to start on a project. In other words, Chapter 18 can be viewed as one possible entry point into the world of domain architectures.

In general, you may need to iterate a number of times before you calibrate a system with the most suitable domain architecture(s). There is no golden or infallible rule that states that one architecture is optimal for a given application. We must remember that we have developed models of the real worlds and that they focus on certain aspects while neglecting others.

In this chapter we shall use the word 'object' in a generic sense to denote something that has structure and contents. It is something with sharp boundaries. In some cases we shall use the synonym entity, information or data when it is more appropriate to do so.

17.2 OBJECT CREATIONAL SYSTEMS (OCS)

The instances in this category all share the feature that objects are created from basic input information. This is the overriding concern and focus. Once these objects have been created they will be used by other systems in various ways. In other words, the roles that the newly created objects play will be determined by the client systems that use them. The main sub-category in OCS is MAN (Manufacturing System).

Object Creational Systems, their specializations and instances are fundamental because they produce data and information for other client systems. What actually happens depends on the particular situation as shown in Figure 17.1 where we have shown how MAN systems work as servers to other domain architecture instances:

- MAN to MAN (pardon the pun): a MAN instance system delivers smaller objects to another MAN instance that in its turn uses these objects as half-products to create even more complex objects. For example, a client MAN system may get half-products from several source MAN systems. The MAN server objects play the role of *half-product* or *product objects*.
- MAN to RAT: in this case an object is created by a MAN system and then presented to a RAT system for verification, scheduling and resource allocation. In this case we can speak of *request objects* that must be processed and tracked by the RAT system. The objects will contain information such as the sender of the objects, the type of request, the ultimate receiver of the request and so on.
- MAN to MIS: a MAN system creates objects that play the role of *transactional objects*. Such objects contain information about low-level system resource usage.

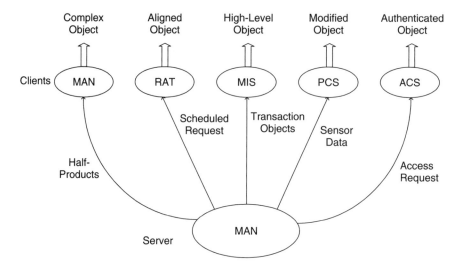

Figure 17.1 Manufacturing system as 'server' to other DA 'clients'.

By low-level we mean that the objects describe which stakeholders use which resources. In general, these transactional objects contain multi-dimensional data that will be consolidated and merged by the MIS system.

- MAN to PCS: a PCS system monitors exceptional situations. In this particular client–server relationship the MAN system plays the role of the sensors that send information to the PCS system to notify it that a setting or value has changed. In this case the objects contain actual values of some entity that the PCS system is monitoring and controlling. In this case we speak of *sensor-valued objects*.
- MAN to ACS: in this case the MAN system creates request or command objects that are then delivered to ACS for processing.

In general, relationships between the systems in Figure 17.1 are many-to-many; a system can be a server to several clients while a system may be a client of several other systems. We must determine the precise multiplicity for our own specific applications.

17.3 OBJECT ALIGNMENT SYSTEMS (OAS)

The main focus with Object Alignment Systems is to associate objects that have just been created (for example) with objects in other systems. Since object-oriented systems are essentially networks of associations and links between objects, we see this category as the 'glue' that binds objects together.

The main sub-category in OAS at the moment of writing is RAT (Resource Allocation and Tracking). Other special cases (for analysis and design objects) are the GOF structural patterns and the POSA system patterns. We are thinking in particular of the patterns called Composite, Bridge, Decorator, Proxy, Façade and Whole–Part.

RAT systems create objects that can be used as input to instances of other domain architectures. Figure 17.2 shows the relationships:

- RAT to Object Reporting Systems: a status-based object is defined as a request object whose coordinates in time and space have been annotated as well as the resource objects that have been assigned to it. Status-based objects (SBOs) are usually low-level in the sense that they have to do with simple organizational units (such as people, a department and suchlike). For MIS systems, the SBOs play the role of transaction objects and SBOs will be consolidated into higher-level objects, while for PCS systems the SBOs will be similar to sensor data.
- RAT to MAN: the output from a RAT system can play the role of *raw data* for a MAN system. This raw data will be converted to some new *product* or *service*.
- RAT to RAT: a RAT system can send data to another RAT system. The client system can track requests at a higher level of abstraction or granularity. We have given some examples in Chapter 7, Section 7.11.

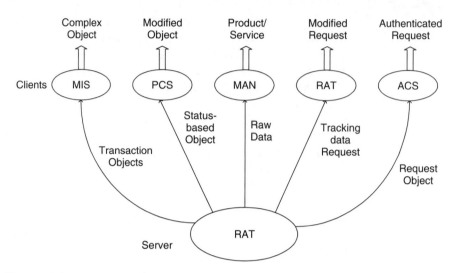

Figure 17.2 RAT system as 'server' to other DA 'clients'.

- RAT to ACS: this is a common pattern. A RAT system produces a request that is authenticated by an ACS system that then gives a go/no-go response to *its* client systems.

17.4 OBJECT BEHAVIOURAL SYSTEMS (OBS)

In contrast to RAT systems (where we are assigning objects to other objects), in this case we are modelling interactions and functionality in systems. Some scenarios can be generated by considering the ISO 9126 characteristics and their sub-characteristics again:

- Suitability: extending the functionality of a system
- Accuracy: ensuring that information is correct and up-to-date
- Security: ensuring that only authorized users have access to a system or part of a system.

In general, the systems in this category are concerned mainly with functionality, whether it is adding functionality to a system or restricting the functionality or operational capabilities of a system in some way.

17.4.1 MIS

These are systems that produce high-level decision-support and reporting information based on algorithms that aggregate or consolidate lower-level transaction data. MIS systems play the role of server as shown in Figure 17.3.

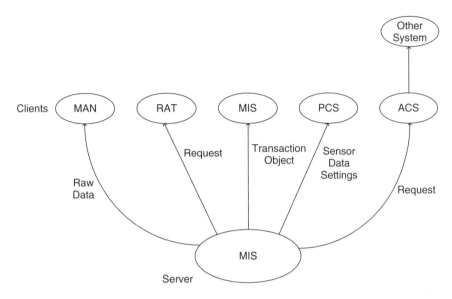

Figure 17.3 MIS system as 'server' to other DA 'clients'.

- MIS to MAN: the high-level data from a MIS system is seen as raw data for a MAN system. This scenario is possible in principle. For example, the MAN instance could be some kind of graphics compiler that converts the high-level data to a new product.
- MIS to RAT: high-level information may be seen as request data to a RAT system. This information can be assigned to resources, scheduled and tracked.
- MIS to MIS: a MIS system may receive information from a number of MIS server systems that play the role of systems that produce transaction data (albeit at a high level) for the client MIS system.
- MIS to PCS: high-level data may represent some kind of sensor data that is input to a PCS system. The latter system must decide what to do (the control part of PCS) once it has received this *out-of-bounds* data. Further, more MIS and PCS systems may cooperate as follows: a MIS sends configuration and download information to a PCS system.
- MIS to ACS: high-level data that is destined for a system is first filtered by an ACS system.

17.4.2 PCS

PCS systems monitor and control critical system parameters. If the value of a parameter reaches a certain critical level some action is executed in order to redress this aberration. PCS systems play the role of server as shown in Figure 17.4.

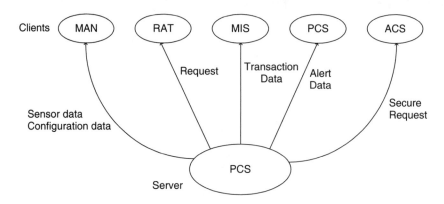

Figure 17.4   PCS system as 'server' to other DA 'clients'.

- PCS to MAN: PCS systems can send real-time sensor data or historical/static configuration data to a MAN system. In this case these data types play the role of the raw data that MAN needs in order to create products and services.
- PCS to RAT: PCS can send a request to a RAT system because it needs some resource.
- PCS to MIS: this is a common situation. For example, several PCS systems send their sensor data or configuration data (these data types will then play the role of transaction data) to a MIS system for consolidation and high-level reporting.
- PCS to PCS: this is the 'watchdog monitoring and controlling the watchdog' option in which the server PCS system is the provider of sensor data.
- PCS to ACS: PCS systems may send commands or requests to other systems but we wish these commands to be screened and authenticated.

17.4.3 ACS

ACS systems restrict access to certain resources. In general, an ACS can be a front-end system to an instance of some other domain architecture as shown in Figure 17.5. In general, we place an ACS system between a client system and a server for a number of reasons (by the way, these are generalizations of the different kinds of Proxy pattern in POSA 1996):

- *Remote ACS*: Client and server systems are in different address spaces or use different data formats. In this case the ACS system encapsulates and maintains information on the locations of server systems. In general, we could create one ACS system per server.
- *Protection ACS*: We protect the server system from unauthorized clients. This is a special case of the Reference Monitor model in Chapter 9.

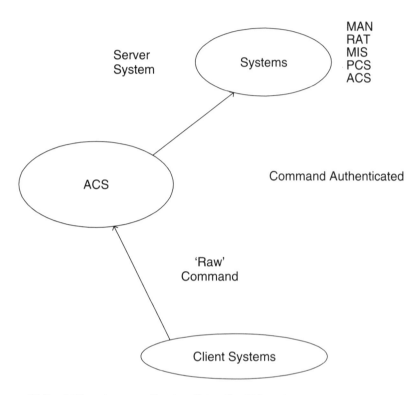

Figure 17.5 ACS system as a 'front-end' to other DA systems.

- *Cache ACS*: Multiple client systems can share results from remote servers. In this case we must extend the basic ACS system with an external stakeholder system that temporarily holds results.
- *Synchronizing ACS*: We can synchronize multiple simultaneous accesses to a server system using this specialization of ACS. This option allows multiple simultaneous client accesses. Only one client can access the server system at any one time.

Other kinds of ACS (proxy) systems are discussed in POSA (1996).

17.5 KEEPING THE DOMAIN ARCHITECTURES DISTINCT AND ORTHOGONAL

In Section 17.4 we discussed how instances of domain architectures cooperate in a kind of client–server environment. We now must discuss how to discriminate one domain architecture from another and to ensure that a specific domain architecture does not fade away or get lost in some higher-level category. After all, the domain architectures are very similar but not the same (an apple is similar to a pear, an orange is similar to a mandarin, but there are differences).

The distinction between the different architectural types can become a bit blurred unless we are eternally vigilant! It is easy to become confused and it may be very difficult to make a choice (which is sometimes even more frustrating than having just one choice or no choice at all!). In order to be sure how to choose the most appropriate pattern, we have provided a number of differences between pairs of domain architectures. At least you will know that your application is *not* an instance of some domain architecture (this will save you a lot of time). For a start, we recall:

- MAN systems create objects.
- RAT systems allocate/assign objects to other objects (resources).
- MIS systems produce reports for objects containing multi-dimensional data.
- PCS systems monitor and control objects by comparing their values with predefined settings.
- ACS systems do not do much as such; instead they contain authorization information concerning which principals have which kind of access to which resources.

These one-liners should be consulted before you start digging deeper.

17.5.1 MAN versus RAT

A MAN system creates objects while a RAT system assigns objects to some other objects that play the role of resources. MAN systems are usually not interested in tracking the life of an object through the system (although there may be exceptions to this rule) whereas RAT systems model what happened to an object, who did what with the object and where the object can be found in space and time.

MAN systems do not usually monitor service-level agreements, response time and other performance issues. The jargon is not in the vocabulary while RAT systems do have this embodied in their context diagram.

The information in Figures 17.1 to 17.5 could be used as input to finding new requirements. In general, instances of certain domain architectures exchange information on a client–server basis. We can then start investigating what the different viewpoints are in this regard. For example, taking the client–server relationship between PCS and MIS in Figure 17.1 in which MIS sends real-time sensor data and scheduled set-point data to PCS, we could examine the following viewpoints (for example ISO 9126) and corresponding stakeholders in relation to that data:

- Reliability of the data
- Functionality (accuracy, security)
- Efficiency (time and resource).

We can then determine how to find new system requirements (the Inquiry Cycle model may be useful here).

17.5.2 MAN versus MIS

At a superficial level, MIS systems create high-level and consolidated objects. However, once created they can never be changed (famous last words ...) and they are then stored in a so-called data warehouse. Furthermore, MIS are concerned with the comparison of *target values* of objects with *actual values* and they produce reports based on these values at various levels of detail. Furthermore, MIS systems allow users to drill down in the data warehouse by using queries. Using this kind of jargon and vocabulary for MAN systems would be out of place.

MIS and MAN systems employ *algorithms* that convert input to output. In the former case the emphasis is on producing multi-dimensional data for querying purposes, while in the latter case the algorithms are concerned with the creation of a product or service that will be used somewhere else.

In short, MAN systems create objects and send them on their way while MIS systems store long-term information pertaining to objects at various levels of detail.

17.5.3 MAN versus PCS

PCS systems do not create objects as such; they monitor the actual values of some attributes in those objects. If the actual values drift too far away from so-called scheduled values (or set-point values as they are called) the PCS system will attempt to activate some actuators in order to redress the imbalance.

17.5.4 MAN versus ACS

ACS systems do not create objects as such but they restrict the kinds and number of objects that may access other server systems. MAN systems create objects, ACS systems define or restrict access to those objects.

17.5.5 RAT versus MIS

MIS systems are concerned with different kinds of data at different levels of granularity while RAT systems tend to track more fine-grained objects in a system. There is no real concern in RAT with consolidation issues; these would be taken care of by a client MIS system (see Figure 17.2 again). For example, we might like to create a report of all outstanding orders for the last month. This functionality should be placed in the MIS system and not in the RAT system, otherwise we will get a bloated system in no time.

17.5.6 RAT versus PCS

These categories are similar in the sense that they monitor objects in a system. RAT systems monitor objects as they 'flow' in a system, as it were, and historical information is gathered on which actors created or modified the object, where the object is and other relevant information. PCS systems, on the other hand, are less dynamic in the sense that we are not interested in tracking objects as they move in multi-dimensional space, but we are interested in monitoring critical values of certain attributes. This is called exception management, a feature that we do not see with RAT systems.

17.5.7 RAT versus ACS

RAT systems are silent on access control issues and are not responsible for defining which subjects or principals have which kind of access to which objects. This is of course the speciality of ACS systems.

17.5.8 MIS versus PCS

There is a lot of commonality between these types. In fact, we can view them as specializations of a general Object Reporting System category. Both describe, document and report the status of the information in systems. In particular, MIS creates all kinds of reports (*ad hoc*, periodic) at all levels of granularity. These reports include both *normal* and *exceptional* cases. PCS systems, on the other hand, tend to produce reports only when something goes wrong (is about to go wrong, in other words an impending major event in the system). Furthermore, PCS systems tend to be small but of course we could have a park/farm (composite) of such systems.

There is one last major difference: MIS systems are good at monitoring information and objects while PCS systems' responsibilities have to do with both *monitoring* and *control*. When an exceptional event occurs in a PCS system it performs an algorithm to activate an actuator that brings the system back to equilibrium again.

17.5.9 MIS and PCS versus ACS

Both MIS and PCS are specializations of Object Reporting Systems. They are concerned with delivering decision-support information to client systems. ACS systems may have basic reporting facilities but this feature is not the main concern.

17.6 SUMMARY AND CONCLUSIONS

In this chapter we have given a summary of domain architectures from two main perspectives:

- How instances of domain architectures cooperate in client–server settings
- Comparing and contrasting pairs of domain architecture types.

This discussion should help you appreciate the real differences between the different types and how they complement each other. Once we have achieved this level of understanding we shall be in a better position to apply them to real-life applications. This is the subject of Chapter 18.

18 Using domain architectures and analogical reasoning

18.1 INTRODUCTION AND OBJECTIVES

In this chapter we develop a number of techniques that help the reader use domain architectures in real-life applications. Our basic assumption and starting point is that we are embarking on a real application whose architecture and requirements must be discovered. Instead of using trial and error methods, serendipity or word-of-mouth experience, we try to formalize the thought process somewhat. In particular, we use domain architectures as a stepping-stone to helping the reader understand the system under discussion (SUD). The author has developed formalisms for documenting domain architectures and their instance systems. The assumption is that they describe a range of real-life applications and we document their essential features using UML notation. We have attempted to apply a number of techniques, from cognitive psychology to the process of classifying the SUD as an instance of some domain architecture, or even comparing it with some other instance system that we (or others) have developed in the past.

This chapter discusses the following topics:

- How to fit the SUD into the most appropriate domain architecture(s)
- Focusing on essential system features as a way of understanding the SUD
- Using domain architectures to instantiate specific SUDs
- Using the best example (*prototype*) of a domain architecture in order to understand the SUD
- Using several *exemplars* in order to understand the SUD.

We stress that there are other ways to solve problems and that the above choices are not exhaustive and may not be suitable in all cases. All we can say is: try it!

In order to keep both feet on the ground, we give a summary of the advantages and disadvantages of the different approaches that help us gain an understanding of the software development process.

18.2 IN WHICH DOMAIN ARCHITECTURE DOES MY APPLICATION BELONG? THE BIRD-WATCHING METHOD

The bird-watching method is a technique for spotting birds of a given species by making a *deliberate attempt* to look for certain features. We learn to recognize the characteristics of the different species. In our case we equate a bird with the system under discussion (SUD) and the species with one or more domain architectures. See Figure 18.1. Our first attention-director method is a technique for determining the most suitable domain architecture for the SUD. First of all, we must enumerate the essential characteristics of the different categories and these will play the role of a set of destinations, as it were. We try to arrive at one destination by examining the SUD and placing it in that category (or categories) that fits the SUD best. In order to reduce the scope, we define a number of key identifiers:

- I: the vocabulary and jargon used
- II: the core process and information flow

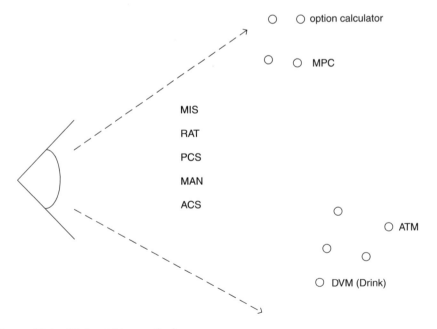

Figure 18.1 Bird-watching method.

- III: the major viewpoints in the system
- IV: Activities and algorithms

We now give the contents of the above identifiers for each domain architecture:

- MIS (see Section 5.4 for more detailed attention directors):
  — I: Decision-support information, consolidation and reporting
  — II: Create reports: transaction data, consolidated data
  — III: Functionality (accuracy, interoperability)
  — IV: Data mining and data drilling; merging.
- PCS (see Section 6.5 for more detailed attention directors):
  — I: Process control jargon (setpoints, process value)
  — II: Sensor readings, actuator output, exceptional management
  — III: Reliability, efficiency, safety
  — IV: Control algorithms, actuator algorithms.
- RAT (see Section 7.4 for more detailed attention directors):
  — I: Tracking, traceability
  — II: Request data, display of request status
  — III: Accuracy, usability
  — IV: Scheduling and planning of requests/activities.
- MAN (see Section 8.4 for more detailed attention directors):
  — I: Raw materials, half-products, products and services
  — II: Raw data, finished products
  — III: Efficiency, suitability
  — IV: Preprocessing, conversion, postprocessing.
- ACS (see Section 9.4 for more detailed attention directors):
  — I: Authorization, authentication, secure access
  — II: Access request, status of request
  — III: Security, usability
  — IV: Checking user credentials.
- LCM (see Section 10.4 for more detailed attention directors):
  — I: The word 'Lifecycle' (occurs in business world)
  — II: New ideas transformed into long-term products
  — III: Traceability, performance and reporting
  — IV: Creation, scheduling and reporting.

In general, you are embarking on a new system and you wish to determine which category is the best fit. You can create a decision table by giving each category a score. Even fuzzy numbers based on your intuition are allowed (the so-called first impression) and the results should steer you in the right direction. The Quality Function Deployment (QFD) method uses this approach and there is a lot of spreadsheet software available to support the decision-making process.

Real-life applications are usually a combination of all of the above categories. In particular, you should apply the technique in this section to the SUD and its external stakeholder systems.

Once you know which category your application belongs to, you can then start exploring more specific and focused questions.

18.3 FOCUSING ON ESSENTIAL SYSTEM FEATURES: THE FRAMEWORK METHOD

The framework method is an attempt to define a framework for the deliberate operation of thinking. We draw up a sequence of boxes where each box is an attention area. We fill each box by thinking about the problem or situation in the terms defined by the box. For example, we use this method to think about domain categories by choosing boxes with the following contents:

- Context diagram
- Core process
- Stakeholders
- System and subsystems.

Each box holds our attention on a specific thinking task. The added value of this method is that we direct our thinking to just one area at a time instead of trying to cover all areas at once. The general picture is sketched in Figure 18.2(a). Each box can be elaborated and other boxes in Figure 18.2(b) suggest this. These boxes represent 'further thinking'. In other words, we can elaborate in depth and in breadth and there is also room for discussions on alternatives (Plan A, Plan B). As such, the boxes do not have any value except just to hold attention for a while. In this way we hope to carry out one particular thinking activity. The end-result is less confusion, with each aspect of the problem getting some attention.

Having devoted some time to one particular aspect of SUD (for example, its core processes or context diagram) helps us in a better understanding of it and we get insights into other aspects. For example, the author nearly always focuses on the following issues during initial customer interviews:

- The core process (what does the system really do?)
- Context diagrams
- The interfaces between SUD and the external stakeholder systems.

In this way the interview remains focused and we know what is to be done after completion of the interview (which usually takes between two and three hours).

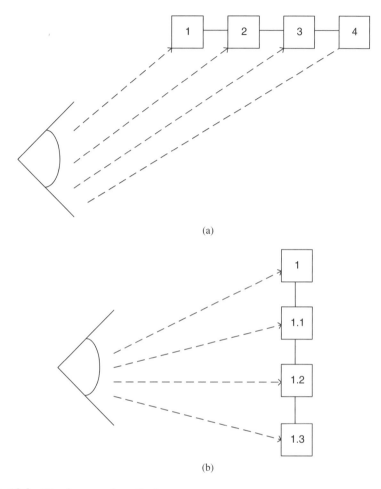

(a)

(b)

Figure 18.2 The framework method.

In general, you can apply the framework method to all structural and behavioural artefacts of the software lifecycle process. See Chapter 3 for details.

18.4 THE DEFINING-ATTRIBUTE VIEW

This view is based on the assumption that the meaning of a domain architecture can be captured by an all-encompassing list of attributes. These attributes are atomic units or primitives that are the basic building blocks of a category. Each attribute is necessary and all of them are jointly sufficient for an instance system to be identified as a member of the category. This is tantamount to saying that a domain architecture is sufficient for discovering the essential properties for *any* SUD (something which I do not believe, because there is no universal model for all systems; some modicum of humility is in order).

Things are very clear-cut; what is and what is not a member of the category is clearly defined and there are clear boundaries between members and non-members of the category. Furthermore, all members are equally representative of the category. Finally, when categories are organized in a hierarchy then the defining attributes of a more specific concept (for example, Drink Vending Machine) in relation to the more general superordinate concept (for example, ACS category) include all the defining attributes of the superordinate. In practical terms, this approach allows us to find the structure and behaviour of SUD by specializing and instancing the artefacts in the corresponding category. For example, ACS systems allow authorized principals to securely access resources (or objects). Specializing this to the Drink Vending Machine problem, we execute the following specialization activities:

- Principals map to customers
- Resources map to physical cans of lemonade/cola
- Authorization database maps to coin unit
- Authentication is realized through coin insertion.

Another example from Chapter 5 is the Acoustic Data List (ADL) system where we specialize the external stakeholder system from the more general MIS category to ADL:

- Transaction Database = sound level meters
- Organization   = operating characteristics of physical equipment
- Permanent Database   = data for equipment usage
- Reference/Schedule   = target/acceptable noise levels
- Sink   = SPL presentation information
- Algorithms   = algorithms that calculate noise levels.

We can apply this specialization process to any artefact for any domain architecture.

18.4.1 Advantages and disadvantages

All models are wrong; some are useful. The defining-attribute view is based on semantic network theory and it has been suggested that humans reason by linking more concrete concepts to more general ones and vice versa. In this book we have already created a hierarchy of domain architectures and their instance systems in Chapter 1 (see Figure 1.2). In general, the evidence against the defining-attribute view outweighs that in favour of it (Eysenck and Keane 2000). Basically, general concepts are unstable and highly context-sensitive. For example, in Chapter 13 we modelled the Elevator Control System as primarily an instance of a RAT category even though it would have been better to have modelled it as a PCS system. That's life! We gain experience by experimenting with hypotheses and modifying our assumptions as new experimental evidence is gathered.

Some other weaknesses are:

- We cannot be sure that we have found essential defining attributes that describe a domain architecture or its instance systems.
- We have five basic domain architectures in this book: are there others and, if so, how do we discover them?

Summarizing, I see some truth in the statement that breaking down a domain architecture into its necessary and sufficient attributes is fundamentally ill-conceived. The defining-attribute is rampant in the object-oriented paradigm: we create classes having very sharp attributes and functions and then we create instances of those classes. This assumption needs revision, in the author's opinion.

18.5 THE PROTOTYPE VIEW

In this section we assume that we wish to find the structure and behaviour of SUD. We may or may not yet have determined in which domain category it fits. Of course, if we already know that it is an instance of, let's say, a MIS category then our life becomes easier.

The Prototype view is based on the idea that each domain architecture has an instance system that is the best example of the architecture because its properties exemplify the essential characteristics of the category. There is no defining set of necessary and sufficient attributes that determines membership in the category. There may be necessary attributes but they are not jointly sufficient. Category boundaries are fuzzy or unclear; what is and is not a member of the category is ill-defined or some instances may slip into the wrong category. For example, we see in hindsight that the Elevator Control System in Chapter 13 should have been modelled as an instance of PCS rather than as a RAT instance.

Instances of a domain architecture may be ranged in terms of their typicality, that is there is a typicality gradient that characterizes the differential typicality of instances in the category (Eysenck and Keane 2000). For example, in the MIS category we grade some instance systems as follows:

- Manpower Control (MPC) system (highest score)
- Acoustic Data List
- Heart Monitoring System
- Simple Digital Watch (lowest score, least typical).

Thus, we choose MPC as being the most typical example in the category and this will be our prototype instance. When you are working on a new SUD you can determine its membership in MIS by the similarity of objects and other artefacts to the category's prototype, in this case MPC. The tactic is to use MPC's artefacts to discover or improve the corresponding artefacts in SUD. Some prime examples are:

- The context diagram
- The subsystems and layered classes
- Stakeholders and viewpoints
- Use cases.

It is possible that a new 'best' prototype will come along in the future to displace the current prototype MPC system.

For the other domain architectures we consider the following instance systems to be prototypes:

- Home Heating System is prototype for PCS.
- Help Desk System is prototype for RAT.
- The Reference Monitor is prototype for ACS.
- Plastic film production is prototype for Lifecycle Model (LCM).

The reader may notice that we do not have a prototype for the MAN (Manufacturing) category. We do have some typical *exemplars*, but we cannot give an example of a system that is typical of the category. We have to be happy with these exemplars and use them to help us find the essentials of SUD.

18.5.1 Advantages and disadvantages

There is a lot of positive evidence to support the prototype account of categorization. There seems to be a universality in people's categorization of certain systems and the structure of categories of systems. It would seem that these categories have a prototype structure. There are a number of disadvantages of this view:

- Not all domain architectures have a prototype (for example, we do not really have a prototype for MAN). This is probably due to the fact that there is endless flexibility in the membership of domain architectures.
- People seem to know about the relations between attributes, rather than the attributes themselves.
- Why do we group instances in one category and not in another? The prototype view provides no guidance in this regard because similarity is responsible for category cohesion. Similarity is not the only mechanism because we form categories, not by basing them on shared attributes but which are nonetheless coherent. For

example, in some cultures animals are grouped into clean (for example, fish and grasshoppers) and unclean (for example, pigs and rats).

18.6 THE EXEMPLAR-BASED VIEW

This view is based on the assumption that a domain architecture is made up of a collection of instances or exemplars rather than an abstract description of these instances as already discussed in Sections 18.4 and 18.5. Instances are grouped together relative to some similarity metric. In this book we group systems by their core processes and the kind of information that they produce:

- MIS: Reports
- PCS: Correction data and exceptional reports
- MAN: Products and services
- RAT: Display status of tracked entities
- ACS: Secure access to resources
- LCM: Entity lifecycle.

All instance systems in a given category have the same core process (however, we must admit that we are stretching the definition at times). For example, the category RAT has the following exemplars:

- Help Desk System (highest score)
- Order Registration System
- Rent-a-Machine (tracking part)
- Discrete Manufacturing
- Call Forwarding
- Risk Tracking
- Elevator Control (lowest score, really a PCS instance).

Figure 18.3 summarizes some stakeholder systems for the following instance systems:

- MPC: Manpower Control System
- SDW: Simple Digital Watch
- HMS: Heart Monitoring System
- ADL: Acoustic Data Lists.

The artefacts are:

- Source: the system where basic input data comes from
- Sink: the client recipient system

	MPC	SDW	HMS	ADL
Source	Used Hours	Pulse from satellite	Patient's characteristics	Noise from Equipment
Sink	Reports	LED	Doctors Screen	Noise Level DB
DWH	Dept. + Proj. Data	Hours + Minutes	Patient History	Historical info on Plant
KB	Verify User	?	Patient Profile	Plant Layout

Figure 18.3 Some stakeholder systems for MPC, SDW, HMS and ADL.

- DWH: data warehouse system containing historical data
- KB: knowledge database that classifies incoming data.

You can use the results in Figure 18.1 to help you think about new instance systems. Notice that the author is not sure about the kind of data in the KB for the SDW application!

18.6.1 Advantages and disadvantages

The main advantage of the exemplar-based view is that there are several instance systems to choose from when trying to discover the attributes of SUD. This could be called the 'safety in numbers' option; if one instance is not a good example then try another one, for example:

- A penguin is an example of a bird.
- A robin is a better example of a bird.

For example, I find the Help Desk System is a better example of a RAT instance than the Elevator Control System, the reason being that I am more familiar with the former system.

The exemplar-based view also preserves correlational information between instances of a category that the prototype view does not. It has also been shown that people use such knowledge in category learning and classification. In normal language, this amounts to saying that we learn by doing lots of examples.

Some of the disadvantages of the exemplar-based view are:

- Like the Prototype view, this view depends on similarity; it does not cope easily with class inclusion questions. For example, sometimes people think in terms of general concepts rather than specific exemplars, as in the truth of the statements 'All birds are creatures'.
- The exemplar-based view has no good account of how abstract knowledge comes into being.

18.7 SUMMARY AND CONCLUSIONS

We have given an introduction to a number of practical techniques to help us integrate domain architectures with the software development process. In a sense we have encapsulated knowledge about classes of applications and we have documented the knowledge using UML notation whenever possible. Domain architectures provide the substrate upon which you can build and understand your own applications. The main techniques are:

- Defining-attribute view
- Prototype view
- Exemplar-based view.

An introduction to bird-watching and the other techniques in this chapter are given in de Bono (1976).

APPENDIX 18.1: ANALOGICAL REASONING AND LEARNING BY ANALOGY

Much thinking is done by analogy. For example, when we face a situation we try to recall a similar situation from the past. Some specific examples are:

- We learn about resistors by thinking about water pipes
- We learn how to fly by thinking about how birds do it
- We study law by examining law cases from the past
- We (should) analyse software systems by looking for similar systems.

A number of authors have developed a so-called theory of analogy (see Hall 1989, Winston 1980) and we discuss some of their main findings in the hope that they can be applied to the work in this book, in particular in our quest to locate and apply domain architectures. Winston (1980) distinguishes between learning and reasoning. On the one hand, learning takes places when analogy is used to generate a constraint description in one domain, given a constraint description in another. For example, we learn Ohm's law by studying water hammer flows in pipes. Lifecycle models for a hardware rental company can be constructed by using our knowledge of a plastics extrusion manufacturing and tracking system.

Reasoning takes place when analogy is used to answer questions about one situation, given another situation that is supposed to be a so-called *precedent*. For example, we can answer questions about a system that monitors disk space usage in a large computer network environment by comparing it with the Manpower Control (MPC) system that monitors man-hours in engineering projects.

We now discuss some aspects of a system to support analogical learning and we give some examples such as the Automated Teller Machine (ATM) and the Drink Vending Machine (DVM). We have constructed a concept map and initial UML class diagrams and let us suppose that we wish to analyse DVM by using ATM as a precedent (in the Winston sense). The most important aspects are:

1. *Importance-dominated matching*: We discover similarity between two situations by finding the best possible match according to what is important in the situations as exhibited by the situations themselves. The assumption in this case is that if two situations are similar in some respects then they must also be similar in other respects. We must place the situations in correspondence. Of course, the two situations will not be the same in all respects. Thus, we will have a combination of paired and unpaired entities. What is the best way to match two situations in general? This is a very difficult question and to reduce the scope we concentrate on the ATM and DVM applications, for example:
   — Compare the viewpoints of ATM and DVM (functional, structural, behavioural)
   — Compare similarities of the phases of ATM and DVM (for example, analysis)
   — Compare the ISO 9126 characteristics of ATM and DVM.
   In general, we can compare ATM software space to determine whether there are similarities in the DVM software space. For example, it is fairly clear that both DVM and ATM have similar authentication units and use cases!

2. *Analogy-driven constraint learning*: This has to do with how a constraint or fact as a by-product of a mapping in one part of a situation in a well-understood domain (such as ATM) can be learned for the new unknown domain. For example, in the ATM problem the customer may enter an incorrect password at most three times, after which the ATM machine is temporarily disabled and the pin card is not returned. Similar security constraints should also hold for the DVM problem. In this way we gain a better understanding of DVM.

3. *Analogy-driven reasoning*: This type of reasoning asks whether a particular relationship holds. Specifically, causes found in a remembered (or documented!) situation can supply suggestive precedents.

4. *Classification-exploiting hypothesizing*: This is the problem of searching in short-term or long-term memory (or documentation in a handbook!) for situations that

are likely to be similar to a new, given situation. Of course, we must find the documented situation that is most relevant to the situation under discussion. We assume that the documented situations will involve the same sorts of things as the new one. There are two mechanisms for searching through a network of possibilities:

— SIMILAR-TO mechanism
— A-KIND-OF mechanism.

For example, a coin unit in the DVM problem is SIMILAR-TO the pin unit in an ATM machine. Furthermore, both units are KIND-OF Authorization Database in an ACS category. Finally, both ATM and DVM at the highest level are themselves KIND-OF ACS systems.

We note that the above mechanisms can be applied at any level, in contrast to the conclusions in Winston (1980) where the mechanisms are not scalable, due to the fact that many people begin the thinking process at the lowest level (in our case, the object or class level). A shift in emphasis is obviously needed. So why not start reasoning at the highest level? The measure of the similarity between DVM and ATM can be defined in the following set notation:

$$\text{SIMILARITY(DVM,ATM)} = f(\text{DVM} \cup \text{ATM}) - f(\text{DVM-ATM}) - f(\text{ATM-DVM})$$

Here, the function f counts the number of occurrences, the symbol $f(\text{DVM} \cup \text{ATM})$ denotes the number of features in ATM and DVM combined, while $f(\text{ATM-DVM})$ denotes the number of features in ATM and not in DVM. A 'feature' in this case could be a value of any artefact.

We conclude this section with an introduction to computational approaches to analogy (see Hall 1989). Hall proposes a conceptual framework that includes the following processes:

1. *Recognition*: Given a target (unknown) problem, find a candidate analogous source. For example, if I asked you to develop a cruise control system for an automobile, which source system would you use?
2. *Elaboration*: This is an analogical mapping between the source system and the target problems, including so-called *analogical inferences*.
3. *Evaluation* of the mapping and inferences in some context of use, including justification, repair, or extension of the mapping. This aspect could be part of the requirements elicitation phase, for example. The requirements analyst must learn the similarities and differences between target and source problems.
4. *Consolidation* of the outcome of the analogy. The added value is that the results can be used in other contexts. For example, having developed the DVM system we may come to the conclusion that the ACS category is in need of an update.

1 The Inquiry Cycle and related cognitive techniques

'We do not know what will happen in the future, but our ignorance is not total. The degree to which we can make useful statements about the future differs from case to case. In this context we identify three categories of uncertainty ... risks, structural uncertainties and unknowables.'

Kees van der Heijden

A1.1 INTRODUCTION AND OBJECTIVES

This appendix introduces a number of simple but effective techniques that help the software development team gain insights into customer requirements. The techniques are applicable in *all* phases of the software development lifecycle. In fact, they are highly effective during design because this is the phase where many implicit and sometime false assumptions lurk.

This appendix develops several techniques to help software people gain a good understanding of what the customer wants, how to ask probing questions and how to handle changes in requirements. To this end, we introduce the so-called Inquiry Cycle model that was developed in Potts *et al* (1994) and which we see as an extremely valuable tool for the IT stakeholders. The model describes the requirements lifecycle and uses a number of questions that help improve communication between the customer and the IT staff. The added value of the model is that it reduces risk and improves communication between the stakeholders that are involved in the software project. This can't be a bad thing.

A1.2 BACKGROUND AND HISTORY

The object-oriented paradigm has been around for more than 30 years. The early years were characterized by looking for objects and classes in the problem domain and then attempting to 'glue' these together into some form of semantic network. The techniques for object discovery were very primitive indeed: search the requirements document for nouns and these will be the objects and classes that you are looking for (see Rumbaugh *et al* 1991). There are two mains risk here. First, large and enterprise systems may have thousands of classes (eventually!) and the simple approach will fail to scale up. Second, the discovered classes may not be correct because the person looking for the classes is not a domain expert or may not be the best person to do the job (for whatever reason). Classes are context-sensitive and different developers will create different structures for the same concept. These problems may be alleviated somewhat if we adopt a more top-down and predictable course of action (as is done in this book) and develop a number of interviewing techniques before we jump into the low-level details of objects and classes. We use the techniques in many of the book's chapters and they represent a bridge between the customer's mental model and the model that is being used by the IT specialist. The gap needs to be bridged if we are to avoid misunderstandings and improve communication between the different stakeholders.

A1.3 AN INTRODUCTION TO THE INQUIRY CYCLE MODEL

The Inquiry Cycle model is a dynamic hypertext model that captures information concerning requirements during the requirements elicitation process. It supports inquiry and scrutiny so everyone knows what information is missing and what assumptions are pending (see Potts *et al* 1994).

The model works as follows. First, a stakeholder writes down proposed requirements in the Documentation phase. It can be an informal wish or need or it could be documented by using use case templates. Second, in the Discussion phase certain stakeholders challenge the proposed requirements by attaching annotations to them in the hypertext models. As we shall see in Section A1.4, part of this process is the application of specific questions. Finally, in the Evolution phase the stakeholders attach change requests to the requirements on the basis of the discussion with other stakeholders. The requirements are refined when the changes are approved.

A1.3.1 Requirements documentation

The Inquiry Cycle model can be used in situations where a requirements document is in place as well as in situations where the document is absent. In this latter case the model provides a systematic and incremental process for writing such a document.

A1.3.2 Requirements discussion

The three main elements in this phase are:

- Questions
- Answers
- Reasons.

Most discussions start because a stakeholder has a question concerning a requirement (Questions). Then some other stakeholder will describe a solution to the problem posed in the question (Answers). A question can generate many answers and each answer may lead to another round of questions. The advantage of answers is that they provide stakeholders with a better understanding of the requirements. It also helps them to come to terms with the fact that requirements may be ambiguous, missing or inconsistent. Finally, the Reasons element has to do with the justifications for the answers. These justifications must be made explicit as they may not be obvious to all stakeholders or, even worse, may represent implicit knowledge. There are various approaches for setting up and conducting requirements discussions; for example, they can take place gradually and informally or in discrete bursts associated with formal review procedures. These issues are outside the scope of this book.

A1.3.3 Requirements evolution

Having completed the requirements discussion we must then make a commitment to either freeze a requirement or change it in some way. Freezing suggests that the requirement will not be changed (at least, not yet). To be able to change a requirement, a so-called change request must be created and should be traced back to a discussion. We should include a description of why the change is needed.

What kinds of changes to requirements do we see during evolution? There are three basic types: mutation, restriction and editorial. A *mutation* request calls for a change or addition to the requirements. The system changes once a mutation request emerges. A *restriction* request, on the other hand, calls for a change to the requirements document, usually in the form of a clarification of the text or a definition. In this way, we remove potential ambiguities and the system is further constrained. However, the system has not been changed and the original intent remains intact. An *editorial* request is a proposal to reword or rewrite a requirement or part of a requirement.

A final remark on stakeholders: they often make assumptions during elicitation. This means that they tend to answer a tacit question about requirements without articulating the question. They seldom justify their assumptions and they often fail to consider alternatives. The requirements analyst should flag all assumptions carefully and should attempt to justify these assumptions.

A1.4 USING THE RIGHT QUESTIONS

The Inquiry Cycle model makes use of a number of questions that are posed during requirements elicitation. These questions trigger discussions. The questions are:

- What-is?
- How-to?
- Who?
- What-kinds-of?
- When?
- Relationship
- What-if?
- Follow-on.

What-is questions request more information about a requirement; we resolve the question by giving a definition. Definitions are usually found in a glossary in requirements documents. Some examples of 'what-is' questions are:

- What is an order?
- What is a panel on a screen?
- What is a validation procedure?

How-to questions ask how some activity, action or use case is to be performed. These questions arise mainly from core processes, requirements and generic scenarios. For example, applying this question to business processes leads to activities and activity diagrams. Some examples of 'how-to' questions are:

- How to create an order?
- How to cancel the action?
- How to change from idle to active modes (state)?

Who questions request confirmation about which stakeholders are responsible for a given action or requirement. Resolution is forthcoming by use case analysis and activity modelling. Some examples of 'who' questions are:

- Who creates and modifies the order?
- Who is responsible for source input data?
- Who monitors the system?

Answers to this type of question ensure that new satellite systems must be created and analysed. For example, the answer to the question 'who monitors the system?' might lead us to deduce that a watchdog system (an instance of the PCS category) should be created. This system monitors all hardware in the current system.

What-kinds-of questions request refinement of some concept. Stakeholders do not usually state what kinds of concepts they work with; they tend to cluster specializations under a more generic and encompassing concept. Some examples of 'what-kinds-of' questions are:

- What kinds of order?
- What kinds of input data and output information?
- What kinds of 'Create user friendly input mechanisms'?

When questions have to do with the timing constraints on an event or action. Some examples of 'when' questions are:

- When is an order created?
- When does input data arrive at the system boundary?
- When is primary output information created?

Relationship questions ask how one requirement is related to another requirement. This discovery may then lead to new constraints between the requirements. For example, two requirements may have positive, negative or zero correlation. By negative correlation we mean that the realization of one requirement will probably ensure that the other requirement will not be realized. Other possible types of relationships between requirements are:

- Requirements overlap (Sommerville and Sawyer 1997)
- Order of requirements execution (for project management).

Some examples of 'relationship' questions are:

- What is the relationship between an order and a product?
- What is the relationship between requirement R1 and requirement R2?
- What is the relationship between the current system and its satellite systems?
- What is the relationship between system X and system Y?
- What is the relationship between artefact X and artefact Y?

What-if questions allow us to discover things that can go wrong in an activity, action or use case. Pursuing this type of question leads to insights into apparently unrelated system features. Some examples of 'what-if' questions are:

- What if the order is not processed on time?
- What if the core process is not performing as expected?
- What if we get 'risky' requirements from the analysts?

Follow-on questions originate from other pending questions. A special case is when one question generalizes another one. This has the advantage that we can accommodate initial stakeholder questions by subsuming them under more general questions. Some examples of 'follow-on' questions are now given. We group them so that you see the original question and then its follow-on equivalents:

- When is an order created?
- What is the lifecycle of an order?

- How to create an order?
- What are the actions to be taken on an order? (first follow-on)
- Describe the lifecycle of an order object (second follow-on)

- What is an order?
- Are you interested in modelling other entities besides orders?

- What is an order?
- Is the order a specialization or a generalization of some other concept?

There is no limit to the number of follow-on questions that you can conjure up. The answers will be invaluable.

A1.4.1 General applicability

The model in this chapter is very general and can be applied in many situations. For example, it can be used during the following phases of the software lifecycle:

- Business processing
- Requirements and Architectural modelling
- Analysis
- Design.

Furthermore, the generic question types can be applied to the entities and artefacts in each phase. For example, let us suppose that we are designing software for the Drink Vending Machine that is documented in Chapter 15 and let us focus on identifying the most volatile hardware, software and customer environments for this problem. To this end, we could pose the following questions and we focus on the specific details of the units that enable the machine:

- What is a coin unit?
- What kinds of coin unit?
- How to operate a coin unit?

- Lifecycle of a coin unit? (follow-on question)
- What is an enabling unit, for example a pin unit?
- What is the relationship between a pin unit and a coin unit?
- What if the coin unit is not functioning?
- How to repair a coin unit?
- What other kinds of enabling unit are there?
- Who is responsible for a coin unit?
- Who is responsible for an enabling unit?
- When is the coin unit used?

And so on. As you can see, the list of questions is infinite. These questions will keep your IT department going for years. Of course, many of the questions may be trivial so that answers to them are either obvious or easy to give.

A1.5 THE LEARNING LOOP

It is important to ask the right questions and this demands a lot of effort. Unfortunately, many people are better at talking than listening. Some people have the answer to the problem before the problem has been understood or posed.

When applying the techniques in the Inquiry Cycle model we should realize that experience and insight are gained incrementally. In particular, the different stakeholders must learn from interviews. To this end, we give a brief discussion of the Kolb 'learning loop' (see van der Heijden 1996). It is a never-ending loop and the main phases are shown in Figure A1.1. The loop starts at the top and is traversed in a clockwise direction. We discuss each phase.

- *Concrete experiences*: We learn from concrete experiences, for example our last software project.
- *Observation and reflection*: We reflect on our experiences. In particular, we tend to compare what we have made in relation to other software projects, for example. The end result of this reflection phase is the discovery and awareness of new patterns and trends in events that we did not see before. As stated by van der Heijden, reflection *'is related to our ability to differentiate between our existing mental model and perception of a different reality'*. Domain categories fit into this context because we compare each new system to be developed with other systems. We discussed this topic in Chapter 18.
- *Formation of abstract concepts and theories*: We develop new theories on how our ideas need to change as a result of observations and our own reflection. We integrate the old mental model with the new reality to form a new theory.
- *Testing the implications of the theory in the new situation*: We use the theories to plan new steps and develop new systems. We test the implications of our theory by taking actions in new situations.

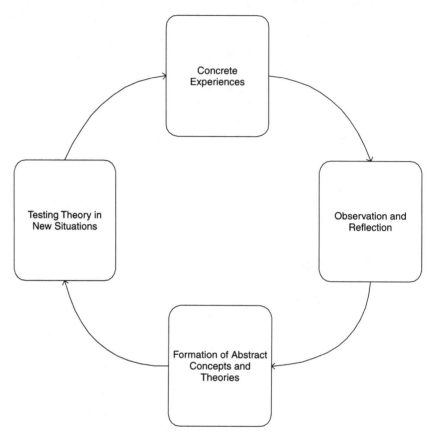

Figure A1.1   The Kolb 'learning loop'.

The added value of the Kolb model is that it describes how people improve at what they are doing by doing, thinking, integrating and testing. Then the loop begins again.

A1.6 SUMMARY AND CONCLUSIONS

We have introduced a number of techniques that help IT stakeholders gain insight into customer requirements and thus help them produce better requirements documentation and eventually software products. They might even help you to become a better requirements analyst. In particular, we presented a list of eight types of questions that can be applied again and again:

- What-is?
- How-to?

- Who?
- What-kinds-of?
- When?
- Relationship
- What-if?
- Follow-on.

The best way to learn how to apply these questions is to use them in real projects with real customers.

Appendix

2 The Presentation–Abstraction–Control (PAC) pattern

> *'Indeed, a culture always defines its pattern of events by referring to the names*
> *of the physical elements of space which are "standard" in that culture.'*
> Christopher Alexander, *The Timeless Way of Building*

A2.1 INTRODUCTION AND OBJECTIVES

In this appendix we introduce the Presentation–Abstraction–Control (PAC) pattern (POSA 1996, Bass *et al* 1998). This is a model that allows developers to decompose a hierarchical system into more specialized subsystems (or *agents* as they are sometimes called). Our main interest in PAC is that we use it to produce a stable architecture for our UML-based applications. The model is particularly useful during the analysis phase of the software lifecycle where classes and objects emerge as entities that realize system requirements and use cases. In fact, we consider the discovery and construction of a stable architecture to be a precondition for requirements and use case analysis. What we are saying is that use cases play a supporting role during analysis and design. The tactic in this book is to set up a strawman PAC model and then improve it using use cases. This is an iterative process in general. The PAC model forms the substrate on which we place the use cases, as it were.

It would seem that the PAC model is not so well known in mainstream UML software development. This is unfortunate because its use resolves a number of usability and maintainability problems that the author has encountered with traditional object-oriented projects.

The structure of this appendix is as follows: in Section A2.2 we give an introduction to the origins of the model and why we are using it. Section A2.3 discusses several strategies for actually decomposing a system into subsystems. This is important because we all agree that decomposition is a good thing but we must develop a repeatable process that tells us *how* to decompose an arbitrary system into loosely coupled subsystems. Section A2.4 discusses how we have applied PAC to document the structure of domain architectures and their instance systems. Numerous examples have been given in Parts II and III of the book. In Section A2.5 we note the relationship between PAC and UML, in particular how Boundary, Entity and Control classes are integrated into the PAC model. This is a vital section because it provides us with a framework on which to hang a number of UML artefacts (such as use cases and sequence diagrams, for example).

A2.2 MOTIVATION AND BACKGROUND

In this section we motivate why we use PAC and how it subsumes traditional OO thinking. We are not replacing object technology by a new paradigm but we augment it with some high-level paradigms and techniques. There is a severe lack of good and proven design models that we can use in mainstream object-oriented technology.

The PAC model was originally documented in Coutaz (1987) and subsequently elaborated in POSA (1996). It was invented for large, distributed interactive systems that consist of multiple cooperating *agents*. Agents specialized in human–computer interaction accept user input and display data. Other agents are responsible for the functionality in the system while others are concerned with error handling and communication with other systems and agents. There is a clear separation of concerns because each agent is specialized for a certain task. It is possible to support horizontal and vertical decomposition with the PAC model.

The reasons for applying the PAC model are described in POSA (1996):

- Agents often maintain their own state and data. However, they must be able to interoperate with other agents.
- Interactive agents must provide their own interface and their respective human–computer interactions may differ. Some users interact by means of a keyboard, while others may interact using a pointing device.
- Systems change over time and it is important that volatile elements are hidden from other agents. This requirement is another facet of the *Information Hiding* principle (David Parnas).

We must take the above forces into account when developing large systems.

An agent has three components in general:

- *Presentation [P] component*: provides the visible behaviour of the agents. This component is for both input and output.

- *Abstraction [A] component*: maintains the data model and has functionality for accessing this data.
- *Control [C] component*: connects the Presentation and Abstraction components. It is a kind of *mediator*. Agents communicate via their control components.

In this book we use a variation of PAC. In this case we use a layered pattern where C communicates with A, and A with P, but there is no link between P and C. This fact should be noted when reading this book because the examples will deploy this particular layering regime.

We mention that objects populate these components. Thus, changes in the object interface or class structure in a given layer should not adversely affect the stability of a layer. This is a good thing because classes and objects tend to change during the life of a software project. The following section attempts to explain why.

A2.2.1 A short history of objects

Classes have their origins in philosophy, logic and cognitive psychology (Eysenck and Keane 2000). In particular, the theory of concepts has been an important influence on the development of the object paradigm. There are a number of theories, one of which is the *defining-attribute view*. This view was developed and elaborated by the German logician Frege (Frege 1952). Frege maintained that a concept can be characterized by a set of defining attributes or semantic features. He distinguished between a concept's intension and extension. The *intension* of a concept consists of the set of attributes that determine what it is to be a member of the concept. This idea is similar to a class in class-based object-oriented languages. The *extension* of a concept is the set of entities that are members of the concept. This idea corresponds to class instances or objects. Some features of the defining-attribute view are:

- The meaning of a concept is captured by its defining attributes.
- Attributes are atomic building blocks for concepts.
- Attributes are necessary and sufficient for defining members of a concept.
- There is no doubt about whether an entity is in the concept; there are clear-cut boundaries between members and non-members of the concept.
- All members of the concept are equally representative of the concept; we cannot say that one member is more typical of the concept than another member.
- When concepts are organized in a hierarchy the defining attributes of the more specific concept (for example, a sparrow) include all the attributes of the super-ordinate concept (in this case, bird).

These features are implemented in many class-based object-oriented languages such as C++, Java and C#. Looking back in hindsight (which is always easy), the author concludes that these assumptions are too restrictive for certain classes of application. There are other object-oriented languages where there is no class concept. Instead, if we wish to create an object we must clone or copy it from an existing prototype object. The Self language is one example of a so-called classless object-oriented language.

A2.2.2 Subsuming object orientation in a broader context

Objects and classes are fine-grained structures in general. A large system may have hundreds or even thousands of classes (and be a cognitive nightmare at that!). Looking for these entities in the earliest stages of the software lifecycle will invariably lead to huge understandability and maintenance problems. Unfortunately, this mindset is still highly prevalent in the literature. It has been proved in other disciplines that controlling complexity should be a goal when embarking on new projects.

Our standpoint is that objects are useful during design but they are not so useful as a technique for helping us to decompose a *system* (and a system is not some kind of 'large' object) into loosely coupled subsystems.

A2.3 DECOMPOSITION STRATEGIES

A system is an entity having structure, behaviour and rules. Eventually, the systems that we discover will be mapped to, or realized by, entities such as objects, components and other data-holding modules with well-defined functionality.

Our approach uses both structural and functional decomposition. We speak about the even more generic term: problem decomposition. This book attacks the twin problems of structural decomposition and functional decomposition. We show *how* to carry out these activities; furthermore, we show how to integrate these two viewpoints. The same idea can be found in Jackson (2001) where Michael Jackson describes his problem frames in terms of frame concerns. A frame concern addresses both requirements and domain issues (see Appendix 3 for a discussion of frames and their relationships with domain architectures). The requirements are mapped to use cases while the domain description will be mapped to class diagrams and other artefacts in UML. Our aim is to discover the main systems in a given problem, the relationships between them and how systems are decomposed into smaller, more cohesive and loosely coupled subsystems. Before we address these issues we first of all enumerate some possible system configurations that crop up again and again when analysing large systems (see Figure A2.1):

- Hierarchical systems
- Collaborating systems

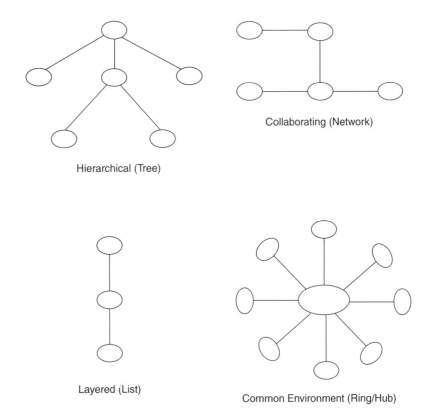

Figure A2.1 Common topologies.

- Common environment systems
- Layered systems
- Combinations of the above four topology types.

Figure A2.1 depicts some examples of such topologies. Each ellipse represents a system (which may itself be decomposed into other subsystems based on a given topology). The lines connecting the systems indicate that the systems are related to each other in some way. In the early phases of the software lifecycle it is sufficient to know that there is something going on between the systems although we are not sure yet what the exact relationship is.

How do we create or discover a topology for a problem? First of all, we start with a fundamental axiom:

Axiom 1: Each business process is realized by a system

This tactic is a good first shot for finding the main systems in the SUD (system under discussion). The core business processes will be mapped to 'key' systems while supporting and management processes will be mapped to 'satellite' systems.

A2.3.1 System decomposition and activity diagrams

We have already stated that each discovered process is mapped to a system. Whether the process is core, supporting or management is irrelevant at the moment. Since the processes depend on each other in some way, this implies that the corresponding systems also depend on each other, mainly due to the fact that one system is a client, server or collaborator system of another system. We already know that a given process is realized by activities. In a sense we can view the process as being partitioned into loosely coupled parts (in this case the activities). The main question that we pose is: can we use the activity diagrams as catalysts for subsystem discovery? In general, we try to discover the subsystems by letting them be the realizations of the major activities in the corresponding process.

There is no magic formula for transforming activity diagrams to subsystems. The quality of the end-result depends on the 'activity granularity', by which we mean the number of activities in the activity diagram (and to a lesser extent the amount of coupling between the activities). Of course, an activity diagram containing 40 activities is difficult to understand and to maintain, and this may be caused by the fact that there are too many low-level activities or that the activity diagram is modelling a large process. In the former case we could decide to merge some activities into bigger ones, and in the latter case we should have a critical look at the business processes in the system again. In general, we see that there is a many-to-many relationship between activities and subsystems. The ideal situation is to model each activity in an activity diagram by a single subsystem. In the case of domain architectures we propose the following axiom:

Axiom 2: Each activity in a process in a given domain architecture is mapped to a subsystem

This axiom has been verified in practical applications and is one of the cornerstones of our development process. Examples are given in Part II.

A2.3.2 System decomposition and context diagrams

In general, real problems have several core, supporting and management processes. Based on Axioms 1 and 2 we should then get a context diagram where each resulting system can be seen. This is shown by an example in Figure A2.2 where the enclosing system S consists of key systems S1, S2 and S3 and satellite systems S7 and S8. It is impossible to model this composite system in one go, so it is advisable to reduce the scale by examining one system at a time. For example, we could analyse the systems that have the highest customer importance or those systems that are the most difficult to realize (for example, because these are technically difficult or there are organizational or political impediments). For example, we could decide to model systems S1 and S2 first. In this case we would need to produce new context diagrams as shown in Figure A2.3 and the whole process would begin again! One

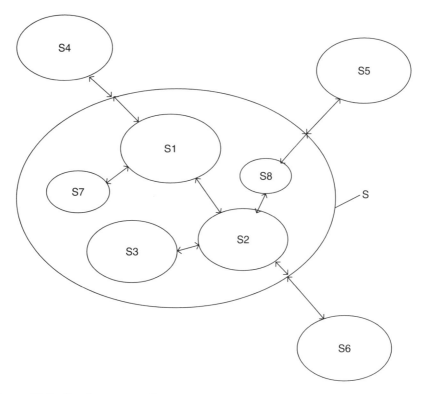

Figure A2.2 Scoping context diagram.

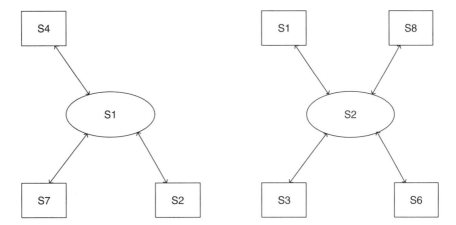

Figure A2.3 Reducing the scope.

of the advantages of this approach is that we can adopt a divide-and-conquer tactic: each system is modelled as a separate entity and is loosely coupled with other systems. It is also advantageous if the contracts and interfaces between the different systems are defined as early as possible.

A2.4 PAC AND OBJECT-ORIENTED ANALYSIS

We stated that systems were related to each other but nothing was said on how these relationships are realized. We now need to address a number of action points:

- A1: The internal structure of systems and subsystems
- A2: How systems actually communicate with each other
- A3: Structuring networks of systems
- A4: The mapping of systems to objects and components.

Action point A1 is concerned with how systems are populated by components. A component is any entity containing data and functionality. We shall see that three types of components populate each system when we use UML.

Action point A2 is concerned with the problem of how systems 'know' about each other and through which 'channels' they communicate. To this end, we introduce the notion of boundary components (or *receptionists* as they are called in Agha 1986). These are the only components in a system that are free to communicate with the outside world. See Figure A2.4 for an example. In Agha's Actor theory the set

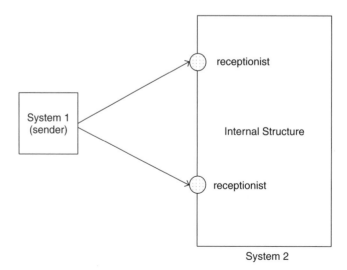

Figure A2.4 Motivating boundary components.

of receptionists may be constantly changing since real systems are dynamically evolving. However, a discussion of how this is realized is outside the scope of this book. If no receptionist is declared for a system then it cannot initially receive messages from external systems. In this book we shall use the term Boundary component instead of the term receptionist because of its acceptance in UML.

Action point A3 is concerned with the problem of configuring a system and its external stakeholder systems by introducing the Boundary components that glue them together. An example is shown in Figure A2.5 for the Manpower Control (MPC) system. MPC is the system under discussion and it communicates with its clients, collaborators and servers by means of Boundary components. This approach increases modularity and hides environmental details from MPC. This is why the Boundary components are sometimes called *environment-hiding components*: they accept messages from the outside world and translate them into internally recognizable data and commands. We can refine Figure A2.5 by realizing that MPC has three subsystems (remember that MPC is an instance of a MIS category). Here's the rub: can we align Boundary components B1 to B5 with a specific subsystem of MPC, thus increasing cohesion and promoting loose coupling? The answer is yes! This is because each subsystem has its own responsibilities and must interact with the external subsystems as well as the top-level MPC system. The refinement is shown in Figure A2.6. We describe Boundary components B1 to B4 as 'local' (because they operate at subsystem level) and these objects provide services to the current system. On the other hand, we place B5 at *top (highest-level mediator)* level and this is a 'global' component because it is in a sense the receptionist to MPC's

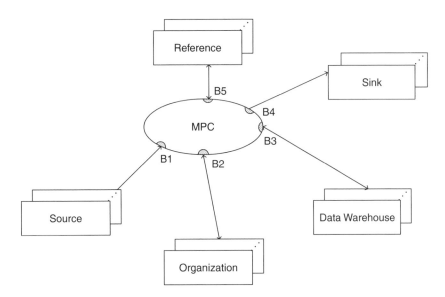

Figure A2.5   Revised context diagram.

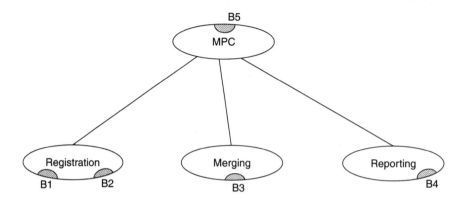

Figure A2.6 Cohesion and Boundary components.

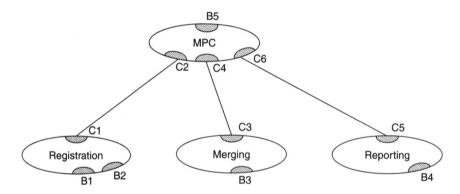

Figure A2.7 Including Control object.

client systems. Thus, the best place to put it is at the top level. This tactic promotes loose coupling. Action point A3 subsumes the problem of structuring the SUD in terms of its subsystems. Then we cannot use Boundary components because by definition they are communication objects with the external stakeholder systems. To this end, we introduce a new type of component specifically for this purpose. This is the class of Control components. An example is shown in Figure A2.7. We name these components by using numbers because we do not wish to start thinking about human-readable names, at least not just yet.

So what have we achieved? We have found how a system communicates with its internal and external systems. There is just one more component type (the so-called Entity components) to discover and then we are finished. We discuss Entity components in Section A2.4.1.

Finally, action point A4 is concerned with the problem of realizing Boundary, Control and Entity components using object-oriented and component-oriented

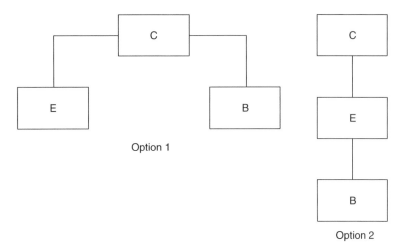

Option 1

Option 2

Figure A2.8 Structural relationships between Boundary, Control and Entity components.

techniques. This is the subject of object-oriented analysis (OOA) and component-oriented analysis (COA), respectively.

A2.4.1 Entity classes

Boundary and Control components have already been introduced. Now is the time to decide where the long-lived data in a system resides. Enter the Entity components! Once we have discovered and documented these components we can then safely conclude that a system's internal structure has been determined. The next problem is to define the structural relationships between the layers. There are two options as shown in Figure A2.8. Option 1 depicts the Control layer as a Mediator between the Entity and Boundary layers while Option 2 produces a strict layered regime. Option 1 has been found useful for interactive applications (for example, Web applications) while Option 2 is a common mini-architecture for process control and embedded applications.

Together, the Boundary, Control and Entity components are called Analysis classes in UML. They were originally used by Ivar Jacobson in his OOSE methodology but they also appear in the work of other researchers, for example at Carnegie Mellon University (Bass *et al* 1998) and the Presentation–Abstraction–Control (PAC) model (see POSA 1996).

A2.5 THE RELATIONSHIP BETWEEN PAC AND UML

Having discussed the three UML analysis classes we now move on to discussing how they are used in larger patterns. The idea behind PAC (see Losavio and Mattes

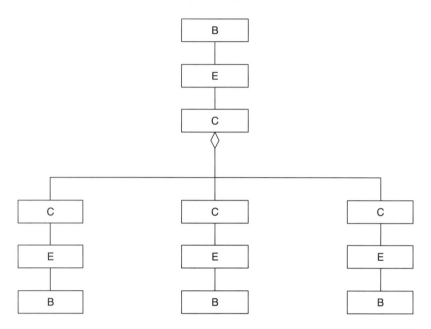

Figure A2.9   Generic class model for a domain architecture.

2000) is that a system can be hierarchically decomposed into a collection of so-called agents. Each agent has its own data and user interface and is able to communicate with both the outside world and other (internal) agents in the system. Thus, each agent has three components:

- Presentation (P): input/output from and to the outside world
- Abstraction (A): entities containing long-lived data of interest in the system
- Control (C): internal communicators with other agents.

We thus see that these three components are in principle the same as the Boundary–Entity–Control (BEC) components in UML. Which terms you should use depend on the context. However, I have not seen any guidelines in the UML literature on *how* to partition a system into BEC agents, while there is literature available on how to partition a system into PAC agents. By the way, the discussion on PAC in POSA (1996) adopts Option 1 in Figure A2.8 when defining the relationships between the agents' components. I sometimes favour Option 2 because many systems are layered, especially real-time (RT) systems.

How do we document a PAC model using UML notation? The answer is very easy to give. We assume for the moment that we are documenting instances of a domain architecture, for example the MPC application. In this case each agent is composed of three components and the relationships between them are described as

UML associations. The top-level agent plays the role of the Whole with respect to its subsystems and hence is modelled as a UML aggregation. This is documented in Figure A2.9 (strictly speaking, we should have described the associations using text, but we have not done this so as not to clutter the diagram).

A2.6 SUMMARY AND CONCLUSIONS

We have presented a medium-grained architectural pattern that forms the bridge between business modelling (in particular, business processes and activities) and UML artefacts. The original PAC model was motivated by the goals of modifiability and scalability. There is a clear separation between presentation and application and each PAC agent is decomposed into three components.

PAC is seen as the next-generation Model–View–Controller (MVC) model (see Bass *et al* 1998, POSA 1996). There is no reason why you *must* use this model as long as you don't end up with a graph of entangled objects. PAC, like all good patterns, lets you separate concerns. It is a means to an end.

Of course, there are many other models in circulation. We have chosen PAC because of its appealing properties for OO projects.

Appendix

3 Relationships with other models and methodologies

'For the Words are these; That all true Believers shall break their Eggs at the convenient End; and which is the convenient End, seems, in my humble Opinion, to be left to every Man's Conscience, or at least in the Power of the chief Magistrate to determine.'

Jonathan Swift

'Every good quality is noxious if unmixed.'

Ralph Waldo Emerson

A3.1 INTRODUCTION

Domain architectures are new because they are reference models that we apply and use in the early stages of the software lifecycle. To my knowledge, no one has come up yet with a set of reusable architectures for UML applications. The offerings are unfortunately a bit thin on the ground. We are interested in modelling the problem domain and we try to disregard design and implementation details in this book (at least, for the moment). Thus, we do not include discussions of the following design issues:

- The detailed structure of subsystems
- How data is created, accessed and stored in databases
- How systems and subsystems communicate
- Multi-threading and multi-tasking issues
- System design or detailed design (POSA 1996, GOF 1995).

We exclude these attention points in this book for two reasons. First, we are interested in defining a stable model that we can show to business users. In other words, we do our best to use the same vocabulary as our business customers. Second, there are a number of good books that do deal with the above design issues.

We now discuss several architectural and design styles that have influenced the current work.

A3.2 INFORMATION HIDING AND THE WORK OF DAVID PARNAS

It has been clear for some time that decomposing a system into subsystems is a good mechanism for improving the flexibility and comprehensibility of a system and shortening the development lifetime (Parnas 1972). Each subsystem forms a separate and independent entity or module. Taken together, the subsystems cooperate to fulfil the system requirements. Parnas introduced the term *modularization* and this corresponds to several partial specifications of a given problem. Of course, these partial specifications must be integrated to realize the responsibilities of the main system.

Some of the features and advantages of modules according to Parnas are:

1. A module can be written with little knowledge of the code in another module.
2. Modules can be reassembled and replaced without reassembly of the whole system.
3. On a management level, separate stakeholder groups work on each module with little need for communication.
4. Maintainability—it should be possible to make major changes in a module without needing a change in other modules.
5. Understandability—it should be possible to study one module at a time independently of the other modules.

Accepting the fact that decomposition is a good thing, we must determine what *criteria* to use when decomposing a system into modules. In other words, what is the driving force behind a system decomposition? To answer this question, a Key Word In Context (KWIC) reference case is examined (see Parnas 1972, Shaw and Garlan 1996 pages 33–39). The KWIC program accepts an ordered set of lines; each line consists of an ordered set of words and each word consists of an ordered set of characters. Parnas advocated a decomposition into modules where each module has knowledge of a design decision that it hides from other modules. Module interfaces or definitions are chosen to reveal as little as possible about the inner workings of the module.

Although Parnas discussed code-level modules in his article, the conclusions are valid for other artefacts. For example, in this book we decompose all kinds of artefacts into more specialized and more tangible ones. Typical examples are:

- Decompose a process into activities
- Decompose a system into subsystems

- Decompose a subsystem into layers of objects
- Decompose a requirement into sub-requirements.

In fact, we can decompose the structural, functional and behavioural artefacts from Chapter 3 in this way and we use the Inquiry Cycle model (Appendix 1) to ask the right questions.

As in Parnas's original paper, the Datasim Development Process has the main advantage that the whole system can be well designed *because* all involved stakeholders understand it. On the other hand, traditional object-oriented class diagrams can be very difficult to understand because they contain many classes and many relationships between them. For example, the Elevator Control System (ECS) case in Yourdon and Argila (1996) has an initial list of about 90 candidate classes! There is no clustering or levelling in this approach, with the result that it is difficult to understand the structure of the system. We show in Part III how to construct class diagrams based on a decent decomposition of the ECS system. Each subsystem hides details from other subsystems, thus making it easier to look at each subsystem separately.

A3.3 THE RUMMLER–BRACHE APPROACH

The Rummler–Brache approach is a method for analysing and documenting the main business processes in a system or organization (see Rummler and Brache 1995). In contrast to traditional functional unit level processes (typically, processes at department level) the authors are concerned with how work gets done in an organization. Furthermore, Rummler and Brache view an organization as an organism that collaborates and communicates with its environment. The relationships are shown in a so-called *super-system map* (this is the business person's terminology for what IT folk call the context diagram).

We take our initial definition of business process from Sharp and McDermott (2001):

A business process is a collection of work tasks, initiated in response to an event, that achieves a specific result for the customer.

The end result of a process might be a physical product or service. It could also be some piece of information. The result is in all cases a deliverable that some customer sees as being valuable. A customer could even be some other process in a network of processes! Thus, a process clearly indicates a result or end state. The customer is the entity that benefits from the process's output. The customer may be internal to the current organization or could be some unit external to it. In this book we model the process as a collection of activities (also known as steps or tasks). A single person or actor usually executes an activity; in some cases several actors could execute it. The activities are interrelated in the sense that they have compatible inputs and outputs. These activities are interdependent. Finally, each process is triggered by some event in the system. Thus, the process is 'inactive' if no triggering event takes place. In a sense we see the event and the process's products as bounding the process. We distinguish between those processes whose deliverables are visible to external customers and those that are not visible to external customers. The main types are:

- Core processes
- Supporting processes
- Management processes.

This classification is based on Rummler and Brache (1995) and has major consequences for the way we view systems and system development. It helps the separation of concerns, keeps us focused on the essential issues and provides a basis for analysis using UML. A core process is one whose deliverables are visible to external customers and it usually spans the whole organization because several functional units are involved in its execution. A supporting process is similar to a core process but its deliverables are for the benefit of internal functional units and customers. Thus, the deliverables are not visible to external customers; however, supporting processes are essential for effective management. Finally, management processes provide support for core or support processes. They do not provide deliverables as such but they are the 'enablers' for other processes.

The two elements, namely business processes and the super-system map, form the starting point for the Architecture Discovery (AD). In particular, the super-system map is the forerunner of the context diagram that defines the boundaries of a system and its relationship with its neighbouring systems. Furthermore, core processes are mapped to 'key' systems while supporting and management processes are mapped to collaborating systems. *In short, the business processes drive the architectural discovery and decomposition activities.* Compare this to current object-oriented thinking; there is no equivalent in the author's opinion.

Summarizing, business processes and the super-system map are essential input to our software process. We have seen in the past that attempting an object-oriented analysis can lead to less than optimal results (see Coleman *et al* 1994, Duffy 1995, where we examined the Petrol Station problem; both solutions adopt an object-centred approach, although in Duffy 1995 there is an attempt to decompose the problem into two loosely coupled subsystems that are populated by objects).

An excellent introduction to process and workflow modelling for software systems is given in Sharp and McDermott (2001). The book contains many examples of how to model systems using process maps (similar to UML activity diagrams) and it also contains a chapter on how to implement processes and process maps using use cases. The assumption here is that use cases are more specific than the corresponding process maps that they describe.

A3.4 MICHAEL JACKSON'S PROBLEM FRAMES

Michael Jackson has introduced the idea of a problem frame in his excellent book (see Jackson 2001). A problem frame is defined as

... a kind of pattern. It defines an intuitively identifiable problem class in terms of its context and the characteristics of its domains, interfaces and requirements.

Some of the reasons why we are interested in problem frames in the present book are:

- They provide us with ideas on how to document domain architectures.
- They are based on a small set of very generic concepts.
- They provide reference models for classes of applications.

In general terms, we say that the concern of a problem frame captures the fundamental criteria of successful analysis for problems that fit that frame. Quoting Jackson, the frame 'specifies what descriptions are needed, and how they must fit together to give a convincing argument that the problem has been fully understood and analysed'. Jackson has identified five basic reusable frames and these can be considered as being instances of a problem frame model. The five forms are:

- *Required behaviour*: some part of the physical world whose behaviour must be controlled until some conditions are satisfied. An example of such a system is a Home Heating System (see Chapter 12).
- *Commanded behaviour*: the physical world is controlled by the actions of an operator. An example is the sluice gate problem (Jackson 2001); this problem is a model of a simple irrigation system.
- *Information display*: systems where we need constant information about the real world. The information must be presented in the required place in the required form. An example is a one-way traffic light system.
- *Simple workpiece*: a tool to allow users to control and edit text or graphics objects on a screen. The objects can subsequently be copied, printed or transformed in some way. An example is a CAD (Computer Aided Design) application.
- *Transformation*: computer-readable input files whose data must be transformed to give certain required output files. The output data must be in a particular format. An example of such a frame is any management information system, for example the MPC system that we analyse in Part III of this book.

These five basic frame types can be seen as special subcategories of the domain architectures because the latter are more general, in structure, functionality and behaviour. For example, we propose the following generalization/specialization relationships:

- Required behaviour is a subcategory of PCS (Process Control).
- Commanded behaviour is a subcategory of ACS (Access Control).
- Information display is a subcategory of MIS (Management Information).
- Simple workpiece is a subcategory of RAT (Resource Allocation and Tracking).
- Transformation is a subcategory of MAN (Manufacturing).

We see that (at face value at least) there is a one-to-one correspondence between the basic frame types and our five domain architecture types. It is possible to compose domain architectures into large assemblies such as Lifecycle Models (LCM) and even multi-LCM models. These models are discussed in Parts II and III of this book. In a similar vein, Jackson (2001) discusses his composite frames and in general advocates decomposing a problem into simple subproblems that *fit* recognized simple frames. Each subproblem has both its own frame concerns as well as fresh composition concerns that merge because of the fact that the subproblems must interface with each other.

Jackson (2001) has some remarks and conclusions on the usefulness (or otherwise) of problem frames and how we should use them. The same conclusions could also hold for domain architectures:

- Problem frames are a way of classifying software development problems.
- They provide a structure for capturing your growing experience and knowledge.
- They help you anticipate the concerns that you must eventually address and put them into context.
- They provide a guide to problem decomposition.

Finally, we can say something about the granularity of a problem frame; it is bigger than that of a class or a GOF design pattern (see GOF 1995) but smaller than any realistic problem. However, a problem frame is big enough to represent a significant portion of the whole problem.

Moving to domain architectures, we shall see that each one can be instantiated to produce a non-trivial system as the chapters in Part III show. Furthermore, the 'concerns' of a domain architecture are documented in a standard manner. As with problem frames, these concerns show what needs to be done in a given situation.

A3.5 THE HATLEY–PIRBHAI METHOD

This was a popular method for analysing real-time systems in the 1990s but its use has diminished somewhat in the last few years. This is a multi-perspective approach that combines data flow decomposition with model components constructed in control- and information-space (see Hatley and Pirbhai 1988). The authors take a hierarchical and iterative view of systems development. In particular, they capture system requirements by viewing a system from three major perspectives:

- The process (functional) model
- The control (state) model
- The information (data) model.

The Data Flow Diagram (DFD) is the primary tool for depicting functional requirements in the Hatley–Pirbhai method. It partitions the requirement into component processes or functions. These functions are connected by data flows to form a network.

The second view is called the control model and describes the circumstances under which the processes from the process model are performed. The control model examines the events in a system and is documented using finite state (FS) machines. Finally, information modelling is the third perspective and is not documented in Hatley and Pirbhai (1988).

We have been influenced by the Hatley–Pirbhai approach in a number of ways. First, it discusses the so-called context process consisting of a single process, terminators (entities outside the context of the system) and data flows. Second, the main process is decomposed or levelled into subprocesses, thus promoting separation of concerns. Summarizing, the usefulness of this method for us is the realization that the context diagrams, data flow and architecture are important when analysing systems.

A3.6 THE GARLAN AND SHAW ARCHITECTURAL STYLES

An architectural style (or idiom or pattern) is a description of an architecture of a specific system as a collection of computational components together with a description of the interactions among these components, the so-called connectors (see Shaw and Garlan 1996). Examples of components are databases, layers, filters and clients. Examples of connectors are procedure calls, event broadcasts and database protocols. Shaw and Garlan propose several common architectural styles:

- *Dataflow systems*: for example, batch sequential, pipes and filters
- *Call-and-return systems*: object-oriented systems, hierarchical layers, main program and subroutine
- *Data-centred systems* (*repositories*): databases, hypertext systems, blackboards
- *Independent components*: communicating processes, event systems
- *Virtual machines*: interpreters, rule-based systems.

These styles are in fact reference models that we apply in the detailed design stage of the software lifecycle. They are discussed in some detail in Shaw and Garlan (1996) and a more detailed account of a number of these styles can be found in POSA (1996) where they are documented in handbook form.

There is little overlap between our domain architectures and architectural styles because the former are mainly concerned with the problem domain (the 'what') while the latter is mainly concerned with the solution domain (the 'how'). It is of course very interesting to discuss how to transform a domain architecture (or an instance thereof) to an architectural style and what the criteria are for such a transformation, but such an endeavour is outside the scope of this book.

A3.7 SYSTEM AND DESIGN PATTERNS

We position the famous system and design patterns of GOF and POSA (see POSA 1996, GOF 1995). The patterns in POSA are concerned mainly with large-scale system design while the GOF patterns are more finely grained and are concerned with class-level patterns. For example, POSA describes how to design large systems in terms of large-grained patterns such as:

- Presentation–Abstraction–Control (PAC)
- Layers
- Blackboard
- Model–View–Controller
- Pipes and Filters
- Microkernel
- Proxy
- Publisher–Subscriber.

The GOF patterns are concerned with the lifecycle of software objects (recall that objects are instances of classes) and the patterns can be clustered into three categories (including *some* specific patterns):

- Creational patterns: flexible ways of creating objects
  — Abstract Factory (creating instances from a class hierarchy)
  — Factory method (creating instances of a given class)
  — Prototype (creating objects as 'clones' of some typical object).
- Structural patterns: defining relationships between objects
  — Composite: recursive aggregates and tree structures
  — Proxy: indirect access to a resource via a 'go-between' object
  — Bridge: separate a class from its various implementations
  — Façade: create a unified interface to a logical grouping of objects
  — Adapter: convert the interface of one class into that of another class.

- Behavioural: how objects send messages to each other
  — Visitor: extend the functionality of a class hierarchy (non-intrusively)
  — State: implement a Harel statechart (see Rumbaugh 1999)
  — Strategy: create flexible, interchangeable algorithms for object methods
  — Observer: define synchronizing procedures between objects
  — Mediator: define a single communication 'hub' in a star of objects
  — Command: encapsulate a function as an object.

It is important to describe the relationship between domain architectures and the other approaches to software development.

We remark that the GOF patterns can be viewed as a special case of a Lifecycle Model (LCM) because we are interested in object lifetime; the main phases are the creation of an object in memory (MAN), placing the object in some structure (RAT) and then monitoring how the object interacts with other objects (MIS). We discuss the lifecycle category topic in Part II.

A3.8 THE UNIFIED MODELLING LANGUAGE (UML)

UML is a *de facto* standard for documenting object-oriented systems and can be used in all phases of the software lifecycle. Without a common standard it would be very difficult to communicate with developers. We assume that the reader has knowledge of UML syntax, in particular the following:

- Class diagrams that use generalization, association and aggregation relationships
- Interaction diagrams (sequence and collaboration diagrams)
- Statecharts (originally due to David Harel)
- Use cases (whatever version!).

We show how to integrate these artefacts into our software process in Chapter 4.

A3.9 VIEWPOINT-BASED REQUIREMENTS ENGINEERING

Although this book is primarily about architecture, we have found it necessary to devote some attention to the behavioural aspects of a system; in this case we discuss how system requirements (both functional and non-functional) are captured, documented and mapped to UML. Of course, we cannot escape use cases because they have become so popular as a mechanism and medium for discussing and documenting system behaviour. In spite of their perceived benefits, we claim that they are not suitable for describing large system behaviour. At the risk of initiating an anti-use case campaign, we note some of the major shortcomings that we have seen during recent years:

- There is no precise definition of a use case in the literature.
- A use case is a specific interaction sequence with the system, not a general requirement; a use case is *not* a requirement.
- Use cases describe functional requirements only.
- Use cases tend to be closely aligned with objects and classes.
- Business users do not understand use cases; these people are more at home with business processes and activity modelling.
- Technically oriented developers usually create use cases; their jargon is not necessarily that of the customer, an unfortunate state of affairs if it happens in your project.

Notwithstanding their shortcomings, use cases do have their place in the behavioural value chain but then during the later stages of the software development lifecycle. In order to align them with business thinking we adopt an approach that stems from the computer science community (see Somerville and Sawyer 1997). To this end, we introduce a number of new concepts that are not (yet) in the official UML standard:

- Business concerns
- Viewpoints and stakeholders
- Requirements.

A business concern is an abstract high-level goal that must be satisfied if the system is to make a contribution to the organization that is *paying* for it. In other words, the system must contribute to the key concerns of the business. We make these concerns explicit. This avoids misunderstanding between sponsors and developers. Examples of business concerns are customer service, system reliability and cost (by the way, how do you create a use case for cost?). A stakeholder is any human or non-human entity that is directly or indirectly involved with, or receives some benefit from, the system. A viewpoint is a difficult concept when met for the first time. It can be defined as an expectation of system behaviour as perceived by some stakeholder group. As such, a viewpoint is a partial system specification. For example, in a safety-critical system, reliability is the viewpoint taken by the law, safety regulators and other organizations. It must be stressed that a business concern is not the same as a viewpoint.

A requirement is a statement of what system behaviour should be without specifying how to realize that behaviour. Some other complementary definitions are:

- Capability that the system must deliver
- Capability needed by the user to solve a problem in order to achieve an objective

- Capability that must be met or possessed by a system to satisfy a contract, standard, specification or other formally imposed documentation.

Finally, a use case is a description of an interaction between the system and its stakeholders. It can be seen as the realization of a requirement.

In general, the chain Business Concern $\rightarrow$ Viewpoint $\rightarrow$ Requirement $\rightarrow$ Use Case is our way of mapping high-level system behaviour to more familiar and more specific use cases.

4 The 'Hello World' example: the Simple Digital Watch (SDW)

'What we have to learn, we learn by doing.'

Aristotle

A4.1 INTRODUCTION

We examine a very simple test case in this appendix to show how the Datasim Development Process works, what the artefacts are and how they are documented. The other examples in this book (in Parts II and III) are similar; they just contain more detailed information and they take longer to read and understand than the problem here.

The source code for this problem (C++ and COM versions) can be found on the Datasim website www.datasim.nl.

We recommend that the reader browse through the sections in this appendix in order to get a first impression of our approach to software development and how it subsumes traditional object-oriented analysis approach. We discover the objects and classes late in the game.

We defend why we see SDW as an instance system of MIS in Chapter 18.

A4.2 FEATURES AND DESCRIPTION OF PROBLEM

The problem is easy to understand and is well known in the literature (see Rumbaugh *et al* 1991 where it was used as an example to show how statecharts work). The description of the problem goes as follows:

SDW accepts pulses (one pulse every second). The pulses are buffered until the number of pulses reaches 60. Then the current time (in hours and minutes) is (re)calculated and the new time is displayed on an output panel. SDW can be configured on a 12-hour or 24-hour time regime. The SDW contains a panel consisting of two buttons for setting the time.

This is the kind of description that you see in marketing brochures as Customer Requirements Specifications (CRS). The requirements analyst must now map this to a form that can be used by UML analysts.

A4.3 GOALS AND PROCESSES

The main goal is to provide a service to the stakeholders who are the major clients of the SDW system (somewhere inside SDW we will create a Watch class that ticks away and displays the correct time every minute). The main processes are:

- Core process: Display time as needed
- Supporting process: Set time.

The core process is the most important one, of course; you buy a watch not to set the time but to be informed of what the time is!

The top-level activity diagrams for these processes are shown in Figures A4.1 and A4.2, respectively. It is clear what the input to and output from each process is. The expanded activity diagram for the core process is shown in Figure A4.3. We identify three main activities:

- Registration: collect pulses and carry on incrementing until a minute has gone by
- Merging: add a new minute to the current time; current time is updated
- Reporting: display new current time on a suitable medium.

Thus, we see that the three activities cooperate in order to realize the core process.

Figure A4.1   Core process in SDW.

Figure A4.2   Supporting process in SDW.

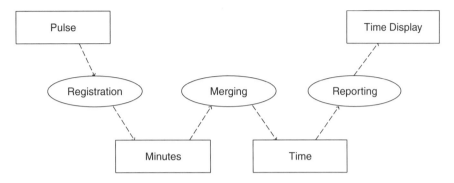

Figure A4.3 Activity diagram for core process.

A4.4 STAKEHOLDERS, VIEWPOINTS AND REQUIREMENTS

The main stakeholder is the person (usually the owner) who wishes to use the services of SDW. In this case it should be possible to read the time (usually on some kind of LED) and there must also be some means by which the owner can set a new time. There are other possible stakeholders, of course; for example, the system that is the source of pulses is a stakeholder. We concentrate on the owner stakeholder in this appendix.

The main viewpoints (ISO 9126 characteristics and sub-characteristics) taken by the owner are:

- Accuracy: the displayed time should produce the desired results and effect
- Usability: the system should be easy to operate and to understand
- Reliability: fault-tolerance. The mean-time-to-failure (MTTF) should be quantified.

These viewpoints will determine what the requirements and use cases will be.

A4.5 CONTEXT DIAGRAM AND SYSTEM DECOMPOSITION

The context diagram is shown in Figure A4.4. There are five stakeholder systems:

- SDW: the system that we are modelling (the 'SUD')
- Pulse Source: the system where pulses come from (one per second)
- Menu: the system that allows the owner to set and change the time
- Data Warehouse: the system that 'stores' the current time in the form <hours>:: <minutes>
- LED: the systems that display the current time in the appropriate format.

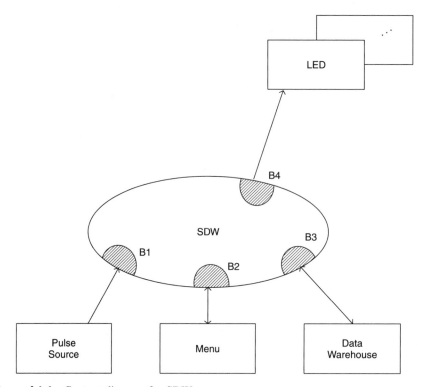

Figure A4.4   Context diagram for SDW.

It is possible to document the information and event flow between SDW and its external stakeholder systems by using system-level sequence diagrams or even collaboration diagrams (Rumbaugh 1999).

In keeping with the approach in this book we decompose SDW into three subsystems as shown in Figure A4.5. Subsystem 'Registration' is responsible for producing minutes, 'Merging' produces time and 'Reporting' displays the time.

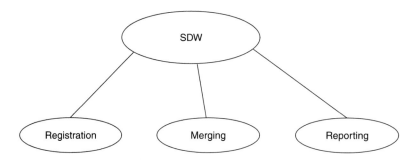

Figure A4.5   System decomposition in SDW.

A4.6 USE CASES

The main use cases correspond to the core and supporting processes in this problem. Recall that the core processes are:

- Core process: Display time as needed
- Supporting process: Set time.

The use cases corresponding to these processes are:

- U1: Update watch in continuous mode
- U2: Set a new time.

We document U1 according to the standard use case template.

Use case name and ID: Display time as needed, U1.
Actors involved: All external systems except Menu.
Precondition: SDW is in operational mode and is accepting pulses.
Description: Pulses enter the system. When the number of pulses reaches 60 (this means that a minute has elapsed) a new time is calculated based on a 12-hour or 24-hour clock. Then the time is displayed on the LED.
Exceptions:
— Pulses arrive out of synchronization (drift)
— Pulse source breaks down
— LED breaks down.
Postcondition: SDW has been updated and new value displayed. Waiting for next bout of pulses.

In general, we map each use case to one or more sequence diagrams where we discover objects and messages. These objects help to build up the class architecture that we discuss in Section A4.7.

A4.7 UML CLASSES

We advocate loose external coupling and strong internal cohesion and to this end we see the Presentation–Abstraction–Control (PAC) pattern as a viable model for object-oriented systems. The initial model is shown in Figure A4.6 where each subsystem in Figure A4.5 has been fine-tuned in order to tell us how its responsibility is realized.

A4.8 STATECHARTS

In principle, each object in the analysis can have a statechart. We take one example, namely the Watch that is the Entity object in the Merging subsystem in Figure A4.6.

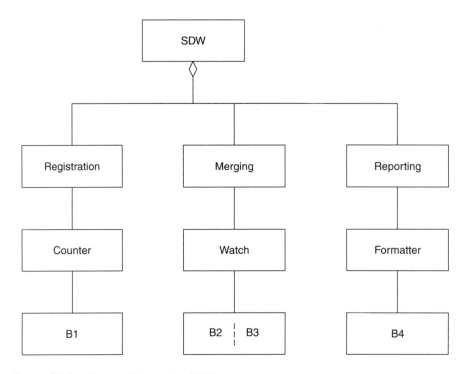

Figure A4.6 Class architecture in SDW.

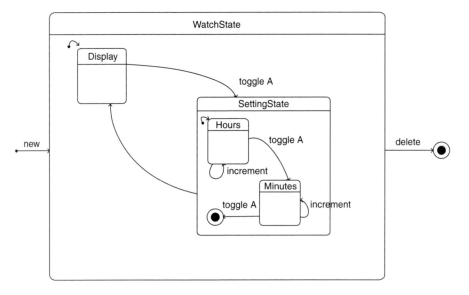

Figure A4.7 Statechart for Watch Entity Object.

Its input and output methods have been found from the corresponding use cases and sequence:

- Method `toggle`: switch modes (for example, from `Display` to `SetHours` and so on)
- Method `increment`: increment hours or minutes (depending on mode)
- Output method `notify(time)`: notify other objects that a new time has been calculated.

The corresponding statechart is shown in Figure A4.7.

Appendix

5 Using domain architectures: seven good habits

We have written this appendix in order to give the reader some tips and guidelines on using and applying domain architectures. There are a number of similarities between the way we document domain architectures and the way that the authors of design patterns (see, for example, GOF 1995) present their work. In fact, GOF's book was the motivator for the structure of the chapters in Parts II and III of this book.

We adapt the guidelines in Vlissides 1996 (which uses the steps in Covey 1994) to understand, learn and apply domain architectures to real-life projects.

Habit 1: Taking time to reflect

It is important to take time off to reflect on what you have done, to distance yourself from your work and to examine it from a different perspective. How often do we see programmers hacking a solution only to realize that the solution is incorrect or sub-optimal? Instead, we should take time off to reflect on our progress. Some tips are:

- Jot down your experiences; you can incorporate them into your pattern documentation later.
- Your experience accumulates if you document your experiences.
- Look at as many systems as you can, for example systems designed by other people.
- Be on the lookout for novel design solutions.

Habit 2: Adhering to a structure

This book documents domain architectures in a structured and consistent way. Our approach describes large-grained systems as opposed to the GOF patterns that are fine-grained and describe class-level interactions. It is interesting to note that the patterns movement was influenced by the work of Christopher Alexander (see Alexander *et al* 1977, Alexander 1979), an architect and founder of the patterns movement. The analogies between architectural structures, the relationships between these structures and the events that take place in them may have been the catalyst to the software patterns movement.

Some tips and observations are:

- We need to decide what structure to use when documenting or categorizing.
- Consistent structure leads uniformly to patterns and categories.
- Less structure means more prose (not acceptable for comparison and reference purposes).

Habit 3: Being concrete early

It is always a good idea to give a concrete example when introducing a new theory or concept. Mathematicians do it all the time. *They constantly switch between the instance and meta levels.* Many articles and chapters in mathematics books have the following structure:

- Definition of some new concepts
- Examples of the concepts
- Lemmas (preparatory results relating to new concepts)
- Propositions and theorems concerning the concepts
- Corollaries ('spin-off' conclusions based on theorems)
- Exercises.

In this book we give numerous concrete examples of domain architectures; in general we give two examples of each one. The advantage of providing examples is that they give the reader a frame of reference for the general problem and its solution. Some tips and remarks are:

- Use lots of examples and counter-examples.
- Be concrete even when you are being abstract.
- Even the most abstract sections may contain examples.
- Be honest: don't forget the potential pitfalls of the categories.

It is important to realize that the categories in this book cannot solve all problems. Some readers may have problems that do not fit seamlessly into the models. There may be several reasons for this, one of which is that the reader's current problem is an instance of some new category that is not in our basic repertoire of architectural types. For example, we have no reference model for decision-support systems or similar problems in Artificial Intelligence (AI) or sub-disciplines thereof.

Habit 4: Keeping patterns distinct and complementary

It is important to distinguish between the different domain categories. If the categories look the same then it will be very confusing. The most important and fundamental classifier or 'separator' for a domain category is the type of information that it produces. The reader can use the following *initial separation mechanisms* to classify applications:

- MIS: produce decision-support information from transaction data.
- MAN: create products and services from raw materials.
- RAT: track requests in time and space.
- PCS: satisfy certain conditions at all times.
- ACS: provide authorized subjects with access to objects/resources.
- LCM: track an entity from its birth to its demise.

These one-liners could be seen as the equivalents of the Intents section in GOF (1995). This section describes the reasons for existence of the pattern or category. Some final remarks are:

- Categories should not overlap (either in scope or in purpose).
- Categories are orthogonal and work synergistically.
- Don't worry if two categories have similar context diagrams and architecture.

Habit 5: Presenting effectively

The quality of your categories is determined by how well you present them. We must take typesetting, layout and writing style into consideration. Categories are complicated enough to deserve a decent presentation. Some hints are:

- The best way to learn is to have a go at writing.
- Break up long sentences and paragraphs.
- Use everyday words and make your story sound natural.

One of the greatest challenges for any author is describing and documenting domain categories in a way that is accessible to others.

Habit 6: Iterating tirelessly

You never get it right first time. Or the second time. The chances are better that you get it right on the third attempt. According to John Vlissides (1996) you won't even get it right the first ten times. This is just another form of continuous improvement or *Kaizen* (see Imai 1986). Some remarks are in order:

- Pattern writing is an on-going and iterative process.
- Patterns do not exist in isolation; they affect one another.

Habit 7: Collecting and incorporating feedback

Finally, 'the proof of the pudding is in the eating'. Categories and patterns are written for others to use and to apply in their own applications. To this end, it is important to monitor how others tackle the problem of applying the categories to real-life situations. In the present author's experience the most difficult activities for our students and customers seem to revolve around the following common themes:

- What is the core process? (There may be more than one!)
- What is the scope and span of the problem?
- Can I explain the essence of the problem without getting bogged down in low-level and irrelevant details?

Programmers and developers tend to be solution-oriented and tend to think and talk in terms of the solution to a problem rather than the problem itself. This can be very confusing (and annoying!) for customers. What we advise is: when you are talking to the customer concentrate on his particular problem and avoid IT jargon as much as possible.

We conclude with some remarks:

- Be prepared for feedback; even negative feedback can represent new requirements and suggestions for improvement!
- Not everyone needs to be a pattern or category writer.
- There will be many more category users than writers.

References

Agha, G. (1986) *Actors: a Model of Concurrent Computation in Distributed Systems*. MIT Press, Cambridge, MA.

Aho, A. V. and Ullman, J. D. (1977) *Principles of Compiler Design*. Addison-Wesley, Reading, MA.

Alexander, C. (1979) *The Timeless Way of Building*. Oxford University Press, New York.

Alexander, C., Ishikawa, S. and Silverstein, M. (1977) *A Pattern Language*. Oxford University Press, New York.

Bass, L., Clemens, P. and Kazman, R. (1998) *Software Architecture in Practice*. Addison-Wesley, Reading, MA.

Bogan, C. E. and English, M. J. (1994) *Benchmarking for Best Practices*. McGraw-Hill, New York.

Booch, G. (1991) *Object-Oriented Design with Applications*. Benjamin Cummings, Redwood City, CA.

Booch, G. (1996) *Object Solutions: Managing the Object-Oriented Project*. Addison-Wesley, Reading, MA.

Buschmann, F. *et al.* (1996): see POSA.

Cohen, L. (1995) *Quality Function Deployment*. Addison-Wesley, Reading, MA.

Coleman, D., Arnold, P., Bodoff, S., Dollin, C. and Gilchrist, H. (1994) *Object-Oriented Development: The Fusion Method*. Prentice-Hall, Englewood Cliffs, NJ.

Coutaz, J. (1987) PAC, an object-oriented model for dialog design. In Bulinger, H. J. and Shackel, B. (eds), *Human–Computer Interaction—INTERACT '87 Conference Proceedings*, Stuttgart, pp. 431–436. Elsevier Science Publishers, North-Holland, Amsterdam.

Covey, S. (1994) *Seven Habits of Highly Successful People*. Simon and Schuster, London.

Cox, D. R. (1974) *Queues*. Chapman and Hall, London.

De Bono, E. (1976) *Teaching Thinking*. Penguin, London.

DEC (1988) *Digital Equipment Corporation Guide to VMS System Security*. Order no. AA-LA40A-TE.

Douglass, B. (1998) *Real-Time UML*. Addison-Wesley, Reading, MA.

Dowd, K. (1998) *Beyond Value at Risk*. John Wiley & Sons, Chichester.

Duffy, D. (1995) *From Chaos to Classes: Software Development in C++*. McGraw-Hill, London.

Eysenck, M. W. and Keane, M. T. (2000) *Cognitive Psychology*. Psychology Press, Hove.

Fowler, M. *et al.* (2003) *Patterns of Enterprise Application Architecture*. Addison-Wesley, Boston, MA.

Frege, G. (1952) On sense and reference. In Geach, P. and Black, M. (eds), *Translations from the Philosophical Writings of Gottlieb Frege*. Basil Blackwell, Oxford.

Gamma, E. *et al.* (1995): see GOF.

Garrido, J. M. (1998) *Practical Process Simulation.* Artech House, Boston, MA.

Gattorna, J. L. and Walters, D. W. (1996) *Managing the Supply Chain.* Macmillan, Basingstoke.

GOF (1995): Gamma, E., Helm, R., Johnson, R. and Vlissides, J. J., *Design Patterns: Elements of Reusable Object-Oriented Software.* Addison-Wesley, Reading, MA.

Gross, R. and McIlveen, R. (1995) *Cognitive Psychology.* Hodder and Stoughton, London.

Hall, R. P. (1989) Computational approaches to analogical reasoning: a comparative analysis. *Artificial Intelligence* **39**(1) 39–120.

Harel, D. and Politi, M. (2000) *Modeling Reactive Systems with Statecharts.* McGraw-Hill, New York.

Hatley, D. J. and Pirbhai, I. M. (1988) *Strategies for Real-Time System Specification.* Dorset House, New York.

Haug, E. (1998) *The Complete Guide to Option Pricing Formulas.* McGraw-Hill, New York.

Hecht-Nielson, R. (1990) *Neurocomputing.* Addison-Wesley, Reading, MA.

Hitomi, K. (1996) *Manufacturing Systems Engineering.* Taylor and Francis, London.

Hull, J. (1993) *Options, Futures and Other Derivative Securities.* Prentice-Hall, Englewood Cliffs, NJ.

Imai, M. (1986) *Kaizen: The Key to Japan's Competitive Success.* McGraw-Hill, New York.

Jackson, M. (2001) *Problem Frames.* Addison-Wesley, Reading, MA.

Jacobson, I., Christenson, M., Jonsson, P. and Övergard, G. (1993) *Object-Oriented Software Engineering.* Addison-Wesley, Wokingham.

Jacobson, I., Booch, G. and Rumbaugh, J. (1999) *The Unified Software Development Process.* Addison-Wesley, Reading, MA.

Jarrow, R. and Turnbull, S. (1996) *Derivative Securities.* South-Western College Publishing, Cincinnati, OH.

Joshi, B. D., Aref, W. G., Ghafoor, A. and Spafford, E. H. (2001) Security models for Web-based applications. *Communications of the ACM* **44**(2) 38–44.

Kinsler, L. E., Frey, A. R., Coppins, A. B. and Saunders, J. V. (1982) *Fundamentals of Acoustics* (3rd edn). John Wiley & Sons, New York.

Kitchenham, B. and Pfleeger, S. L. (1996) Software quality: the elusive target. *IEEE Software* **13**(1) 12–21.

Kruchten, P. (1999) *The Rational Unified Process: an Introduction.* Addison-Wesley, Reading, MA.

Lee, V. and Pranja, D. G. (1995) *Children's Cognitive and Language Development.* Open University Press, Milton Keynes.

Leveson, N. (1995) *Safeware: System Safety and Computers.* Addison-Wesley, Reading, MA.

Leveson, N. G. and Heimdahl, M. P. E. (1994) Requirements specification for process-control systems. *IEEE Transactions on Software Engineering* **20**(9) 684–707.

Losavio, F. and Matteo, A. (2000) Multiagent models for designing object-oriented distributed systems. *Journal of Object-Oriented Programming (JOOP)*, June.

Miller, G. (1956) The magic number seven, plus or minus two: some limits on our capacity for processing information. *Psychological Reviews* **63** 81–97.

Nichols, B., Buttlar, D. and Farrell, J. P. (1996) *Threads Programming.* O'Reilly & Associates, Boston, MA.

Novak, J. D. and Gowin, D. B. (1985) *Learning How to Learn.* Cambridge University Press.

Pallu de la Barriere, R. (1967) *Optimal Control Theory.* Dover, New York.

Parnas, D. (1972) On the criteria to be used in decomposing systems into modules. *Communications of the ACM* **15**(12) 1053–1058.

POSA (1996): Buschmann, F., Meunier, R., Rohnert, H., Sommerlad, P. and Stal, M., *Pattern-Oriented Software Architecture: a System of Patterns*. John Wiley & Sons, Chichester.

Potts, C., Takahashi, K. and Antón, A. I. (1994) Inquiry-based requirements analysis. *IEEE Software* **11**(2) 21–32.

Rumbaugh, J. (1999) *The Unified Modeling Language Reference Manual*. Addison-Wesley, Reading, MA.

Rumbaugh, J. *et al.* (1991) *Object-Oriented Modeling and Design*. Prentice-Hall, Englewood Cliffs, NJ.

Rummler, G. A. and Brache, A. P. (1995) *Improving Performance* (2nd edn). Jossey-Bass, San Francisco.

Saaty, T. L. (1961) *Elements of Queueing Theory with Applications*. Dover, New York.

Schmidt, D., Stal, M., Rohnert, H. and Buschmann, F. (2000) *Pattern-Oriented Software Architecture: Patterns for Concurrent and Networked Objects*. John Wiley & Sons, Chichester.

Schmidt, D. S. and Huston, S. D. (2002) *C++ Network Programming*, Vol. 1. Addison-Wesley, Boston, MA.

Selic, B., Gullekson, G. and Ward, P. T. (1994) *Real-Time Object-Oriented Modeling*. John Wiley & Sons, New York.

Sharp, A. and McDermott, P. (2001) *Workflow Modeling*. Artech House, Boston, MA.

Shaw, M. and Garlan, D. (1996) *Software Architecture: Perspectives on an Emerging Discipline*. Prentice-Hall, Englewood Cliffs, NJ.

Smith, B. J., Peters, R. J. and Owen, S. (1985) *Acoustics and Noise Control*. Longman, London.

Sommerville, I. and Sawyer, P. (1997) *Requirements Engineering: a Good Practice Guide*. John Wiley & Sons, Chichester.

Umphress, D. A. and March, G. D. (1991) Object-oriented requirements determination. *Journal of Object-Oriented Programming*, winter special issue 'Focus on Analysis and Design', 35–40.

van der Heijden, K. (1996) *Scenarios: The Art of Strategic Conversation*. John Wiley & Sons, Chichester.

Vlissides, J. (1996) Seven habits of successful pattern writers. *C++ Report* (Nov./Dec.).

Wilmott, P. (1998) *Derivatives*. John Wiley & Sons, Chichester.

Winston, P. H. (1980) Learning and reasoning by analogy. *Communications of the ACM* **23**(12) 689–703.

Wooldridge, M. (2002) *Multi-Agent Systems*. John Wiley & Sons, Chichester.

Yourdon, E. and Argila, C. A. (1996) *Case Studies in Object-Oriented Analysis and Design*. Prentice-Hall, Upper Saddle River, NJ.

Yourdon, E. *et al.* (1995) *Mainstream Objects: an Analysis and Design Approach for Business*. Prentice-Hall, Upper Saddle River, NJ.

Index